THE ROUGH GUIDE TO

PCs & Windows

There are more than two hundred Rough Guide travel, phrasebook and music titles, covering destinations from Amsterdam to Zimbabwe, languages from Czech to Vietnamese, and musics from World to Opera and Jazz

www.roughguides.com

Rough Guide Credits

Written, designed and typeset by Peter Buckley and Duncan Clark
Series editor: Mark Ellingham
Production: Julia Bovis

Publishing Information

This second edition published September 2004 by
Rough Guides Ltd, 80 Strand, London WC2R 0RL.

Distributed by the Penguin Group

Penguin Books Ltd, 80 Strand, London WC2R 0RL
Penguin Putnam, Inc., 375 Hudson Street, New York 10014, USA
Penguin Books Australia Ltd, 487 Maroondah Highway,
PO Box 257, Ringwood, Victoria 3134, Australia
Penguin Books Canada Ltd, 10 Alcorn Avenue,
Toronto, Ontario, Canada M4V 1E4
Penguin Books (NZ) Ltd, 182–190 Wairau Road,
Auckland 10, New Zealand

Printed in Italy by LegoPrint.

448pp includes index
A catalogue record for this book is available from the British Library.
ISBN 1-85828-897-5

THE ROUGH GUIDE TO

PCs & Windows

written by
Peter Buckley and Duncan Clark

Contents

get yourself connected

software

keeping it purring

contexts and resources

index

Introduction

where to begin

Over the last two decades or so, the **personal computer, or PC,** has revolutionized the way we go about things. And though the high-tech bubble has been and gone, a knowledge of computers is more useful and important today than ever before. Not only is computer literacy a prerequisite in many areas of **employment**, it's also a skill that can prove incredibly useful and rewarding at **home**. As well as being invaluable for number-crunching and document editing, the modern PC can also help you access the unimaginable wealth of information and communication possibilities of the **Internet**. And that's not even to mention its potential for music, video, images and games.

Whether you're thinking of buying your first computer, planning to upgrade an old machine or just out to hone your skills, this book should help. We start right at the beginning and assume no prior knowledge, but besides the basics about buying and using a PC, you'll also find scores of **tips and tricks** as well as everything from the nitty-gritty of how a PC functions to advice on how to build your own PC. We were surprised, in fact, by just how much we were able to squeeze into such a small book. And where we haven't had room to expand, we've suggested websites where you can find out more.

But before moving on to all that, let's answer a few basic questions about PCs and Windows.

What's a PC? And what's Windows?

In the broadest sense, a PC is any personal computer – a computer designed to be operated by an individual. However, the term is generally used in a more specific way: to describe a computer running the **Windows** operating system.

An operating system, or OS, is the underlying software that acts as a bridge between a computer's hardware (its physical bits), its application software (programs such as word processors or image editors) and its user (you). No computer can function without an operating system, and Windows, produced by the giant computer firm **Microsoft**, is the one found in the vast majority of the world's computers. Microsoft don't have much to do with PC hardware – which is made by an endless list of different companies – but their complete dominance of the operating system market adds up to a highly controversial monopoly (see box).

That's not to say all personal computers run Windows. There are others, such as **Linux** (see p.238), which can run on the same hardware as Windows. And there are computers which have different operating systems *and* different hardware, the best known example being the **Apple Mac** (see p.4). But these machines, though they are certainly personal computers, aren't usually known as "PCs".

The hardware of the modern Windows-based PC is based on a machine produced by IBM in 1981, which was called, inventively enough, the **IBM-PC**. And in terms of their basic structure, today's PCs aren't actually too dissimilar from that pioneering machine or its immediate successors. But for users the difference couldn't be greater. Modern personal computers can handle huge volumes of data at an unbelievable **speed** – we're talking about millions of computations per second. This changes everything: playing computer games, for example, no longer means bouncing a small flickering square around a two-dimensional box, but going head-to-head with Serena Williams in a meticulously detailed 3D cyber-court.

Breaking (free from) Windows

Microsoft's stranglehold on the operating system market is so strong that writing an introductory guide to computing inevitably means including an introductory guide to Windows. That's what we've done in this book, but don't take this as a Windows recommendation: there are various good reasons for shunning Microsoft's flagship product. For one, there's security. Since nearly everyone in the world uses Windows, it's the operating system that malicious programmers focus on – hence the smug look on the faces of Mac or Linux users when yet another virus is taking the Net by storm. Second, there's the ethical question of supporting Microsoft. Besides a history of making massive political donations in the US (allegedly to help buy off politicians who intend to shut down their monopoly), the company is famous for using its monopolistic position to crush competitors and even new technologies that threaten its dominance – just as you'd expect of a huge corporation legally obliged to consider its shareholder before the good of the computing world. Third, there's the cost. Most stores don't even sell computers without Windows pre-installed, but don't fool yourself that you're not paying for it – it accounts for between five and twenty percent of the price of most PCs on the market. The main alternative (aside from Apple Macs) is Linux, which is genuinely free and, many would say, infinitely better. However, in reality Linux is not as simple to use as Windows – not yet, at least – so it's difficult to recommend to computer newbies. But if you fancy giving it a go, see p.238 for more information.

The other major difference it that personal computers are incomparably more user-friendly than ever before. Gone are the days when using a computer involved learning cryptic languages; today, thanks to intuitive operating systems, it's incredibly easy to harness the power within these plastic shells. And we're no longer limited by location – with lightweight laptops and even handheld-sized computers, you can do what you want, where you want.

What can you do with a PC?

Modern PCs can do everything you'd imagine and a whole lot more. They're still very good at the kind of jobs they've long been associated with – writing well-presented **letters and documents, balancing the books** and so on – as well as other office tasks such as **organizing appointments** and maintaining **databases**. But for most home users, other capabilities are far more important.

First there's the **Internet**, perhaps the most exciting thing ever to have happened in the computing world. More than just a porthole for nerds, the Net can be pretty much whatever you want it to be: newspaper, shopping mall, bank, educational tool or just a pretty cool way to spend a few hours broadening your horizons. You can use the Internet to almost instantly retrieve information on anything from anywhere. A PC connected to the Internet will also help you to keep in touch. **Email** enables you to communicate swiftly and inexpensively with long-lost friends and distant relations. You could even take advantage of a webcam and make face-to-face **video phonecalls** to anyone with a similar device anywhere in the world.

Whether you buy a custom-built PC or a family package, the chances are that your system will have astonishing multimedia potential. Perhaps you fancy creating a **home recording studio**. Or converting your old vinyl collection into an archive of digital music files, so you can burn them onto CD or put them on a portable MP3 player. And it's not just music. With a **scanner** you could create a digital album of all those fading photos in the attic or the stack of your toddler's paintings under the stairs, ready to email to your friends or relatives (not that they'd necessarily thank you for it). or you could **craft a website** to show the world what you're about, or even use your computer as a **video editing suite** and create an art-house masterpiece complete with special effects and soundtrack, ready to burn onto DVD or distribute via the Net. And then there's **gaming**. Whether you want to spend long nights trekking through the Amazon jungle with Lara Croft or solving complex spatial puzzles, the PC is for you.

Although technology is moving at an unbelievable pace, R2-D2 is still a long way off – computers can't think for themselves and only operate within strict parameters laid down by us humans. But that's no bad thing: realizing that your PC is just a loyal servant who happens to be rather good at mathematics can be very liberating. And though PCs have come a very long way in the last decade, it's **easier to catch up now than ever before**. So long as you view your computer as an ally and not an enemy, using it should be both productive and enjoyable.

How this book works

The first part of this book provides you with everything you need to know when **buying PCs, parts and peripherals**: where to get them, what to look out for and how to decide what you'll actually need for the kind of computing you're aiming to do. Also in this section you'll find the lowdown on what a PC consists of and how its various components work – before long you'll know your RAM from your ROM and you'll be waxing lyrical about buses, buffers and burners.

Chapters 5 to 13 whisk you through the **Windows operating system**. We cover the basics, but also introduce you to a barrel-load of tips and tricks to help you get the most out of your operating system. So whether you're new to Windows or already familiar with its tools, menus and buttons, you're sure to learn a lot. As well as covering the latest version – Windows XP – we also deal with Windows Me and Windows 98. Even if you're using an antiquated Windows 95 machine, most of what we say will still apply.

In chapters 14 to 16 you'll learn how to set up a **home network** and get to grips with the **Internet**, while chapters 17 through 22 present a roll call of some of the best **software** titles around, tips on keeping your PC working as it should, a **troubleshooting** section to pull you out of deep water should things go wrong and a detailed guide to **upgrading** your machine.

We've tried to keep the book as user-friendly as possible, but if you do find yourself flummoxed by the odd bit of techie jargon, turn to the **Glossary** (p.355) to get a concise and digestible definition – if nothing else, you'll be much better at Scrabble after reading this book. And if we succeed in whetting your appetite, the **website directory** chapter (p.399) will point you towards some of the best, and most entertaining, PC-related sites on the Web.

How this book works

The first part of this book provides you with everything you need to know about buying a PC, parts and peripherals, where to get them, what to look out for and how to decide what you'll actually need for the kind of computing you're going to do. Also in this section you'll find an introduction to what a PC consists of and how its various components work together, so you'll know your RAM from your ROM and you'll be able to [illegible] bytes, buffers and busses.

Chapters 5 to 13 walk you through the Windows operating system. We cover the basics but also introduce you to a [illegible] of tips and tricks to help you get the most out of your operating system. So whether you're new to Windows or already familiar with its tools, menus and layout, you're sure to find a lot here. As well as covering the latest version – Windows XP – we also deal with Windows Me and Windows 98 [illegible] Windows 95 [illegible].

In chapters 14 to 16 you'll learn how to set up a home network and get to grips with the Internet and e-mail. Chapters 17 to 22 [illegible] software [illegible] keeping your PC working as it should, a troubleshooting section to pull you out of a [illegible] when things go wrong, and a detailed guide to upgrading your machine.

We've tried to [illegible] the book as [illegible] as possible, but if you do find yourself flummoxed by the odd bit of techie jargon, turn to the Glossary [illegible] for clear and concise definitions. [illegible] much better [illegible] after reading this book. And [illegible] the website directory chapter [illegible] will point you towards some of the best and most [illegible] PC-related sites on the Web.

from purchase to power-up

01

Buying a PC

what, where, how

If you want to buy a PC, this chapter will help you decide what you want and where to get it. But if you haven't got time to digest all this information – or you're already standing in the checkout queue of your local PC store – there are a key few points well worth bearing in mind:

▶ Never buy a top-of-the-range PC unless you absolutely need it. They're disproportionately expensive.

▶ No computer is future-proof, but some are more upgradeable than others.

▶ High-street chains charge more than online retailers.

▶ Don't be seduced by packages including stuff you don't need or peripherals you are likely to replace soon.

▶ Where possible, buy with a credit card.

Decision 1: To upgrade or to buy new?

If you already have a computer, you might be wondering whether to give it a revamp or to buy a new machine. It's certainly possible to vastly improve an old PC by upgrading it – and we've devoted a whole chapter to the subject. Your computer is only as good as its weakest link, and it may well be that one thing is holding back its overall performance. But be cautious – you don't want to invest too much money, time and effort in an old machine that has inherent limits. As a general rule, if you're currently running **anything less than a Pentium II system**, upgrading might be more hassle and cost than its worth, but it depends on your specific requirements and system. For more on upgrading, see p.311.

If your system has trouble working with several applications simultaneously, grinds to a halt when faced with a stack of windows, fails to run taxing software or struggles with image editing, the chances are that you need some more **RAM** (see p.33). It could also be the case that your system would speed up considerably with a more powerful **processor** (see p.27), though this may necessitate a new **motherboard** (see p.31). This is a pricier exercise, but could still work out better for your wallet than getting a new machine. Replacing or adding a **video card** (see p.45) may well improve sluggish video and gaming performance, and a better **sound card** (see p.46) should do the trick if your PC's audio is not up to scratch.

If you are **running out of hard drive space** for accommodating software and files, think about getting a second drive to run alongside the first. All these upgrade options are covered in far greater detail in Chapter 22.

Decision 2: PC or Mac?

One thing you have to decide before you buy a new computer is whether to go for a PC or a Mac. But beware – this subject carries a lot of emotional baggage, and you're likely to find yourself on the receiving end of an impassioned rant if you request the opinion of either a PC or Mac devotee. This book only deals with PCs, but for those of you who aren't sure of the difference, or haven't yet decided which way to jump, here's the lowdown.

PCs are manufactured by an endless list of firms but they invariably come installed with the **Microsoft Windows** operating system, which means they all work in the same way and can run the same programs. There are alternatives to Windows (see p.238), but when people say "PC" they're generally talking about PC with Windows. And these account for the vast majority – comfortably more than ninety percent – of the home computer market.

Macs, on the other hand, are made by a single company – **Apple** – and run Apple's own **Mac OS** operating system. Hence at any one time there are only a certain number of models to choose from. Macs

been around since the start of the home computer era, but they've also long been favoured in certain industries, including **publishing** and **graphic design**. As such, they've also been marketed as the "creative" person's computer, and, uncoincidentally, they've become famous for their **slick design** (see the iMac pictured on p.5). And this slick design extends to the operating system, current versions of which are infinitely nicer to look at and use than Windows.

It used to be the case that PCs and Macs were almost completely incompatible: they ran different software, and you couldn't easily move information from one to the other. These days, however, most popular programs are available for both (though following gaming trends is undoubtedly harder with a Mac), and files created on one "platform" can usually be opened on the other. So you can write a document on your PC and open and edit it on a friend's Mac, generally without any huge problems.

One difference between PCs and Macs is **what you actually get for your money**. A Mac generally costs about thirty to fifty percent more than a PC with equivalent specs, and the advertised price may not even include a monitor, let alone a printer and scanner. The extra expense also extends to upgrading and repairs. You don't always have to go for Apple-made devices when expanding your kit, but in some cases (Wi-Fi card for laptops, for example), this is the only option, and you can expect to pay double what you would for the PC equivalent.

Overall, then, PCs are better value in terms of pure firepower, but Macs are nicer to look at and arguably nicer to work with, and they're the de facto standard in certain industries. If you can't decide what to go for, do your own research: test drive both systems in a computer store, and perhaps do some reading online. Eavesdropping on obsessively brand-loyal nerds jousting in Web chat forums can actually be quite entertaining.

For information about the latest Apple options, go straight to the source:

Apple www.apple.com

Decision 3: Desktop, laptop or something else?

Portable computers were once the executive toys of high-flyers who wanted to play Tetris on aeroplanes, but as they've become less expensive and more powerful, increasing numbers of people are choosing them. Today, you can get a turbo-charged **laptop** that's less than an inch thick and more than capable of replacing a traditional desktop machine. And there are variations on both the desktop and laptop themes, such as **tablet PCs** (see p.12), **mini PCs and handheld**, which will literally fit in your pocket (see p.10), and **media centres**, designed to acts as a PC, stereo and TV in one (see p.12).

Laptops vs desktops

Though the cost of **laptops** – which are also commonly referred to as **notebooks** – has fallen dramatically in recent years, they're still considerably more expensive than equivalent desktop systems. But in return for the extra cash you get a PC you can **use anywhere** within or outside the home. With a laptop, you can set up a **wireless network** and surf the Web in the garden or front room, instead of the study or spare room; you can use the same machine both at home and **at work** (perhaps even plugging into the company network); you can take your work, photos, music or projects with you when you travel; and you can hide your computer away in a drawer when you're not using it.

Here are some trade-offs and considerations you'll have to grapple with when choosing between a laptop and a desktop:

▶ **Horsepower and features** A laptop is nearly twice as expensive as a desktop machine with comparable performance and features. And because everything has to be made as small as possible, the workings are generally less efficient – so even if the advertised specs of a laptop and a desktop are identical, the desktop will generally be faster.

▶ **Hot, hot, hot** There's a lot of stuff crammed into a laptop and, as with a desktop, much of it gets very warm, especially with high-performance machines. But cooling a laptop is a tricky business. The fans and vents are small and, depending where they're located on the casing, you may even find that prolonged lap-use of a high-power machine is uncomfortable, if not painfully hot. However, there are new liquid-cooling technologies such as IsoSkin on the horizon that may change all this.

▶ **Keys, pointers and screens** Laptops have miniaturized keyboards and usually come with a small touchpad or rubber pointing device that you operate with your finger instead of using a mouse. This setup takes

PC cards

PC cards – or **PCMCIA** cards, as they're also known – allow laptop users to add extra pieces of hardware to their computers quickly and easily. Though only about the size of chunky credit cards, all sorts of devices are available in this mini-format, from Wi-Fi adapters for wireless Internet access (see p.49) to surprisingly spacious hard drives (allowing large files to be backed up or moved from one machine to another). Many external pieces of hardware such as CD writers can be attached to laptops via a cable with a PC card on the end. Older laptops normally have two slots, whereas newer, thinner machines tend to have only one, but they make up for it with an integral modem (see p.48), so you won't have to use up your only slot to get online. You can even get PC card bays that allow you to use these miniature devices with a desktop system. There are three sizes of card: types I, II and III.

some getting used to, and if you also use a regular keyboard and mouse you'll undoubtedly find the laptop controls frustrating. However, it's very easy to connect a mouse and full-size keyboard to the machine when you're working at a desk, especially if you have a docking station (see box). Laptop monitors are also generally smaller, though if you don't mind forking out, there are many 17" models now on the market. And you can hook up most laptops to bigger external monitors, either directly or through a docking station (if you're planning on doing this, check what maximum resolution the laptop supports, or you may end up with the same number of pixels simply spread out over a larger area).

▶ **Expandability** Laptops, because of their size, leave you with fewer expansion options than desktops, and getting under the hood is often no easy task – so upgrade surgery may not be something that you can do yourself. That said, many modern laptops feature removable hard drives, easily accessible RAM slots and bays that will accept a variety of devices like CD writers and DVD drives, so expanding is far less of a problem than it used to be. Most systems also feature slots for PC cards (see box opposite).

▶ **Games, graphics, video and music** Gaming, image, video and music-making used to be unsuited to laptops because of their small screens, inferior graphics potential and lack of PCI slots for decent sound and video cards. But modern high-spec laptops are more than capable of all these tasks. They can work with image and video straight out of the box, and they can become the hub of a home recording studio via an external sound-card alternative that plugs in via USB (see p.53).

Docking stations

If you plan to use a laptop as your main PC and expect to take it out of the home regularly it's worth considering getting a **docking station** or **port replicator**. This piece of hardware sits permanently on your desk, with all your peripherals – printer, scanner, mouse, keyboard, monitor, etc – plumbed into it. Whenever you bring your laptop home to roost it simply slots onto the station, giving an instant connection to the rest of your hardware.

▶ **Reliability** Though they're getting hardier by the month, computers don't particularly like being lugged around, dropped in puddles and restarted while you're navigating rapids in a dinghy. Because of the extra punishment they often receive, laptops are more likely to go wrong and die than desktop systems. And when they do, they're far more expensive to repair or replace. So make sure the warranty is comprehensive and that you regularly back up your work (see p.288).

▶ **Selecting a machine** Because of a laptop's size, a specific brand may have only a certain number of configuration options, and building your own isn't an option. While a desktop system will allow you the freedom to customize a machine to any specification under the sun, you'll have to shop around to get a best-fit laptop.

▶ **Loseability** Laptops are often stolen, and many home-contents insurance policies don't cover them. You may be able to pay extra to get a laptop included, either just in the house or for when you're out and about – though the premiums might make you wince.

Sub-laptops

If a standard laptop is too bulky for your purposes, you could go for a lightweight, ultra-slim model, but you'll pay a considerable sum for the privilege. The other option, which makes a lot of sense if your portable computer is to be used alongside a desktop PC, is to go for a **sub-notebook** or **mini PC**. These save space by having a smaller screen and dis-

pensing with internal CD and floppy drives (these drives are often included, but because they're external you can leave them at home if you want). Some sub-laptops – such as Vulcan's FlipStart (pictured) – are as small as the book you're currently holding.

Vulcan http://minipc.vulcan.com

Handhelds and smartphones

If a sub-notebook is too expensive, look into **handhelds** (also called **PDAs**) and **smartphones**. These are no substitute for a real PC, but they provide certain functions when you're out and about. Many people use their handheld or smartphone primarily as a fancy **electronic diary**; you can connect it to your desktop at work, for example, and instantly update your schedule. But many handhelds, and all smartphones, also have Net access and often include a full Web browser – great for checking your email on the move.

Some of these devices run a slimmed-down version of Windows (called **Windows CE**), though many other systems are available. There are many applications available, both commercial – such as chopped down versions of Word and Excel – and open source (see **HandHelds.org**). However, don't expect to do much typing on a handheld. Some have a full but absolutely tiny QWERTY keyboard, while others most feature a little **stylus** (pen) instead of a keyboard: you write on the screen and the computer recognizes your scrawl and inserts the appropriate letter.

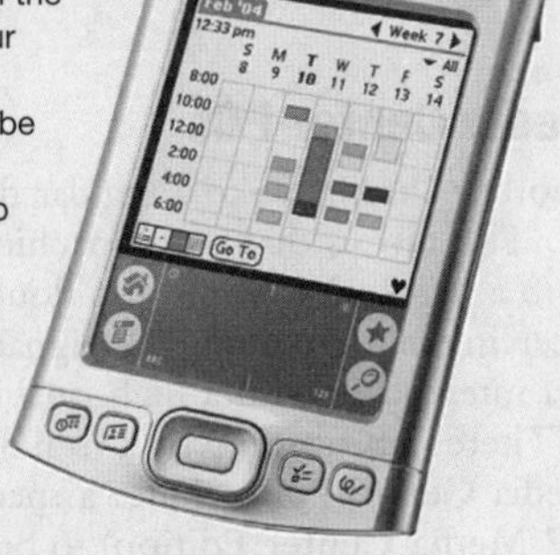

Handhelds and smartphones can also be used to play games, listen to music and read eBooks. And you can hook them up to a standard computer – via a cable, or wirelessly, with Bluetooth or infrared – and automatically download the news from the Web every morning. You'll never need to buy a newspaper again.

BrightHand www.brighthand.com
HandHelds.org www.handhelds.org
Windows Mobile www.microsoft.com/windowsmobile

Tablet PCs

Another variation on the laptop theme is the **tablet PC**. These are basically high-spec laptops which have special **touch-sensitive screens** that can be flipped over to turn the computer into a virtual writing or drawing pad. Most recent tablet PCs run a special edition of Windows XP, which includes software for handwriting recognition, note-making and other relevant things. As you might expect, tablets are currently used mainly by graphic artists and boardroom executives. But it seems inevitable that all laptops will eventually be tablets.

Find out more at:

TabletpcTalk www.tabletpctalk.com
Windows XP Tablet PC Edition www.microsoft.com/windowsxp/tabletpc

Media Center PCs

Another alternative to a regular desktop or laptop is a **Media Center PC**. The idea is that these machines do everything you would expect from a regular PC while also doubling as a media hub for the home – receiving and recording TV signals (no more need for a video or TV) and integrating with a high-quality speaker system (no need for a hi-fi). There's no reason why a "standard" computer can't do all this, but a Media Center PC includes a special version of Windows (**Windows XP Media Center Edition**) to bring the various elements together, as well as a remote control. And numerous third-party companies are beginning to offer movie and music "on-demand" services specifically aimed at the XP Media Center platform.

To find out more, including a list of companies producing Media Center PCs, visit:

Windows XP Media Center www.microsoft.com/windowsxp/mediacenter

It remains to be seen whether the next "standard" version of Windows will contain similar features.

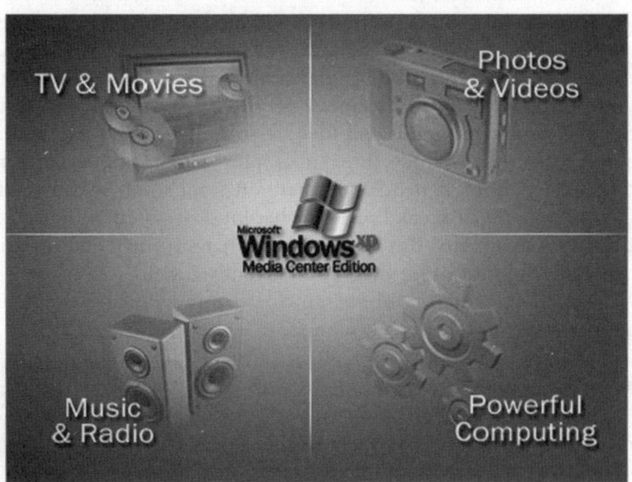

Designer and space-saving desktop PCs

The PC market has begun to rise to the aesthetic challenge set by recent Macs. Not all PCs are ugly beige boxes any more – you can now get ugly colourful boxes too. And there are many space-saving PCs available: some simply offer a smaller, sleeker case, while others cram all the guts of the machine into the base of a slimline monitor. These often look great, but tend to be overpriced and offer fewer upgrade options. So unless you can't bear to be without a design classic, beige is (generally) best.

Decision 4: How much firepower?

If you've already decided that you need a PC, you've probably put some thought into what you want to do with your new toy and where you want to do it. Don't lose sight of these considerations – if you do, it's easy to end up with a high-end PC that you don't really need, or, conversely, a slow computer padded out with a pile of low-end peripherals and redundant software.

Whatever you buy, much of the cost will be determined by the speed of the **processor** or **CPU** (the computer's brain: see p.27), the amount of **memory** or **RAM** (which determines how many things the machine can deal with at any one time: see p.33), and the size of the **hard drive** (where programs and files are stored: see p.37). How much firepower you need in these three areas, plus which other factors you need to worry about, depends on what you want to do with the PC.

Following is a quick breakdown of what kind of system you need for various types of activity. But bear in mind that you may end up using the machine for a lot more than you currently intend.

For detailed information about any of the individual components mentioned, turn to Chapter 2 (see p.23).

▶ **Word processing** Even advanced word processing is child's play for a modern PC, so if all you want is a 21st-century typewriter, don't splash out on a multimedia monster. If you're a serious typist, your money would be better spent on an ergonomic keyboard, a quality printer and a comfy desk chair.

▶ **The Internet** All home PCs ship with a built-in dial-up modem, so you won't need to buy anything extra to connect to the Internet, except possibly an extension cable to reach a phone socket. If you're planning on getting a fast **broadband** connection (see p.198), you'll need a

tip

As a general rule, unless you really need a super-fast system, aim for something with a processor roughly half to two-thirds of the current max available. Above this level, every extra megahertz of speed gets increasingly expensive. Below it, and your system will probably seem out of date before long.

separate broadband modem, but you might get one free when you sign up, so don't buy one with your computer. Whatever your connection, you **don't need a high-spec computer to surf** the Web, send emails, and so on, but if you plan to get into video phone calls, streaming audio and the like, a slow machine will prove frustrating.

▶ **Handling images and video** Pretty much all modern PCs are fine for messing around with images and photos, and watching DVD movies. But if you plan to edit your own video, manipulate poster-size pictures, or work with 3D animation, you'll need lots of **RAM**, a fast **processor**, a **video card** with ample onboard memory and a decent **monitor**. For video editing you'll also want an **IEEE 1394** ("**Firewire**") port for connecting a digital video camera; a **DVD-R** drive for putting your creations on disc; and perhaps also a TV-out socket for hooking up your computer to the TV. Does the system come with a **printer**, a **scanner** or a **digital camera**? These may be useful at first, but if you're likely to replace them with better models soon, they may make for a worse, not a better, deal.

▶ **Gaming** Modern computer games push PCs to the max, so if gaming is something you intend to get into, you'll need a high-end machine. The CPU has to be fast, the RAM plentiful and the video card powerful. You'll also need a joystick that you like the feel of, and a decent monitor and speaker system will enhance the experience.

▶ **Working with sound** If audio is going to be your main concern, you need to think about the capabilities of the PC's **sound card** and **speaker system** – and you'll also want a hefty hard drive and a fast CD burner. If you're a musician looking to build a virtual recording studio, see p.48.

▶ **Multitasking** If you like to do lots of things at once, you won't want to have to close one application to get another working at a respectable speed. No modern computer will struggle to run, say, email and word processing software simultaneously, but if you want to have numerous multimedia programs running at the same time, you'll need **lots of RAM**.

Decision 5: What to buy, where to buy?

Once you know roughly what kind of computer you're after, it's time to compare specific models. **PC magazines** come in handy here, especially if you can find one doing a comparative test of systems in your price range (which usually isn't too difficult, as in any one month, one mag will be seeking the "best budget system" currently available, one will be after the best package for, say, £500 or $500, and another will be looking at the high-end options). However, bear in mind that PC journalists – who don't actually have to actually hand over money for the systems they're reviewing – might rubbish a machine simply because it happens to perform some ludicrous task 0.034 seconds slower than something they prefer.

If possible, try to **get online**. With our website directory (see p.399) to hand, you'll be able to compare prices and buy via the Net: either directly from the manufacturers or via an online computer store. Though you may hear horror stories about shopping online, the Web is in many ways the ideal place to shop for a PC. Not only can you gather information, compare machines and gawp at cool animations of laptops opening and closing, but you can do so unhindered by pushy salesmen and sneering jargonites. You can also read reviews by other customers, both of companies and specific systems.

If you're concerned about using your credit card on the Web, you could do your research online and then place the order by phone. However, bear in mind that entering your details via a webpage is typically less risky than handing your card to a waiter in a restaurant.

In most cases the despatch of your goods will be swift and efficient, though it's worth asking around to see if any of your friends have had good or bad experiences with a particular firm.

If you can't get online or you fancy a test-drive, visit a store. The large **PC superstores** are good places to find all-inclusive deals, though they're not necessarily the best source of advice. **Small dealers**, on the other hand, will be able to furnish you with either a customized machine or a wide range of specific components for upgrades and self-builds (see p.311), and they may be more helpful if things go wrong. If you're feeling brave, go to a **computer fair** – everything from cables to complete systems can be picked up at rock-bottom prices. To find a fair nearby, look in the local newspaper, or search online:

Computer Fairs (UK) www.computerfairs.co.uk
Computer Fairs (US) www.computerfairs.co.uk/usa-computer-fairs.html
Computer Fairs (Aus) www.computerfairs.co.uk/aus-computer-fairs.html

Computer Fairs Information™
market auction forum news

Is the brand important?

Certain companies have well-deserved reputations for producing consistently high-quality computers. But with a PC it's the stuff inside the case that's important and with some of these companies you'll pay a bit extra just for the name – an equivalent PC from a smaller retailer might cost you less. Sometimes the extra money will buy you better components – and therefore more impressive performance – but the overall quality can only really be gauged from a comparative review. In some ways, after-sales service is more important than the manufacturer.

After-sales service

When buying, it's also worth thinking about the kind of support you'll get if things go wrong. A **warranty** of one to three years is almost always included in the price, though be sure to check whether it's an **on-site** (OS) or **return-to-base** (RTB) arrangement. With an on-site warranty, the company will come and repair the computer at your

Secondhand PCs

PC technology moves so fast that you may be able to pick up a machine that was state of the art a couple of years ago for surprisingly little money. With a bit of luck you can seek out a respectable Internet-ready Pentium III system, say, for less than a quarter of the price of a new, off-the-shelf Pentium 4 package. However, buying secondhand from an individual – from an ad in a paper or at an Internet auction – involves a considerable **element of risk**, as you're unlikely to get a warranty or any after-sales service, so you'll have little comeback if it turns out to be a complete turkey. Many professional secondhand dealers and PC refurbishers, though, do offer a guarantee.

Whether you're buying a machine privately or from a dealer, **make sure you see the thing working** before you hand over any money. If you have a friend who's familiar with computers, drag them along: they will help you ask the right questions and spot any obvious flaws. But even with the best advice in the world, buying a secondhand PC is still a gamble. Here are a few things to check or bear in mind:

▶ **Check the specs** Assuming the PC is running Windows 95 or later, you can make sure that the advertised specs are genuine in the **System Properties** dialog box, which you can open by right-clicking **My Computer** on the Desktop or in the Start menu and selecting **Properties.**

▶ **Wear and tear** Don't judge a book by its cover – you may get a great deal on a machine that is perfectly functional despite a dull screen, suspect mouse or duff keyboard. These components are easy to replace: monitors are quite expensive but new mice and keyboards can be picked up dirt-cheap.

▶ **Under the hood** If you can, have a look inside the machine to find out how much room you'll have for upgrades (see p.311): a little extra memory or a new hard drive could bring an old machine up-to-date.

home and take it away if they can't solve the problem, but return-to-base means it's up to you to get the machine to wherever it's going to be fixed. This is fine if you bought it from a local shop – you can easily drop the poorly PC off for surgery – but if you purchased it online or direct from a manufacturer you may find yourself having to pack it up and pay for it to be posted across the country, with little chance of getting the thing back within a month.

The **warranty** can speak volumes about the machine and the supplier. If a company is reluctant to throw in at least one year's on-site support, you should wonder why. It could be because they're cutting costs and passing the savings on to you, but perhaps they think the computer is likely to go wrong. Or maybe they're determined to sell additional cover at an extra charge. Most retailers offer some kind of **extended care plan**. These are fine if you're after peace of mind, but they are usually outrageously over-priced. And do you really need a five-year warranty? You may well have replaced the computer before it even expires. And, even if not, one or two repairs will usually work out less expensive than the cover plan.

Building your own PC

One final option for getting yourself a computer is to buy the ten or so necessary components and put the machine together yourself. If you have the confidence to try this, you can **save some money**, you'll almost certainly **learn a great deal about computers** in the process, and you can make the machine exactly to your own specifications using high-quality components. Though not for the technologically shy, building a PC is much **easier than it sounds** – all you really have to do is slot the bits into place. As long as you're OK at fiddly operations, you have a knowledgeable friend you can call if you get stuck and you don't mind having no guarantee or after-sales support, building your own computer is a serious option – and potentially a highly satisfying experience. If you're considering taking this path for financial reasons, get the components from a mail-order supplier or a computer fair, where they can be purchased at rock-bottom prices; otherwise you won't save much money. And bear in mind that you'll also have to get hold of any application software you may want as well as an operating system like Windows, which is usually pre-installed on an off-the-shelf PC. If you're tempted by the idea of building your own computer, turn to p.340 to read more.

Technical support phone lines are also usually offered with a new computer. Though the idea of having a number you can call if you need advice on anything from starting up your word processor to serious troubleshooting sounds inviting, many of these services are alarmingly costly – in the UK, at least – so always **check the per-minute charge**. If you have a patient friend or relative who knows the basics, you'll get a quicker and more sympathetic response if you phone them instead. Besides, with this book in hand, you should be able to cope with most of the difficulties you'll encounter on your passage to PC proficiency.

And finally: A few buying tips

▶ Where possible, **pay for a PC with a credit card**. This way, you'll be protected if any damage occurs in transit or the company goes under before the machine reaches you.

▶ Don't get excited about **large bundles of software** thrown in with a new machine – they're usually advertised as being worth as much as the computer itself, but often consist of such useful programs as a marine encyclopedia. And you can download a surprising amount of truly useful software – including excellent free alternatives to Microsoft Word and Office – from the Web (see p.259).

▶ If space is a consideration, you may be tempted by a **PC in a small case** (a mini-tower or special design), but before you choose such a model bear in mind that it may not have many spare bays or PCI slots (see p.31) for expansion in the future.

▶ If you're serious about multimedia, avoid systems with **integrated graphics and sound**. This means that instead of a separate **video card** (see p.45) and **sound card** (see p.46), these elements are built into the motherboard, and are probably pretty crummy. Theoretically you can always "disable" the in-built sound or graphics and add decent cards in the future, but occasionally can cause problems.

▶ Find out what sort of **RAM** a machine harbours – anything less than **DDR RAM** is unacceptable (see p.33).

▶ Though you may come across a genuine bargain, it's worth being a little bit suspicious of all-in systems at absolutely rock-bottom prices. Corners may well have been cut: the **power supply** or **case** may be poor quality, for example, or you simply may find something strange like the **hard drive pre-partitioned** into more than one separate drive (you can sort this out but it will be a bit of a pain; see p.336).

▶ Don't spend money on things you don't need. This may sound obvious, but it's incredibly easy to get drawn in by fancy gizmos when all you're really after is a simple but powerful PC and the software essentials.

▶ **A few numbers don't tell you everything about the power of a system**: components and specifications not mentioned in an advert may well have a dramatic effect on performance. A hard drive may be huge, for example, but it may also be slow at reading and writing data. If you really want to get the best computer, you need to understand a bit more about the components themselves – so read on into the next chapter.

▶ If buying a laptop, check out its wireless networking functions. You can always add Wi-Fi and Bluetooth later (see p.228), but if it's built in you won't have to splash out on any extra hardware, and you won't have annoying adapters sticking out of your machine.

02

Anatomy of a PC

take a look inside

This section takes you on a tour inside the belly of the PC, explaining what the various hardware components do and, in the simplest possible terms, how they do it. You'll also find buying advice to help you choose new components, whether for upgrading an existing machine, building a computer from scratch, or simply making an informed decision about an off-the-shelf model. Though you can easily use a PC without this knowledge (if that's what you want to do, turn to Chapter 4), having a basic idea of what makes a PC tick – quite literally – will make you feel much more in control when using or troubleshooting your system. Also, it's pretty fascinating stuff. Really.

Cross section of a PC

The diagram below shows you how the main components are laid out inside a typical PC. Of course, things might be slightly different in any individual machine (many, for example, have sound, graphics or a modem built into the motherboard, and so lack the expansion cards shown). And, when it comes to snazzy, unusually shaped PCs, things

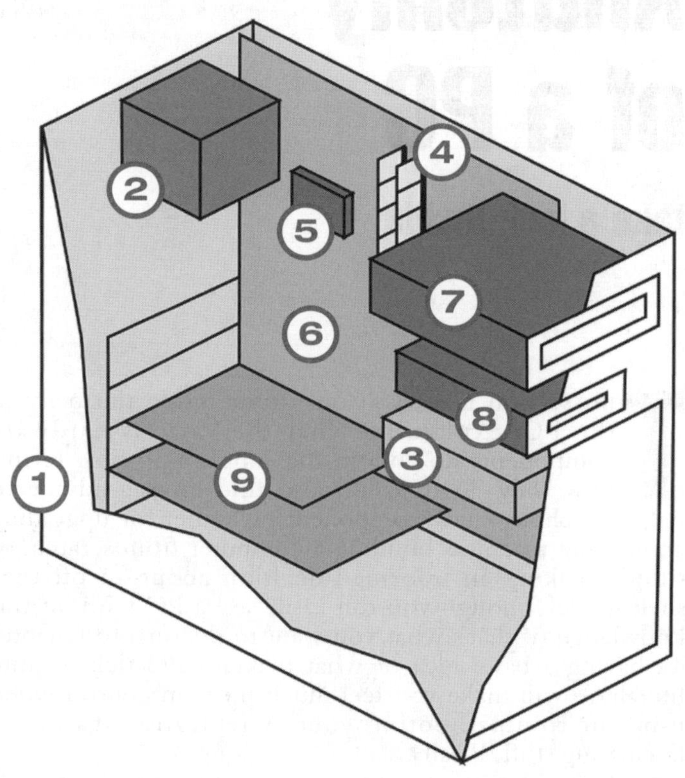

may be laid out completely differently. Still, most home computers look very much like the one shown here, once you get the hood off.

You'll find more information about the various components throughout the rest of this chapter.

▶ **1 Case** The box in which all the bits live.

▶ **2 Power supply** with a built-in cooling fan.

▶ **3 Hard drive** The place where all your programs and documents are stored when not in use (and, sometimes, when they are in use).

▶ **4 RAM** The "short-term" memory where programs and documents stay while you're using or working on them.

▶ **5 Processor or CPU** The brains of the computer, which does most of the actual computing.

▶ **6 Motherboard** The large circuit board to which the other components are connected.

▶ **7 CD/DVD drive** Reads, and often writes, information to CDs and/or DVDs.

▶ **8 Floppy drive** Reads and writes files from or to floppy diskettes.

▶ **9 Expansion cards** Circuit boards, such as video cards, sound cards and modems, which add functionality to the system.

Case and power supply

The **PC case**, or **chassis**, doesn't just house all the other components. It's home to the **indicator lights**, those little blinking LEDs on the front of the machine that show you whether the PC is switched on, whether the hard drive is in use and so on. It contains one or two **fans** to keep everything cool. And, though they are technically separate components, a case usually comes pre-fitted with a **power supply**, which needs to be reliable (cheap ones can fry systems) and powerful enough for the machine (300 watts is essential for most modern setups).

The main case consideration, however, is size. Most modern PCs come with an upright **tower case** rather than a flat **desktop case**, and there are various sizes of tower: mini, midi and full. Though many people want their PC to be as small as possible, **a small case can limit expansion**. Each case has a certain number of **bays** – parking spaces for internal components – some of which you can see from the outside (DVD, floppy drives, etc), and some that are hidden away (mainly for hard drives). If there are no spare bays, you may end up frustrated if you want to install a new piece of kit a few months down the line. Also, certain modern expansion cards are very long; they simply won't fit in a small case.

The case also determines **how the machine looks**, and over the last few years PC cases have been appearing in all sorts of shapes and colours – it's no longer a matter of having light beige or dark beige. Though designer cases aren't always part of PC packages, if you're having a machine custom-made or you're building one yourself, you can choose from a wide range.

If you're looking to upgrade an old machine, your current case may well be fine as long as it has enough room to house any new hardware that you want to add. If you're going to change the **motherboard**, however, you'll need to be sure that the case and power supply connection will accommodate the new board's **form factor** (see p.32).

The vital organs

Moving inside the case, let's first look at the fundamental components of the PC: the bits that deal with actual number-crunching, the short-term storage of information currently being worked on (such as programs that are running) and the distribution of data between all the other internal components. No PC can exist without them.

Processors

The processor, which is also known as the **microprocessor**, **chip**, **CPU** or **central processing unit**, is the brain of a PC – the part of the computer that actually computes. It's a silicon chip containing millions of tiny electronic **transistors** that, like switches, open and close, manipulating electronic code according to logical instructions. Everything you do on your PC, from typing a single letter to rendering a high-quality image, is dealt with by the processor.

The speed of a processor – the number of computations the chip can make in a second – is measured in **hertz**. A processor rated at 500 **megahertz** can make about half a million calculations a second, and a 2.5 **gigahertz** model can handle around five times that. The speed of the processor is perhaps the single biggest factor in determining the power and price of a PC, and it's this hertz tag that's plastered over most computer ads. But be warned: the machine with the fastest processor is not always the fastest computer.

There are two reasons for this. First, the specifications of other components are highly significant (the quantity and speed of RAM, for example, and the access time of the hard drive). There's no point having the fastest processor in the world if the rest of the machine can't keep up. Second, the hertz rating doesn't tell the whole story about the speed of a processor: one type of 3 GHz CPU might perform tasks faster than a different 3 GHz model because of its internal architecture. Even seemingly identical chips may be slightly different: two chips may be advertised as "Athlon 2 GHz", say, but if one was made more recently it may have a faster **front side bus** (fsb), which determines the speed at which data can travel in and out of the processor.

If trying to work out which processor to go for, there is one golden rule. Unless money is no object, **never buy the fastest one on the market**, because you could get something only marginally slower for significantly less cash. And by the time software is available that will utilize a super-fast processor's power, the chip will have become annoyingly cheap. Most users will get optimal value in terms of power and future-proofness by choosing something roughly **half the speed** of the fastest available.

Processor wars – the story so far

Intel (short for **Int**egrated **El**ectronics) have been the biggest name in processor manufacturing since the beginning of the PC revolution. They created the 4004 chip – the first microprocessor – and have been at the forefront of design ever since, dominating from the early 1990s with their flagship range of **Pentium** processors. Their only serious competitor in recent years has been **AMD** (Advanced Micro Devices). This Texan company was once employed by Intel to produce chips on its behalf, but AMD developed their own processor – based on Intel's design – that was more powerful than anything in their employer's catalogue. The two companies have been head-to-head ever since. AMD tend to offer better value for money, but Intel are still the market leaders, partly thanks to strong customer loyalty and a pretty little jingle.

There are other chip manufacturers around, such as **Transmeta,** who produce the energy-saving chips for PDAs and the like (their chips include **Crusoe** and **Efficeon**). But, for standard desktops and laptop computers, the market is still basically a two-horse race.

Tech Info

Digital information

All information is either analogue or digital – humans see, hear, touch and taste analogue information, but modern computers work exclusively with digital. People often get confused about the difference, but it's actually very simple. **Analogue** information has an unlimited set of values. Take a light bulb with a dimmer switch as an example: when you look at the light bulb and turn the switch, you see infinite degrees of brightness between the bulb being off and the bulb being fully on. What you're seeing is analogue information – a perfectly smooth transition from dark to light.

Digital information, on the other hand, has a limited number of values. You could only describe the same light bulb as digital information if you defined a set number of possible states. You could describe it as having two states (the bulb could be on or off), three states (bright, dim or off), or a million (really bright, ever so slightly less bright and so on). Regardless of the number of states, though, the transition from dark to light will be stepwise, rather than smooth.

If you look at a photo stored on a computer it may look pretty convincing, but if you zoom in closely enough you'll find that the picture consists of a certain number of tiny little coloured squares, called **pixels**. The more pixels the photo is made up of, the better it will look. On a traditional printed photo, though, which is analogue, you could keep zooming in and in with a microscope and never find any little squares. Likewise, when you speak, you produce analogue sound, with infinite variation of volume and tone. But the moment you record your voice on a computer it becomes digital information; when you play it back it will still sound like you, but your voice will have been simplified, now having only a limited number of loudness and tone possibilities.

All this paints digital information in a fairly negative light: as just an approximation of the real world. But all digital information can be **reduced to numbers,** and this gives it two huge advantages. One, it allows us to harness the power of computers (analogue computers did once exist, but were inherently doomed). Two, once something is reduced to a number, it can be copied and recopied without ever changing, so the information will never deteriorate. You can copy a digital recording of your voice from computer to computer and it will stay exactly the same. Analogue information, for all its supposed subtlety, changes slightly every time it is copied. If you record your voice onto an analogue medium like a cassette tape, each time you copy it from tape to tape the quality will get worse.

Processors: what's out there

Here's a quick overview of the most important PC processors on the market at the time of writing, newest first.

▶ **Pentium M (Intel)** Released in 2003 and overhauled in 2004, the M series is a completely redesigned version of the Pentium III. It was created as a highly energy-efficient CPU for laptops, but it looks certain to form the basis of Intel's future desktop chips, too. At the time of writing the Pentium M forms part of the **Centrino** setup: a term used by Intel to describe a combination of an M processor and wireless networking functions.

▶ **Pentium 4 (Intel)** Released at the turn of the millennium, the Pentium 4 was a totally new design from Intel, and it still dominates the desktop market. It's very good for demanding multimedia tasks such as 3D gaming, streaming audio and video encoding, though not necessarily any better than the usually less expensive Athlon.

▶ **Athlon (AMD)** The first chip to reach a speed of 1 gigahertz, the Athlon (or K7) was originally released to compete with the Pentium III. However, it can handle much higher speeds (over 3 GHz), and various new models, such as the Athlon XP and Athlon 64, have improved on the original, keeping it at the cutting edge. Probably the best-value chip for high-end machines.

▶ **Pentium III (Intel)** The fastest chip available until the Athlon came around, the Pentium III is no longer top of the range, but is functional enough for most non-intensive applications.

▶ **Duron (AMD)** This is a cheaper and only marginally less powerful version of the Athlon. It is an extremely good-value processor, usable for everything other than the most demanding applications.

▶ **Celeron (Intel)** The Celeron is a less powerful version of the Pentium chips, and was designed for use in low-budget machines. It's perfectly capable of most simple tasks, but isn't ideal for multimedia – nor is it as good value as the Duron, the equivalent AMD chip.

What was out there...

If you are looking to buy a secondhand machine there are several other processor types which, though no longer manufactured, are likely to pop up again and again in the small ads. A **Pentium II** – or a **K6**, the AMD equivalent – is perfectly capable of simple tasks such as word processing and Web surfing, but will be sluggish with multimedia. Any older than that (such as Pentium MMX and Pentium Pro) isn't really worth the time of day. You can pick one up practically for free and use it to surf the Net, but don't expect a pleasant experience.

Motherboards

The motherboard, also called the **mainboard**, is the large printed circuit board in a computer that everything else plugs into. If the processor is the brain of a PC, the motherboard is the central nervous system, connecting the CPU with all the other components. Though these large boards don't get mentioned in most computer ads, they are central to a system's **performance and upgradeability**, because they determine what type of hardware can be attached. They also affect **system stability** – computers with decent motherboards tend to crash (temporarily freeze up) less frequently.

The motherboard is full of slots, sockets and ports. There are external ones (see p.56) which stick out of the back of the PC's case for connecting peripherals such as a mouse, keyboard and printer. But there are also internal ones hidden away inside the machine: a slot or socket for the processor, slots for **RAM** chips (see p.33), a floppy disk drive connector, and various slots – **AGP**, **PCI** and **ISA** – for sound cards, video cards, modems and more (see p.44). Hard drives, CD and DVD drives are connected either to **IDE** ports on the motherboard or via a special **SCSI** card (see p.39). At the heart of the board, controlling the flow of data between all these inputs and outputs, is the **system chipset**, which acts like a super-complex traffic-light system.

As well as all these connections, the motherboard also houses: the **BIOS** (**b**asic **i**nput/**o**utput **s**ystem), a set of special codes which tell a computer how to start up and interact with the operating system (see p.237); the **system clock**, which uses a vibrating crystal to control the speed of the PC's operation; and the **CMOS** (**c**omplementary **m**etal-**o**xide **s**emiconductor), which, powered by a little battery, stores the date, time and various bits of information about the hardware setup. Furthermore, many modern motherboards have sound, graphics, networking and modem functions built in.

Motherboards come in various different sizes and layouts called **form factors**, and they are only compatible with cases and power supplies of the same form factor. **ATX** is the current standard, though unique form factors are being used more and more for the production of space-saving PCs.

If you're buying a pre-built PC, you won't get much choice when it comes to the motherboard – usually you won't even be told what brand or type it is – but there are a few things worth asking. If you're concerned about upgradeability, you should find out what type and

speed of **RAM** (see below) the board takes and the maximum amount it can hold. And ask about the **maximum processor speed** that the board can handle in case you ever want a faster CPU. Make sure there are a few spare PCI slots – essential for adding all sorts of hardware, from sound cards to network adapters.

If you're doing a major upgrade of an old PC or building a machine from scratch, you'll need to make sure that you buy a motherboard which is **compatible with your processor** of choice in terms of model (such as Pentium 4 or Athlon XP), connection (socket 7 or slot A, for example) and speed. Also consider the speed of the chipset and the IDE ports, and favour boards made by the **big-name brands**; not only do they tend to come with better manuals and be made to higher standards, but **BIOS upgrades** will be available on the Internet in case any design flaws are discovered in the future.

RAM (Random Access Memory)

RAM is a computer's **short-term memory**, and it allows the machine to get on with its tasks without constantly having to go to the hard drive to retrieve data. Imagine that when you open an application such as a word processor your computer is setting the table for dinner: it goes to the cupboard (the hard disk), takes out cutlery and plates (the application) and lays them out on the table (the RAM). When you begin typing your document it's like putting food on the plates. The more RAM your PC has, the more applications and files it can handle at any one time – and using a computer with inadequate RAM is like trying to serve a banquet on a coffee table.

The amount of RAM that a computer has is measured in megabytes (MB), and is usually a multiple of 32: 64 MB, 128 MB, 256 MB, 1024 MB, and so on. For a computer to run a modern operating system such as Windows XP, 64 MB of RAM is required, but 256 MB is a much more realistic minimum. For really taxing applications, 1024 MB or even more is desirable.

RAM stands for **Random Access Memory**, which describes the way in which any bit of information can be accessed immediately – unlike with a **sequential access** system, such as a video cassette, where you have to go through the data in sequence until you reach the bit you want. RAM is neatly packaged onto small circuit boards about the length of your finger. Along one edge is a row of little metal teeth, or **pins**, which slot into the motherboard (see p.31).

Nearly everything you do on a PC involves data being transferred between the RAM and the processor, and the faster the data moves back and forward, the more powerful the system can be. You can have the fastest processor in the world, but if the RAM and the motherboard can't keep up then you won't be able to exploit its full potential. Accordingly, various types of RAM have been developed over the years, capable of coping with ever-increasing transfer rates.

Most PCs from around 1997 and before use a type of **DRAM** (Dynamic RAM), such as **EDO** and **FPM**. From then until around 2002, the standard was **SDRAM** (Synchronous Dynamic RAM), which is quicker than the older types and comes in three standard speeds: 66, 100 and 133 megahertz, referred to as PC66, PC100 and PC133 respectively. Some PCs are still sold with this standard SDRAM, but most now feature **DDR SDRAM** (Double Data Rate SDRAM), which is a similar technology but effectively doubles the data transfer rate, and comes in various different speeds. If you're buying a new PC, or components to put one together, **don't settle for anything less than DDR SDRAM**.

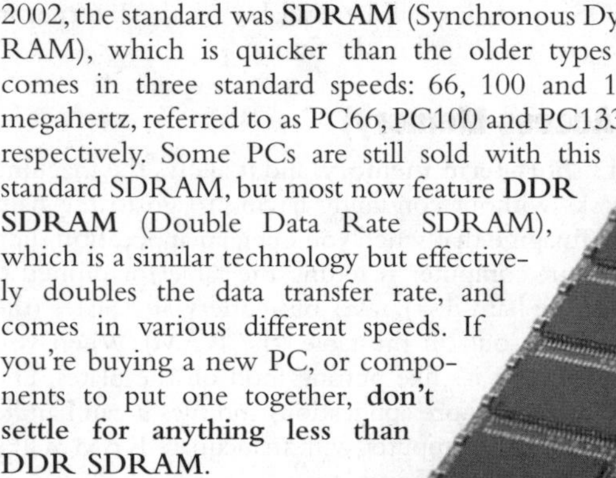

If you want to improve your PC's performance, adding more RAM is often the most effective and inexpensive way to do it, especially if you are struggling to run big applications or lots of programs simultaneously. It's surprisingly easy to install RAM yourself, though you have to make sure you select the correct type for your system. For upgrade instructions and more on the different types of RAM, turn to p.315.

Tech Info

How RAM works

Let's say you're typing the letter "D" into a word processor. The instant this happens, your computer sends tiny bursts of electricity to one of the millions of grid locations within your RAM via microscopic strands of conductive material etched onto the chip. At each of these "address points" is a minuscule **transistor** switch which, when turned on, allows the electricity to charge an energy-storing **capacitor**. When your computer retrieves the data, it recognizes the capacitor's state as either 1 or 0 bits (see p.36): a charged capacitor represents 1 bit, while an uncharged capacitor represents 0 bits. This binary information is grouped into eight-digit strings to represent a single **byte** of data. Our letter "D" is memorized across eight capacitors that read 01000100 (this equals the decimal number 65, which in the globally shared ASCII language represents D). When your computer is turned off, the RAM is returned to its blank state – all the charges drain away and the **data is lost**.

Disk drives and storage

Now it's time to look at the bits of the PC that are used for storing and reading information. Some, like floppy drives, read from and write to removable disks, while others, such as the hard drive, use special internal disks that cannot be taken out. Both of these two store and read data as **magnetic charges**, but there are also various types of **optical drive**, which use light to read from and write to CDs or DVDs.

Not every PC will have all the disk drives and storage devices discussed below, but they can all be added relatively easily. And, though they're most commonly found inside a PC, they can also be added as **peripherals**: external devices that plug into your PC via a cable rather than being housed within the case (see p.51).

Binary, bits and bytes

Humans tend to use the **decimal number system**, which has ten different figures: 0, 1, 2, 3, 4, 5, 6, 7, 8 and 9. The basic language of computers, however, is **binary**, which uses only two figures: 0 and 1. Any number can be expressed in either system, but it will look different. In decimal, a three-digit number consists of three "columns", which (from right to left) represent how many ones there are, how many tens and how many hundreds. The decimal number 132, for example, represents one hundred, three tens and two ones – one hundred and thirty-two in total. In binary, however, the columns mean (from right to left) 1, 2, 4, 8, 16, 32, etc. The binary number 1101, therefore, represents one eight, one four, no twos, and one one – thirteen in total. So binary 1101 is the same as decimal 13.

There are various reasons why computers work in binary. First, computer memory and processors work with transistors, which are effectively little electronic switches which can be "on" (charged with electricity) or "off" (uncharged). These states can be used to represent the 0s and 1s of binary. Also, the binary system leaves less room for error. Electronic signals sometimes get a little bit "fuzzy" or "dirty"; if an electronic signal meant to represent "1" comes in with a little bit more or less power than it should, the computer can have a pretty good guess that what it meant was "1". But if there are more numbers (such as 0, 1, 2, 3, 4 and 5), a dirty signal that was meant to mean 4 could be confused for a 3 or a 5 relatively easily.

The size of a piece of computer data is described in terms of the number of 0s and 1s it takes up. A single 0 or 1 (a single "column") is described as a **bit**, and eight bits make one **byte**. The size of a document or program is always described in terms of bytes.

1 kilobyte (1 KB) = roughly 1000 bytes

1 megabyte (1 MB) = roughly 1000 kilobytes

1 gigabyte (1 GB) = roughly 1000 megabytes

1 terabyte (1 TB) = roughly 1000 gigabytes

So if a hard drive has a capacity of 100 gigabytes, it means it can store 100 billion bytes, which is 800 billion zeros or ones – more than 125 for every person in the world.

Hard drives

The hard drive or **hard disk** (referred to as **C:** in Windows) is the storage depot of a computer – where all the programs and documents are kept. Generally, hard drives are pretty reliable components, providing safe accommodation for your valuable data, but things can go wrong – so it's worth regularly **backing up your files** (see p.288). And because the PC's operating system resides on the hard drive alongside all your other files, if the drive goes wrong you may not even be able to turn on the machine.

If you're looking to buy a new hard drive – either to supplement an existing one or as part of a whole new system – the most obvious and significant consideration is **capacity**. Usually measured in **gigabytes** (often abbreviated to **gigs** or **GBs**), this tells you how much data a drive can hold. Whether you need a high-capacity drive depends on the kind of documents you usually work with. Text documents take up barely any space – a 10 GB drive, for example, could hold the complete texts of around 10,000 novels – so if you're only going to use your computer as a glorified typewriter, you won't need a massive hard drive. Bear in mind, though, that software also occupies space and that you'll probably end up using your machine for more than you thought, so don't settle for anything less than 40 GB and go bigger if possible. If you're the sort of keen computer user who likes to install every program or game you can get your hands on, a decent-sized hard drive is essential. Other drive-fillers are image, video and sound files – so if you intend to store the family photo albums or an MP3 music library (5000 average-sized MP3 files, for example, will occupy around twenty gigabytes of drive space), you can't really have too much room.

If you're buying an extra hard drive for your current system, a standard **internal** model is relatively inexpensive and doesn't require an extra power supply. Installing a new one isn't generally that difficult, but it can be tricky and it does require you to take the case off the machine and perform some minor surgery (see p.330). If you don't feel up to this, any computer shop will do it for you relatively cheaply. Unless your computer has a special SCSI adapter, you should go for a drive with a standard **IDE** – or **ATA** – connection.

If there's no room left inside your PC or you want to be able to move your hard drive between computers, you could consider an **external drive** (see p.70). These are more expensive, sometimes need their own power supplies and generally come with either a USB or FireWire connection. Here are the other factors to consider when choosing a new hard disk.

Tech Info

Inside a hard drive

The hard drive is one of the few components in a modern PC which is actually mechanical – it consists of moving parts – and this makes the speed and accuracy with which it works all the more incredible.

Despite the term "hard disk", a PC hard drive usually contains not just one disk but three, four or more, all stacked up like records in an old-style jukebox. On each side of each disk, or **platter**, is a **read-write head**, which looks like a little record-player arm and stylus. The disks spin about 100 times per second (hence that whirring noise when you open a file) and the heads hover somewhere in the region of a millionth of an inch away from their surfaces, moving back and forward with phenomenal precision to read and write the files. Data is stored as tiny **magnetic charges**, which are created on the special ultra-fine coating of the disks. The amount of information stored on a standard modern hard drive is remarkable, but prototypes are currently being developed which can store as much as 100 GB – around 20 billion words of text – on one square inch of disk surface, so expect pocket-sized reference libraries soon.

A hard drive is completely sealed in its own metal box, because even the tiniest dust particle could play havoc with its delicate mechanism. The bottom of the box is a printed circuit board called the **logic board**, which controls the action inside.

▶ **Physical size** Also called **enclosure size.** This one's simple: 3.5" internal drives are standard for desktop machines and 2.5" internal drives are standard for laptops.

▶ **Data access time** Measured in milliseconds (ms), the data access time is a general measure of drive performance: a shorter time means the drive can read and write information more quickly. It is affected by various factors including **seek time** (the average time the drive takes to find a file), **spindle speed** (the speed at which the disks spin around) and **data transfer rate** (the rate at which the drive can send and receive information). A high-speed drive makes a PC a bit faster and more efficient, especially for those who like to challenge their machine with real-time tasks such as live audio recording.

▶ **Cache** Measured in megabytes (MB). This little memory chip stores the information most recently recovered from the drive, so it can be re-accessed almost instantaneously. The more the better.

IDE vs SCSI

IDE (also known as **ATA**) and SCSI (pronounced "**scuzzy**") are the two most common ways of connecting internal hard drives and CD/DVD drives to a PC. IDE devices are much less expensive and can be attached to the IDE ports found on all modern motherboards. Most boards have two ports, each of which can hold two devices, making a total of four – and more ports can be added with an expansion card if required. In ready-made PCs, the hard drive and CD/DVD drives are invariably connected via IDE.

A single SCSI port – internal or external – can handle many more devices than an IDE port, and SCSI is also marginally better than IDE in terms of maximum data transfer. However, there are no SCSI ports built onto standard motherboards, so you need a special expansion card to attach a SCSI device, and this makes everything a bit more expensive. Also, the performance difference is very small (especially with the more recent fast-transfer versions of ATA, such as **Ultra ATA** or **UDMA**, and **Serial ATA**) so you'll need very high-speed drives and a fast system to notice any improvement in performance with SCSI.

For home PC use, it's easier and cheaper to stick with IDE.

CD drives

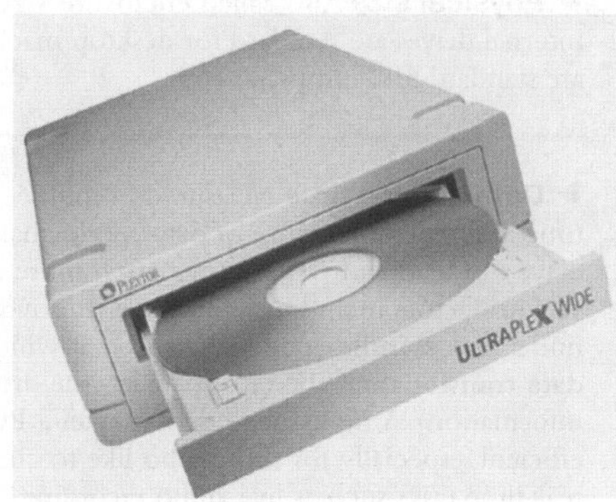

When they became standard around a decade ago, CD drives heralded a breakthrough in home computing. Before they emerged, software and other large files had to be distributed on floppy disks, and a single CD can hold around 500 times more than a single floppy – usually 700 megabytes as opposed to one and a half. These drives also allowed computers to play back music CDs for the first time.

At first, CD drives were "read-only" devices, meaning they could take information from CD-ROMs (meaning Read-Only Memory), which can be used for everything from software and encyclopedias to gardening manuals and foreign language courses. These days, however, most CD drives are **burners** (also called **CD writers, CD-R and CD-RW drives**) and can not only read normal CD-ROMs but also write, or "burn", information onto special types of CD. This is great for backing up data and transferring large folders between computers, duplicating CDs, and burning music discs for use on a conventional hi-fi.

Most CD burners can write information onto two different types of disc. One in the **CD-R** (CD-recordable), which are extremely inexpensive to buy, can be played back in standard music CD players, but can only be written to once: you can't alter the data once it's been written. The second is the **CD-RW** (CD-rewriteable). With these, you can write data and "rewrite" over it again and again, but the discs are slower to burn, more expensive to buy, and usually cannot be read by an audio CD player (though special music CD-RWs are available).

CD drives typically connect to the motherboard via an IDE port, and also have a **digital audio output** that links directly to the sound card for music playback. They're inexpensive to buy and pretty easy to fit (see p.324), so if you're lacking a decent burner you shouldn't have a problem adding one. When buying, there are a few factors and features worth considering. The most important is speed (see box). The others include:

▶ **Internal or external?** Though most people go for an internal drive with a standard IDE connection (see p.39), you could consider an external drive. Though they're more expensive and might need their own power supply, external burners can be used with a laptop or desktop machine, or moved between PCs.

▶ **Buffer size** The buffer size allows the drive to think ahead a little, reducing the chance of failed discs resulting from so-called "buffer underruns". 4 MB or more is preferable, though less is OK if the drive has BurnProof technology.

▶ **BurnProof and SMART-BURN** These technologies greatly reduce the chance of CDs being ruined halfway through recording because the flow of data has been interrupted. Especially useful if you have a slow PC.

▶ **Overburning** Allows you to squeeze a tiny bit more information onto each CD.

CD and DVD drive speeds

Optical drives – DVD and CD – are advertised as being of a certain **speed**, such as "**32x**". This tells us how many times faster they read or write than the speed at which conventional audio or video discs are played. In the case of CD burners, you usually see three numbers, such as **12x 8x 32x**. Generally, the first number refers to the rate at which the drive can **write** onto a CD-R, the second refers to **rewriting** onto CD-RW and the third refers to **reading** from a CD-ROM. Occasionally these numbers are the other way around, but the biggest figure is always the reading speed, and the smallest the CD-RW writing speed. To give you an idea of what the numbers actually mean, a 12x writing speed drive will take around five minutes to burn an average album-length audio CD.

DVD drives

Though they look the same as normal CDs, DVDs work in a different way and can store much more data: between 4.7 and 17.1 gigabytes, depending on whether they're recorded single- or double-sided, and whether each side has one or two **layers**. DVD stands for **digital versatile disc**, though the phrase **digital video disc** is often used because at the moment these high-capacity discs are primarily used for storing and playing back movies.

DVD drives were originally "read-only" units, which only allowed you to extract information from existing DVD-ROM discs and play standard DVD movies, either on your computer monitor or by hooking up to a television, which is possible if you have a **TV-out** or **S-video** socket on your video card (have a look on the back of your machine next to where the monitor plugs in).

However, as with CD drives, older DVD drives have been superseded by **DVD burners**, which are able to write to special recordable DVD discs, and which are now shipped as standard with most decent PCs. Unlike CDs, however, there's a confusing number of different types of recordable DVD discs on the market. Here's the low-down on the main standards.

▶ **"R" & "RW"** As with CDs, a DVD labelled "R" (recordable) can be written to only once, while a "RW" (rewriteable) DVD can be written to many times – up to around 1000. The latter, however, are more expensive and more likely to prove incompatible with other DVD players.

▶ **DVD-R/RW vs DVD+R/RW** Most DVD burners are designed either to use "standard" DVD-R and DVD-RW discs, or a newer, alternative standard called DVD+R and DVD+RW. Both systems are fine, but each has certain advantages ("+" discs, for example, don't require time-wasting "finalizing" after burning) and different compatibility issues (each being incompatible with around five percent of household DVD players). The ideal, then, is to get a drive that can cope with both systems. These are now very common, and are usually labelled **DVD±RW** or **DVD+-RW**.

▶ **DVD-RAM** Now less common than the above, DVD-RAM discs can be written to around 100,000 times. However, they're incompatible with most drives and usually come in protective plastic cases, a bit like floppy disks (though the newer versions look more like standard DVDs).

If you have an old PC without a DVD drive or burner, you can buy one pretty inexpensively and fit it without much hassle. As with CD drives, this basically involves simply screwing the unit in place and connecting the power and IDE cables (see p.39). However, check the speed of your computer's processor before purchasing: if it's slower than around 500 MHz, you'll probably need a special **DVD playback**

Combo drives: CD-R and DVD in one

Many optical drives combine a DVD player/burner with a CD burner. Typically known as "combo" or "multi-format" drives, these are good value and provide all the CD and DVD functionality you need. However, some people prefer to have separate CD and DVD drives, as this is more convenient when it comes to copying information from one disc to another, and because it allows you to use one drive while the other is in the processing of burning.

expansion card to be able to watch DVDs, and it might be worth thinking about upgrading your processor and motherboard.

When choosing a specific drive, the things to look out for are similar to those for CD burners, with **speed** being the primary concern (see p.40). You might also look into **combo drives** (see p.43) if you could do with a new CD burner or you don't have space for an extra drive.

Floppy drives

Most PCs still come with a floppy drive for reading from and writing to old-fashioned 3.5" disks called **floppy disks, floppies** or **diskettes**. The disk itself is housed in a square plastic case, which makes it pretty sturdy. And, once a floppy is formatted (see p.298), which prepares it for duty, it can be used again and again; you can write files to the disk and delete them at will. But floppies are slow, unreliable and have a meagre storage capacity. A standard **high-density** (HD) disk can hold 1.44 megabytes of data on its magnetic surface – around 10,000 times less than some DVDs.

There are, however, other higher-capacity diskettes on the market that have built upon floppy technology. These include the Imation Corporation's **SuperDisk** and the much more commonly used Iomega **Zip** (see p.69).

Expansion cards

Expansion cards are rectangular pieces of circuit board that slot onto a computer's motherboard. They usually deal with a specific type of task such as graphics, sound or Internet connections, and have a rear panel that protrudes from the back of the PC in order to provide **ports** (sockets) for attaching relevant devices. A video card has a port for attaching a monitor, for example, whilst a modem expansion card has a port for connecting a telephone cable. Some cards are very common and found in most modern PCs, such as **modems**, **video cards** and

sound cards (though these functions are very often built into the motherboard). But there are many other types that you could choose to add if and when you require them, such as a **TV card** to let you view television on your monitor, or a **network card** to let you hook up to another computer. There are also cards that exist just to add extra sockets to your system, such as **USB2**, **FireWire** or **SCSI** (see p.54).

There are three main types of expansion cards, and each fits into a different type of slot on the motherboard: **AGP**, the fastest, is specifically for video cards; **PCI** is used for all types of cards; and **ISA** is an older type which is pretty much obsolete today. The most common types of expansion cards are described below. Equivalent devices are also available as external units, or as **PC cards** for use with laptops.

For information about fitting a new expansion card, turn to p.321.

Video cards

A PC's video card, also known as the **graphics card** or **video adapter**, is the piece of hardware that translates computer data into a picture signal and sends it to a monitor. Though this was once a relatively simple task, today's three-dimensional graphics-intensive games and applications require a powerful piece of kit capable of handling enormous amounts of data.

Video cards traditionally slot into one of the motherboard's **PCI slots** (see p.31), but because of the sheer volume of data that passes between the card and the processor, modern cards use a newer slot-type called an **Accelerated Graphics Port** (AGP).

If you're buying a new PC, ensure that it actually has a video card: some lower-end computers come with **integrated video** (video capability built into the motherboard), which is generally pretty pathetic and sometimes a pain to disable if you want to upgrade. When choosing a card you will need to consider several variables. First, **video memory**: a card with more memory can display more colours, at a higher resolution and with a faster refresh rate (the speed at which the image on the screen is replaced). You can scrape by on as little as 8 MB of onboard memory, but if you intend to do any serious 3D gaming or watch DVD movies, 64 or 128 MB is desirable.

When it comes to choosing a particular model, you should also focus on the card's **chipset**, its built-in processor – the difference between two cards made by different brands but with the same chipset is often quite slim. Check out the latest magazine reviews to find out which card is best suited to your needs and price range.

If you want to use your PC to view DVD movies on a regular television, be sure the card has **TV-out** or **S-Video** (though, if not, special external devices are available for turning your monitor socket into a TV-out). Other features found on some video cards include built-in **TV receivers** (see p.50), ports for connecting **digital camcorders** (see p.74) or **digital monitors** (see p.62), and **double-display outputs** for attaching two monitors to a single PC simultaneously.

If you're buying a new video card to upgrade an elderly PC, make sure the motherboard has an AGP slot before shelling out.

Sound cards

Except for the little beep that the machine makes when it starts up, the sound card is responsible for the sound coming out of and going into a PC. It turns digital data from the computer into an analogue sound signal

to be sent to speakers, and turns analogue sound from an input – such as a microphone – into digital computer data. The basic spec of a sound card is expressed as a number of **bits**, which refers to the quality of the digital to analogue converters, or **DACs**; the higher the number of bits, the higher the sound quality – though any higher than 16-bit and you're unlikely to notice too much difference. Two other basic considerations are whether a card is **Sound-Blaster compatible** (important if you want to play games) and whether it's **full duplex** (can record and play back sound simultaneously, which is useful for Internet phone calls and music-making). Also check out the type of **synthesizer** a card uses to create sounds – **wave table** is better than **FM** – and look at what **input and output sockets** it has. Most have three "minijack" sockets for speakers, headphones and a microphone, but some high-quality cards have many more.

For most users a simple sound card will be perfectly adequate – especially if you plan to listen to the sound it makes through the tinny little speakers which come as standard with most PCs. But those who are seriously into music or gaming may want to go for one of the many higher-quality cards on the market. Gamers could opt for a card with **3D audio**, which can be connected to a **surround-sound speaker system** to bring certain games to life. If you want high-quality music reproduction from CDs or MP3 files, go for a 16-bit card, and consider

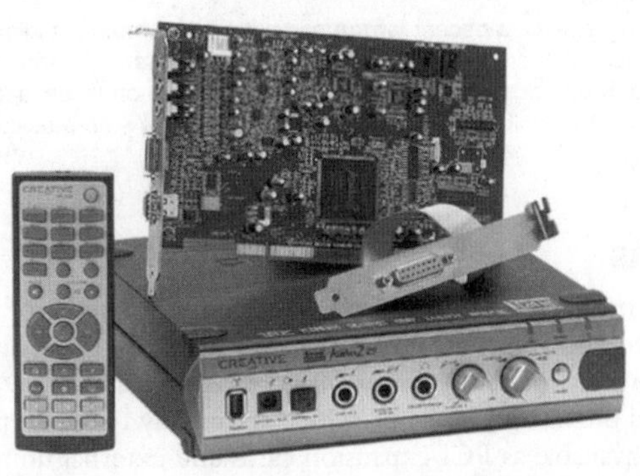

whether there's a **line out** to connect the PC to a hi-fi, or an **optical out** for digital connection to a MiniDisc recorder. If you think you'll be regularly connecting and disconnecting things to and from your sound card, you may want to invest in a card with a **front panel unit**, which lives in one of the bays on the front of your PC's case, providing easy access to many of the sockets.

Building a home recording studio

If you plan to make your PC the hub of an effective home recording studio, you'll need a powerful PC with lots of RAM and a high-quality, 16-bit or better, full-duplex sound card. When choosing a card there are many considerations to take into account. You'll probably want **MIDI ports** for hooking up to keyboards, **phono-lead sockets** for connecting to an amp, and possibly **SP/DIF** ports for linking to a DAT recorder or effects rack.

If you want to deal with samples, get a card with lots of onboard RAM, or consider buying a card that utilizes your system RAM. And if you're interested in recording a whole band, go for a **multi-in card**. These allow you to record several microphones or instruments simultaneously onto separate tracks. You can then edit the tracks individually just like in a real recording studio. Many multi-in cards, and some others, come with either a separate "breakout box" of inputs or a unit that slots into an empty drive bay on the front of your machine; either will save you from having to dig around behind the PC whenever you want to plug something in. Finally, you'll need some **music software** – see p.272 – though decent sound cards often come bundled with a pretty good selection.

These days, even a decent **laptop** can act as a recording studio. External USB devices that do the same jobs as a sound card and perhaps even include a mixing desk, are widely available. For more on these, and all other aspects of PC music hardware and software, visit www.pc-music.com

Modems

Short for **mo**dulator-**dem**odulator, a modem is the piece of a PC used to connect to the Internet. There are various types, the main distinction being between standard "dial-up" modems (built into every recent computer) and broadband modems, which are usually bought separately. Both types are available as PCI expansion cards and external units (see p.198), and there are also special PCMCIA models for laptops (see p.8).

The speed with which modems relay information is measured in **bits**, which shouldn't be confused with **bytes** (see p.36). Standard dial-up modems – which translate digital information into an analogue wave, and vice versa, so that computer data can be transmitted down a telephone line – can theoretically download (receive) information at a rate of 56,000 bits per second (56 Kbps) and upload (send) information at a rate of 33.6 Kbps. However, in reality most regular phone lines struggle to shift this amount of data, especially at peak times, when telephone networks are busy.

Broadband modems – which come in DSL, cable and satellite models for different types of connection – can shift data hundreds of times faster than dial-up ones. However, the actual speed you will achieve is limited by the access plan you sign up for: 512 Kbps (ten times faster than a dial-up connection) is currently the most common broadband speed for home users. See p.198 for more on broadband, or check out *The Rough Guide to the Internet*.

Network and Wi-Fi cards

As we will discuss in Chapter 15, there are two main ways to connect computers together in a LAN (local area network). One is with **Ethernet** cables, and the other is wirelessly with **Wi-Fi**. Modern motherboards usually have an Ethernet socket built in, but if you want

to add either Wi-Fi capability or an Ethernet port to a PC, you'll need to buy a suitable adapter. These are relatively inexpensive and are available in the usual range of forms: internal PCI expansion cards, external USB units and PCMCIA for laptops.

For more information about home networking, including routers (which distribute information between PCs and devices on a network) turn to p.227.

TV cards

A TV card allows your computer to double as a multi-functioning television. They usually come as stand-alone PCI or AGP expansion cards, though video cards with integrated television capability are now quite common. You plug a TV aerial into the socket at the back of the PC, a built-in tuner finds the channels and the card adjusts the picture signal to make it suitable for a computer monitor. With a decent screen and card, the resulting picture quality is excellent – equal to or better than most televisions. And if you have a good speaker system, you can achieve high-quality stereo, or even Dolby surround-sound.

As well as giving you a high-quality image, most TV cards also allow you to do loads of useful, or at least fun, things: record clips or still images onto your hard drive, plug in a video camera, or watch lots of channels at once. They can even be used to receive music in MP3 format and, in the case of cards with digital receivers, they allow you to watch digital stations without buying a special decoder box. One reason for the increased popularity of TV cards is the existence of illegal software that allows the user to unlawfully receive TV stations that should be paid for.

Short of ports?

If you lack certain types of ports on your system – such as USB2 or FireWire – or you simply want more of them than you currently have, you can buy an expansion card to provide them. These are relatively inexpensive, easy to install (see p.321) and offer a neater and cheaper alternative to an external port hub (see p.55).

03 Peripherals

stuff that plugs in

Peripherals are computer devices that live outside the PC's case, and they come in all shapes and sizes, from diminutive key drives to large printers and monitors. This chapter looks at the most important categories of peripherals, as well as the various types of connections and cables used to plug them in, such as FireWire and USB2. You'll find advice on what functions and features to look out for when buying, as well as information, in some cases, on how they work. Thanks to Plug and Play technology (see box overleaf), once you've chosen a peripheral it's likely to be incredibly easy to install: take it out of its box, plug it into the appropriate socket and away you go. If your installation experience isn't quite this smooth, you may want to refer to the Troubleshooting chapter (see p.293).

What's on that CD?

In addition to an instruction manual, peripherals almost always come with one or more CDs. These contain software to make the device work: **utilities** that allow you to operate it and **drivers** to tell your operating system how to control it. For simple peripherals you may not need to use the discs at all, as recent versions of Windows have many software drivers built in. However, you still may need to install the software if you want your new toy to perform all its functions. For example, if you buy a mouse with a scroll wheel and two extra buttons, you should be able to plug it in and use it straight away with the Windows default settings. But if you want to set the buttons up to execute non-standard tasks, you'll need the extra software.

Sometimes you'll also get some free applications with a peripheral, either on separate CDs or bundled in with the utilities and drivers.

Plug and Play

Tech Info

Plug and Play, or **PnP**, is a term used to describe computer devices that immediately recognize each other when connected, without any manual driver installations, physical jumper settings and other techie things. For PC users, this means you can literally just plug in a peripheral and it should configure itself and be all ready to go. The term first appeared as a Microsoft protocol used in Windows 95, though it was soon used to describe equivalent capabilities in other platforms such as Mac OS. In the early days, it was a very unreliable system, and deservedly earned the nickname "Plug and Pray", but today it's pretty reliable, and has developed into an industry-wide system called **Universal Plug and Play** (**UPnP**), which builds on Internet Protocols to allow networked devices (eg a digital camera and a printer) to immediately work together. Combined with the advent of USB and FireWire connections, all this has made adding extra kit to PCs easier than ever before.

Ports and plugs

Peripheral devices connect to PCs in many different ways, using different types of cable and attaching to different types of port (sockets on the computer). You will often have to decide which kind of connection to opt for when you choose a device. In some cases it will make very little difference, but in other cases it pays to choose carefully, as some connection types are faster, more convenient and more future-proof than others.

Always make sure you have the necessary ports for a device before you buy it, but if you do find yourself with a connection problem, don't fret: the cable or adapter you need is almost certainly out there somewhere. And expansion cards are available to add extra ports to your PC (see p.44).

Some peripherals use a dedicated port (PS/2 mouse and keyboards, for example, or VGA monitors), but in many cases you can also expect to be faced with a choice between one or more of the following types:

▶ USB and Hi-Speed USB2

USB, which stands for Universal Serial Bus, is currently the most common connection type for peripheral devices. This clever and easy-to-use technology allows you to attach anything up to 127 peripheral devices to your machine via a single port, either through a hub (like a junction box) or a multi-head cable. Major advantages of USB are that you can **hot swap hardware** – add and remove devices without shutting down your system – and that practically all recent PCs have the necessary ports. Devices can also draw a certain amount of electricity through USB ports, though power-hungry devices will still need their own power supply.

Original USB connections, now dubbed "USB1", are pretty slow: they can only transmit data at around 12 Mpbs (megabits per second), which is fine for most devices but not ideal for high-speed peripherals such as DV camcorders and external hard drives. However, the newer version – Hi-Speed USB2 – is 40 times as fast (480 Mbps), and most new machines come with USB2 ports as standard. USB1 and USB2 are fully compatible: any USB device can be plugged into either, but the speed will be limited to 12 Mbps if either the device or the port is USB1.

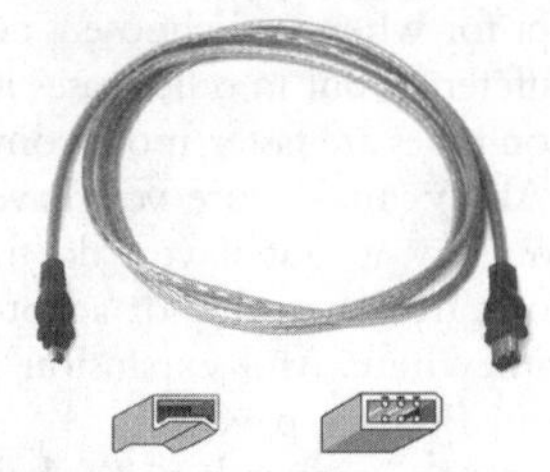

▶ **FireWire/IEEE 1394** Developed primarily for Apple Macs, but now widely used on PCs, FireWire – also known as **IEEE 1394** – is roughly equivalent to USB2, shifting data at up to 400 Mbps and allowing hot swapping of devices. It has become a standard connection for digital video devices, and is also ideal for external hard drives and backup devices. Sony developed their own version of FireWire called **iLink** (which usually uses a smaller 4-pin port and doesn't allow power to be provided from the PC to other device).

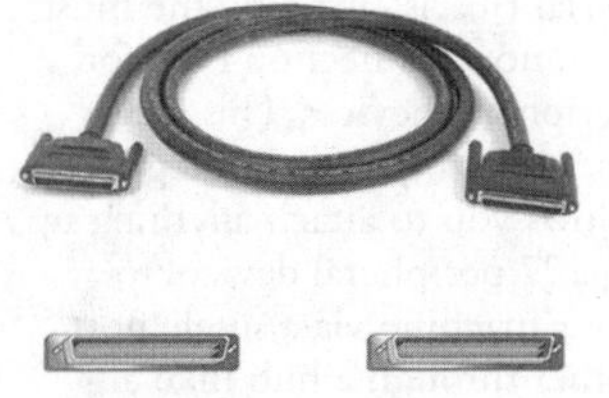

▶ **SCSI** (Small Computer System Interface). The various flavours of SCSI are still used for various high-spec devices, though the system is becoming less common as FireWire and USB2 provide similar speed and flexibility but more convenience. SCSI doesn't come as standard in PCs, so you'll need an internal SCSI interface card to get the port. This adds to the price, though some devices do come with a SCSI card thrown in. One 50-pin SCSI port can control quite a few **daisy-chained** peripherals (devices strung together "in series", each device connected to the next).

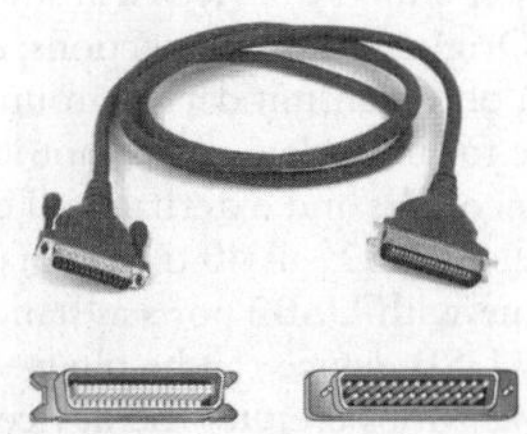

▶ **Parallel** The standard for printers until USB came along, parallel leads have long, flat 25-pin plugs secured by two little screws. They're a bit bulky and awkward but do the job perfectly well.

Hot swap safely

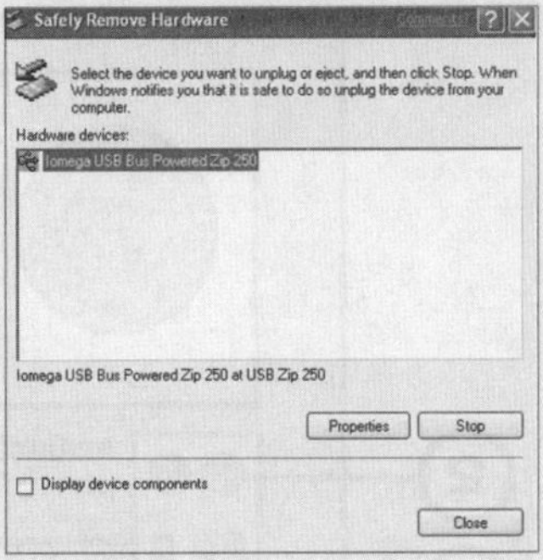

Even though USB "hot swappability" means that you can add and remove devices without having to turn off your system, Windows XP and Me still expect you to follow certain procedures when unplugging USB devices so that they know to stop trying to communicate with them. In the Notification area on the Taskbar, look for the little icon which displays a diagonal green arrow hovering over a grey slab. Right-click it to reveal the **Safely Remove Hardware** dialog box, which contains a list of unpluggable devices. Select the device you want to unplug and then click the **Stop** button. You'll soon get a message giving you the all-clear to pull the plug.

Hubs, switch boxes and plug adapters

There are numerous products on the market – many of which are inexpensive – that can turn a single port into a multi port, or convert one type of plug into another (adapters). **Powered USB hubs** are great for running several devices simultaneously through a single USB port, while **parallel switch boxes** let you alternate the usage of a single port between two or more peripherals. In short, for practically every wiring conflict you encounter there's sure to be a small plastic solution. To find it, check out the hardware retailers listed on p.403 or go straight to a manufacturer such as Belkin:

Belkin www.belkin.com

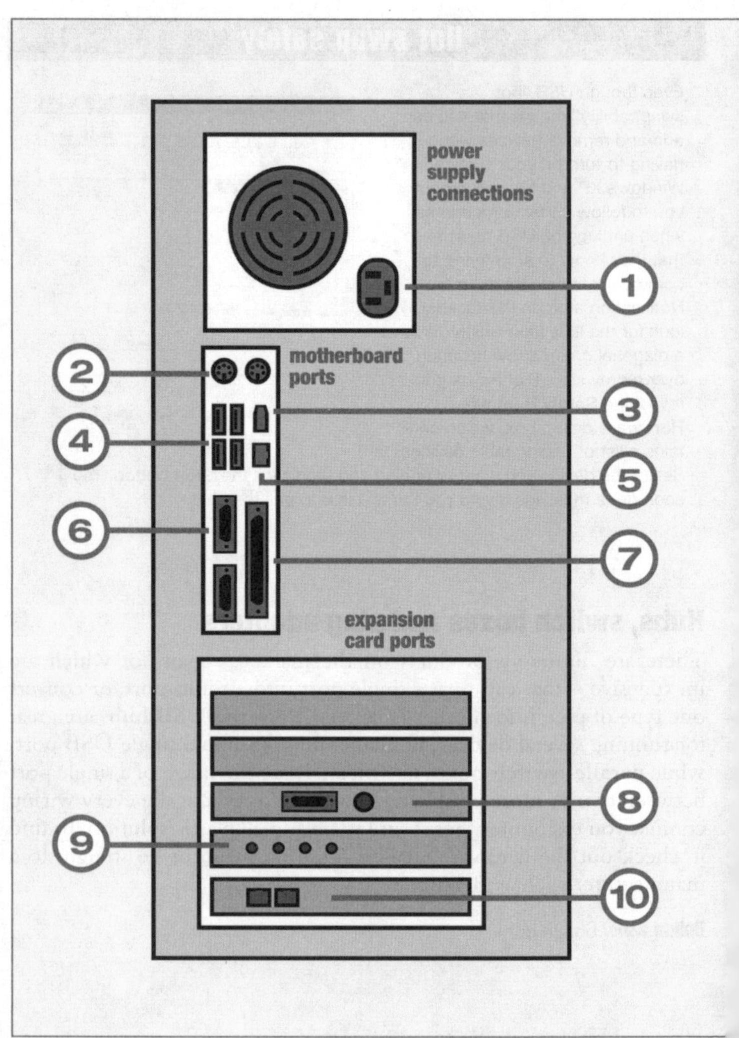
power supply connections
motherboard ports
expansion card ports
1
2
3
4
5
6
7
8
9
10

PC ports and sockets – a typical setup

This diagram shows the back of a typical modern PC. Note, though, that each machine is slightly different, and some ports may be either missing or in a different place. Specifically, many PCs lack the expansion cards shown and have the ports of the sound and/or graphics cards, as well as the modem, built into the motherboard. Conversely, some motherboard lack FireWire and Ethernet and an expansion card is necessary if you want to add these ports.

▶ **1 AC power** Connects your PC to the mains either directly or, preferably, via a surge protector. Usually has a master power switch next to it.

▶ **2 Mouse and keyboard ports** These 6-pin "Mini Din" or PS/2 sockets are generally colour-coded: purple for keyboard, green for mouse.

▶ **3 FireWire port** For DV cameras and external hard drives.

▶ **4 USB ports** Used for all types of peripherals. Additional USB ports can sometimes be found on the front of a PC case, or added via a hub or card.

▶ **5 Ethernet port** for networking with other computers (see p.227).

▶ **6 Serial ports** Secures with two screws; used for old, pre-USB peripherals.

▶ **7 Parallel port** Secures with two screws; used for printers, though most recent printers can also/only connect via USB.

▶ **8 Video card ports** Always includes a VGA socket to connect to a monitor; may also include a digital monitor socket, TV-out, S-video and more.

▶ **9 Sound card sockets** Usually includes four mini-jack sockets for mic, line-in, line-out and headphones; may also feature photo, optical and SP/DIF ports.

▶ **10 Modem ports** Features a phone jack, and possibly also microphone and speaker sockets and more.

The core peripherals

Keyboards

Until recently, all PC **keyboards** looked much the same: tilted grey-beige panels with a specific set of keys. But in the last few years they've become much jazzier, coming in all sorts of shapes and colours. They still feature the same basic set of keys – which includes a number pad, a row of function keys and a QWERTY letter layout – but many also now have **hotkeys** for common tasks such as controlling the computer's CD player, opening an email program or connecting to the Web. These are all things you can do easily with the mouse, but many people like the single-push convenience of a dedicated keyboard function. Another handy key – though also a frightening indicator of Microsoft's global domination – is the **Windows key** (see p.184), which opens the Windows Start menu and can be used for various shortcuts (see p.186). Most new keyboards feature it, but it's worth checking to make sure it's there – it's the one with the flying window icon on it.

For most people, the keyboard that comes with a new PC should be fine. And if it breaks – usually when someone spills a cup of coffee on it – you can buy a new one very cheaply. If you're a serious typist, however, you'll probably want to invest in something more comfortable to

use and which has appropriately springy keys. You may also want to try out an **ergonomic split keyboard**, which has keys for the right and left hands separated and angled to allow for a comfortable arm position. If you're a pathological wire-hater, you may consider spending extra and getting a **cordless keyboard**. You plug a little receiver into the back of the PC and the keyboard, powered by a battery, beams your keystrokes to the receiver unit by infrared or radio waves – making your desk that little bit tidier. These are often sold in a set with a cordless mouse.

Keyboards attach to the back of a PC through either a dedicated 6-pin PS/2 keyboard socket (old PCs have a slightly bigger socket, but cheap adapters are available for fitting a new keyboard) or a USB port. PS/2 keyboards save you using up a USB port unnecessarily and, on older versions of Windows, are more reliable if you have a systems breakdown (since drivers aren't required). USB, however, is a little more flexible and future-proof – many modern laptops, for example, already lack PS/2 ports.

Mice and more

The **mouse** is a brilliantly simple PC input device. You hold it in your hand and manoeuvre it around on a desk or mouse mat, and a little on-screen pointer matches your movements. The standard mouse has two little buttons on its top, which you "click" to select something on the screen. To make your rodent do what you want, you'll need to become fluent in the simple language it understands: that of **left-clicks**, **right-clicks**, **drags** and **double-clicks** (see p.88). Many newer mice also come with a **jog wheel** for "scrolling" through documents, and **extra buttons** that can be set to perform specific tasks in different applications: you could use them, for example, to copy and paste text (see p.191) or move forward and back between webpages.

The mechanics of a traditional "ball" mouse are uncomplicated: as you move it around, the heavy rubber ball that pokes out from the underside moves too, and that motion is transformed into an electronic signal (via rollers) and sent to the computer. The problem with this is that, in the space of covering miles and miles across your desk, the ball can get rather grimy, making the mouse sluggish and unresponsive. This is easy enough to solve with a good scrub (see p.294), but if it keeps happening you might consider upgrading to a ball-free **optical mouse**, which bounces a laser around to track the mouse's movements, and hence has no mechanical parts to get clogged with dirt. Optical mice are also better at working on surfaces which aren't perfectly horizontal or even (eg carpets), but they can be annoying when used on reflective surfaces, which can confuse the laser.

A further option is a **cordless mouse**, which is powered by batteries and sends an infrared or radio signal to a little unit that plugs into the back of the PC. These are great if you don't want your desk cluttered up with wires, but they're also more expensive.

Mice usually connect to either a **PS/2 mouse port**, a **USB port** or (on very old machines) a **serial port** – all of these are perfectly good. Some mice come with an adapter that allows you to connect to different ports.

If the humble mouse doesn't float your boat, there are other pointing devices on the market that do pretty much the same thing, such as:

▶ **Trackballs** These come in various shapes and sizes, and to all intents and purposes are ball mice lying on their backs – you use your fingers to move the large protruding ball. Though some people swear by them, trackballs are not as intuitive as regular mice, so try before you buy.

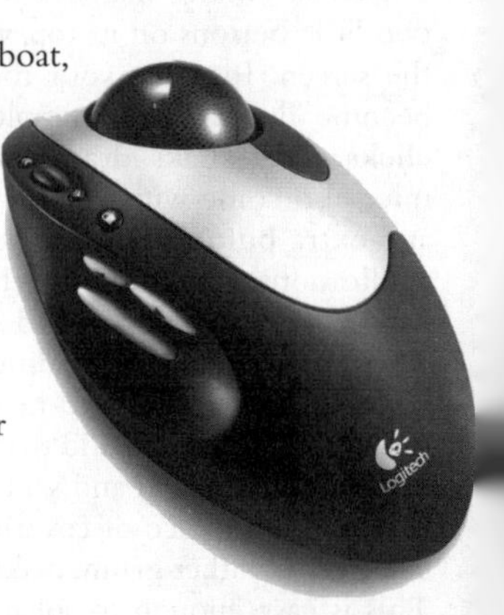

▶ **Graphics tablets** Also known as drawing tablets or digitizing pads, graphics tablets look similar to a rectangular mouse mat but are able to read the movements of a stylus (like a pen) and a puck (a multifunctional mouse used for tracing). Connecting to a PC either via a cable or wirelessly, these high-tech devices are often used by graphic designers, cartographers and illustrators, but aren't especially suited to general PC use. For more, visit a manufacturer such as **www.wacom.com**

www.wacom.com

▶ **Touchpads** It's not a very popular choice, but you can also purchase "touchpads" – the little touch-sensitive pads used on laptops – as external peripherals for desktop PCs. Much more common is plugging a normal mouse into a laptop.

Monitors

In years gone by, computer monitors (also called displays) were either **monochrome** – displaying a single foreground colour against a darker background – or **greyscale**, like a black-and-white TV. Today they can display many millions of colours, and they've also drastically changed in shape and size, with **flat-panel LCD screens** superseding chunky television-like **CRT** models. There are also newer and more expensive options such as **plasma** screens and **monitor/TVs**.

These various categories of monitor are discussed below, but whichever type you go for you'll have to choose what size to go for. This is partly down to the physical size and shape: the diagonal width of the screen, usually measured in inches, and whather it's a standard or widescreen shape (the latter being good for using graphics applications with many palettes, as well as watching DVD movies). However, equally important is the maximum resolution: pictures on a monitor are made up of a grid of pixels (dots), and so a small screen with a high **resolution** can actually fit more information and create a clearer image than a bigger screen with a lower resolution.

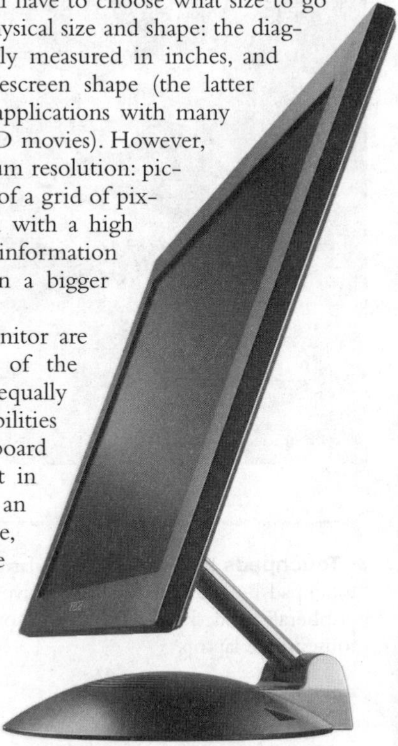

The specs and size of the monitor are obviously key to the quality of the images that you see. However, equally important are the graphics capabilities of the **video card** or motherboard (see p.31), so there's little point in buying a top-end monitor for an old PC, or vice versa. For example, a monitor may be able to cope with a resolution of 2048x1536, but if the video card can only produce 1280x1024, this potential is wasted.

Flat panel displays

Also commonly refered to as LCD screens (liquid crystal display, see box), flat-panel displays are now an affordable alternative to the standard CRT monitor, reflected by the fact that many PC packages include one as standard. Their main advantages are that they take up much less room on a desk (their "footprint" is smaller), they use far less energy than a CRT, emit far less brain-melting radiation and they don't flicker. However, low-end LCD screens often produce a rather dull image when compared to an equivalently priced CRT display, and many have a limited **viewing angle** – the picture becomes impossible to see if you're not looking at it from directly in front.

These days, most flat displays have **TFT** (thin film transistor) screens, which are even more compact than older LCDs. And many also have a digital as well as an analogue input. Digital monitors are generally better

Tech Info

How LCDs work

All **liquid crystal display** (LCD) screens, like those found on flat-panel displays and laptops, consist of a grid of pixels (the dots that make up the image). Within each pixel are tiny red, green and blue **diodes** known as **phosphers** which light up when electricity is passed through them. Every colour you see on screen is created by different combinations of these red, green and blue diodes.

In older LCD screens the electricity is transmitted via two grids of electrodes, with the diodes sandwiched inbetween. Electricity is passed to each pixel in sequence by turning electrodes on and off – this is called a **passive matrix**. This all happens so fast that the eye sees a smooth continuous image even though each pixel is not continually stimulated.

In an **active matrix** display electricity is supplied to the phosphers continuously, rather than as a cycling pulse; this is done with transistors rather than electrodes. The result is that the phosphers spend far more of the time actually being lit, and so the eye sees a far brighter, clearer image. It also means that every time the screen "refreshes" it only needs to worry about altering the state of phosphers within pixels that are actually changing.

Thin film transistor (TFT) screens are a type of active matrix LCD technology with, you guessed it, a very thin film of transistors.

but they tend to be pricier and require a compatible video card (see p.45).

Flat panel displays often come with fancy extras: built-in speakers and microphones aren't anything to get too excited about, though a USB hub built into the display's base may prove very useful. There are even models with built-in webcams for video conferencing.

CRT monitors

CRT monitors are extremely bulky compared to their flat-screened cousins, but they are much cheaper to buy, usually have larger screens and can handle higher resolutions than similar-sized LCDs.

When buying a CRT screen, you'll be told the monitor's **nominal size** (15", 21", etc), which refers to the diagonal distance from corner to opposite corner; but beware, as the **viewable image size** is usually around an inch less. Some dealers quote both specifications, so when comparing screens double-check to see exactly what you're comparing. Also, look out for **Trinitron** or **Diamontron** tubes, which have flatter screens and boast superior image quality and minimal glare.

When shopping for CRT monitors, one key factor is the **refresh rate**. Measured in megahertz, this tells you how many million times the screen can refresh the image each second. Don't go for anything less than 85 MHz, but there's no need to go crazy – anything faster than 100 MHz will make little difference for most tasks. Note that the maximum refresh rate varies according to the resolution setting, so make sure you check the rate at the resolution you intend to use.

Monitor TVs

Any monitor can function as a television if you fit your PC with a TV card (see p.50). However, this doesn't make an ideal substitute for a real TV, not least because you have to have turn on your computer in order to access the TV. If you want to use a computer as your main TV, then, a better option is a monitor with a TV reciever built in. These come with a remote control, can function when the PC is turned off, and feature a scart connection for connecting to a video or other TV-related device.

Alternatively, look into a fully integrated Windows Media Center setup (see p.12).

Plasma screens

Plasma monitors look pretty much like regular LCD displays, but the technology behind them allows for larger screens (up to around 70") and extremely bright colours. However, they're currently prohibitively expensive for home use.

Scanners and printers

Printers

Printers allow you to bring documents, images and webpages from your computer into the real world, so you can scribble on, fax, post or frame your work, just like in the bad old days. Unsurprisingly, these are among the most popular of all computer peripherals, and they've come a long way in the last couple of decades. Choosing a home printer no longer means deciding between a **daisywheel** and a **dot-matrix** – today, for relatively little money, you can buy something capable of producing high-quality colour photographs or churning out hundreds of pages of text per hour. There are so many brands and models on the market that the choice can seem daunting, but once you've asked yourself a few basic questions about what

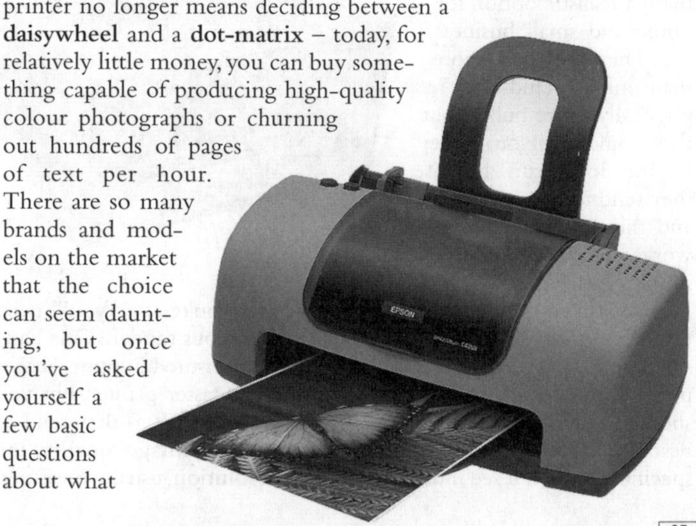

you want to use the printer for, everything becomes much clearer. If you only intend to print the occasional letter and a few colour images, you can pick up something suitable for the price of a meal for two. And most PC packages come with such a model thrown in. But if you plan to create high-quality photos, produce documents in large quantities or print onto large sheets of paper, you'll need to invest in something better.

The first decision is whether to go for an **inkjet** or a **laser** printer. Practically all home users opt for an inkjet: they're cheap, small and good for a variety of uses; practically all of them print in colour; and many can produce photo-quality images. However, if you want something capable of handling an intensive workload you should have a look at laser printers – the fast, smudge-free, high-quality type used in most offices. Both black-and-white and colour models have become significantly cheaper over the past few years, making them a realistic option for home and small business use. They still cost more than inkjets (and they're physically more bulky) but they could save you money in the long run because they tend to be very durable and the cost per page usually works out cheaper once you factor in ink replacement.

Once you've decided which type of printer you're after, you'll need to weigh up the specifications and prices of various models. One consideration is **printing speed**, which is usually measured in **ppm** – pages per minute. Generally a faster figure means a faster printer, but you should always take these numbers with a pinch of salt as they tend to describe a best-case scenario. When it comes to **image quality**, the specification you'll see most commonly is **resolution**, usually measured in **dpi** (dots per inch). A high dpi rating is essential, but resolution alone is not an accurate measure of image quality: other factors, such as the **number of ink colours**, also play a part. Most printers mix all their colours from the four "CMYK" inks (**c**yan, **m**agenta, **y**ellow and blac**k**), but printers with six or more produce truer and deeper colours. And then there's the quality of the **printing heads**. Inexpensive printers often have inferior heads, which can create uneven textures and inconsistent colours, either straight out of the box or after a couple of months' use. The only way to judge a printer properly is to see an example of its printout. If shops in your area don't have examples on display, reading reviews in magazines or on the Internet is the best way forward.

As well as speed and quality of image, it's worth considering what extra features a printer offers. Some can handle lots of different paper sizes, for example, or come with a **feeder reel** so you can print uninterruptedly onto a long sheet of paper. Photo enthusiasts may want a printer with **edge-to-edge capability** or a **memory card slot**, which allows you to print the pictures from your digital camera without even switching on your PC (and sometimes even preview them on a little LCD screen). Some printers even have a built-in scanner (see p.68).

Before you make your final selection, check out the price of replacement cartridges: an apparent bargain may be expensive in the long run if you have to fork out lots of cash every time you run out of ink. If you intend to print out multiple copies of colour images regularly, consider getting a printer that has separate cartridges for each colour, an innovation first introduced by Canon. This way, if you print out ten

Tech Info

How printers work

Inkjet and laser printers work in totally different ways. An inkjet moves printing heads over the page line by line, using heat or force to push tiny quantities of ink from minute nozzles onto the paper. Laser printers, on the other hand, work like photocopiers. They use a laser (or another form of light) to produce a charged image of a page on a cylindrical drum. The drum is rolled through a pool of special toner, which only sticks to the charged areas of the drum. Heat and pressure are then used to transfer the toner from the drum to the paper.

copies of a photo dominated by a rich blue sky, for example, you can replace the blue ink without having to throw away whatever is left of the other colours.

The main printer brands include:

Canon www.canon.com
Epson www.epson.com
Hewlett Packard www.hp.com

Scanners

A **scanner** (or **optical scanner**) is a device that allows you to copy photos and printed documents into your PC so that you can email them to friends, create archives or just mess around with them using a graphics application (see p.266). A scanner digitizes whatever is on a piece of paper into a **bitmap** – an image made up of a grid of points, or pixels (see p.73). Using **optical character recognition** (OCR) software, which most scanner packages now include, you can even turn printed type into computer text and edit it in a word processor.

You can get handheld scanners that look and work like highlighter pens, saving the text as they're passed over a line of type, and there are even printers that double up as scanners. But the most popular type is the A4-size **flatbed scanner**, which is as easy to use as a conventional

All-in-ones: printer-scanner-copiers

If you want to be able to photocopy, or if you simply don't have room for a separate printer and scanner, check out some all-in-one printer-scanner-copiers. These can work out relatively inexpensive when compared to separate machines, and many also offer fax facilities. But they are pretty cumbersome, and you have more to lose if something goes wrong.

photocopier: you place your document on the flat glass scanning bed, close the lid, press the button and off it goes. Flatbed scanners are inexpensive and are regularly included in PC bundles.

Cheap or thrown-in models are fine for most tasks, usually featuring the standard resolution of 600x1200 **dpi** (dots per inch) but versions offering higher quality are available. As with other devices, try to see a scanner in operation before you buy it, to be sure it produces a good image and isn't excruciatingly slow. It's also worth checking that it doesn't have a raised lip around the glass bed, as this can make it hard to scan sections of documents that are larger than A4.

Most scanners connect through a USB port, but not all draw their power directly from the USB cable. This is preferable, as it means you don't have to mess around with a separate power supply.

Removable storage

Zip drives et al

One family of removable storage media are cartridges that look like conventional floppies and work in a similar way, but which hold a lot more data. The most popular type is the **Zip** disk, which is produced by **Iomega** and comes in three formats: 100 MB, 250 MB and 750 MB. Not to be confused with the **zipping** process of file compression (see p.124), the **Zip** disk is a high-capacity floppy diskette and which is only compatible with a special Zip drive (available as an internal or external unit).

Zip disks can be useful for backing up files and data but, overall external hard drives offer far more capacity for your money. And though Zip disks are great for transporting or posting files to a friend with the appropriate drive, CDs do just as good a job, are easy to burn, and are universally recognized.

Iomega's family of products also includes the far more capacious **Rev** drive, which takes 35 GB and 90 GB cartridges. However, you can achieve basically the same results with an external FireWire hard drive – so compare prices and read a few magazine reviews before you buy. For more, see:

Iomega www.iomega.com

External hard drives

A few years ago external hard drives were bulky monolithic devices which required their own power supply and were pretty much tied to your desktop. Some large-capacity drives are still weighty and desk-bound, but today there are also small, light, FireWire or USB2 powered units (around the size of this book) that offer between 40 GB and 80 GB of storage, making this the most quick and convenient means of **backing up or transporting data**. As with internal hard drives (see p.37), the primary consideration when buying is capacity, but if you intend to use it out and about, also consider weight, dimensions and robustness (Lacie's Pocket Drives, for example, feature a defensive rubber bumber around their edges).

Note that hard-disk-based MP3 players such as iPods (see p.78), can also function as portable hard drives.

Lacie www.lacie.com
SmartDisk www.smartdisk.com

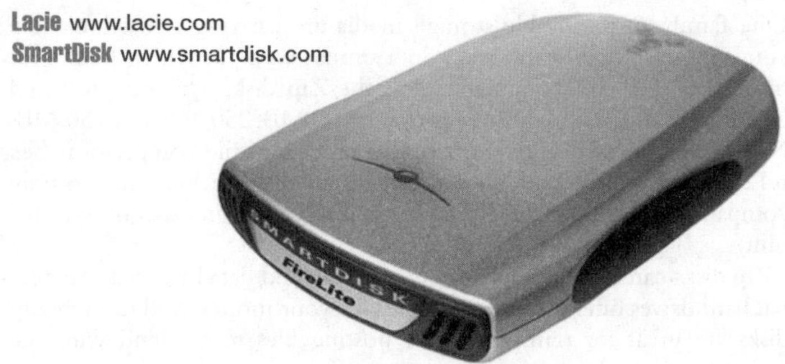

Flash drives

External hard drives are ideal for large files and backing up your whole system. But for transporting documents between home and the office, moving photos between different computers in your house, or for backing up a few essential things that you'd like to always have with you, a **Flash drive** is the way to go. Also known as **key drives** or **thumb drives**, these are vey inexpensive USB storage devices that are small enough to fit on a keyring. They don't require cables or batteries: simply slot one directly into an empty USB port and an icon for the drive will pop up in My Computer, ready to receive or serve up files.

Each key drive contains a small Flash memory chip: the same kind of memory that comes on digital-camera cards. Most drives have a capcity of between 32 and 512 MB at the time of writing, though higher-capacity models come out every few months.

Lots of companies produce key drives – try the online stores listed on p.403.

Cameras

Digital stills cameras

Digital stills cameras (as opposed to digital video cameras) have taken the world of photography by storm in the last half-decade. They look much like old-style analogue cameras, but where the latter capture and record images using film, digital cameras store them as as digital code on a reusable memory chip. This chips usually reside on tiny removable cards, which are known as a **Flash memory** or **SmartMedia card** and which come in a range of storage capacities (usually between 32 and 512 MB at the time of writing).

When the card is full, or whenever you fancy it, you hook up the camera to your PC (usually via a USB port) and download the photos to your hard disk. If you like the results, you can store, edit, email or print your pictures; if you don't, simply delete them.

Digital cameras have numerous advantages over conventional cameras. For example, an **LCD display** on a digital camera's back allows you to set up shots without using the viewfinder and to review photos as you take them, deleting the duds as you go. And because you're not wasting any money on film or developing, you can be as trigger-happy as you like.

With a middle-range digital camera, a decent printer and some photo-quality paper, you can produce very impressive results that will rival those from an average analogue camera and print shop. And if you don't want to invest in a good printer, you can always take your camera to a developing centre and ask them to print images for you – either a whole batch or an individual photo.

When choosing a digital camera, one key consideration is **resolution**, which is usually measured in megapixels: the number of dots, in millions, which make up the maximum-quality image. A million dots sounds like a lot, but only cameras of around 2.5 megapixels or more come anywhere near analogue picture quality. However, read reviews before buying (see p.401), as digital resolution isn't the only factor that will determine image quality.

The number of pictures that you can store on a device depends not only on the memory card used, but on the resolution of the images being taken: the higher the resolution, the more memory is needed to store a single image. Most cameras will offer several different picture qualities, so when you compare image capacity claims, be sure you're comparing like with like.

Most digital cameras have some kind of zoom function, and you will often be quoted magnification specs for both **optical** and **digital zooms**. Ignore the latter (a digital zoom simply enlarges the pixels in the centre of the image to generate a new picture with a lower resolution) and focus on the optical zoom figure. Also check for extra features such as self-timers, remote controls, modes for manual aperture amd focus control, and the availability of different lenses.

Tech Info

Bitmaps

Digital cameras and scanners are used to transfer images into a format understood by computers. They work by translating a "real" analogue image into a **bitmap**, a digital image consisting of a grid of points. How realistic a bitmap looks depends on its **resolution** (the number of points on the grid) and the number of colours and tones recognized (the **colour depth**). A **monochrome** bitmap is the simplest type, each point being represented by just one piece of data: 1 bit means the point is filled, 0 bits means the point is empty. **Greyscale** and **colour** bitmaps, however, are more complex, as each tone and shade needs its own unique string of 1s and 0s to distinguish it from every other. The more colours that can be recognized, the longer the strings need to be – a bitmap in **true colour** uses 24 bits (0s and 1s) to describe each point.

The bitmap files that you'll come across most frequently will have the following **file extensions** (see p.112) on the end of their names: **BMP** (the Microsoft Windows bitmap format), **GIF** and **JPEG** (the bitmap file formats commonly found on the Internet), and **TIF** (the format favoured by profession-als, as it can accommo-date scanned images of any size, resolution and colour depth).

Webcams

Webcams are little digital cameras designed to sit on the top of your monitor, staring unremittingly at you while you work. They are primarily used for making video phone calls – streaming images of you onto the Internet (see p.197) – but they can also be used to record photos and video pictures straight onto your PC's hard drive. Some even have their own **Flash memory**, allowing you to take them out to be used just like a regular digital camera.

When shopping for a webcam, check out resolution and, if possible, see various models in action to judge the quality of the images generated on-screen. Cheaper ones often deliver grainy and generally poor-looking pictures. Like other digital cameras, most connect to your PC via a USB port, and some also feature a microphone (handy for video phone calls).

Digital video (DV) cameras

The final member of the digital camera family is the **DV camcorder**. Though these are still pretty expensive items, prices are dropping fast. You can record in one of two ways: either via a cable plugged into your PC (which passes information straight into your hard drive) or, more commonly, onto **mini-DV tape** in the camcorder, to download later or play back through a regular television.

When choosing a DV camcorder find one that has **DV-in** capability, which gives you the option to export footage from your PC back to the camcorder's DV tape. This is important, because digital video will fill your hard disk very quickly if you have nowhere else to put it – 90 minutes of digital video will eat around 20GBs. Also look out for a model with a decent-sized colour LCD screen, good sound quality (12-bit or better), a variety of both analogue and digital ports, the capacity to take stills photographs, and a **digital image stabilizer** to help you keep your footage wobble-free.

If you intend to get serious about digital video, you'll need a high-spec PC with a decent video card and a sizeable hard drive. For fast transfer between camera and computer, go for a camera with a **bi-directional FireWire port** (if you don't have a FireWire port on your PC, you'll need to add one with the appropriate expansion card). You should also consider what kind of **editing software** you want to use (see p.271).

Multimedia peripherals

Microphones

PCs often ship with a **microphone**, which can be used with **voice recognition software** (you speak and the computer types), for recording snippets of sound to play back or email to friends, or for making video phone calls. Most computer microphones are pen-sized devices on little stands and can be plugged into the appropriate socket on the back of your machine, though sometimes they're built into a headset or integrated into another component such as a monitor or a webcam.

Most are pretty low quality and can be picked up very cheaply. There's little point in buying anything more expensive unless you want to use it for recording music – in which case, bear in mind that the quality of the sound will be limited if you have a poor sound card (see p.46).

Speakers

Until fairly recently, a computer's audio output consisted of little more than the occasional beep and the whirr of a hard drive, but as multimedia capabilities have increased sound has become a serious concern, and PC **speaker systems** have grown to reflect this. As more and more users are playing games, music and movies, tinny little speakers are rapidly giving way to impressive surround-sound systems.

The speakers that come with most systems will be fine for most basic needs, so if you can't be bothered with all this high-fidelity stuff, stick with them. And even if your PC didn't come with any, you can buy a budget pair for the price of a bottle of wine. But if **playing music** is your primary concern – either from CDs or downloaded MP3 files – and you have a decent hi-fi nearby, you should consider hooking it up to your computer. As long as the hi-fi has a spare input (usually labelled **Aux**), this is the cheapest way to get quality sounds out of a PC. All you need is a cable to make the connection: usually a stereo minijack-to-phono lead will do the job.

Serious gamers and DVD fans may not be satisfied with the paltry two channels that stereo provides, however, and investigate **surround-sound speaker systems** instead. Often thrown in with multimedia PC packages, these systems have a number of small speakers (between two

and six) with a subwoofer for bass, and they do an impressive job of reproducing the cinema experience, with bullets flying past your face and explosions rocking your swivel chair. These setups usually come with an amplifier that doubles as a **Dolby Digital decoder**, turning the PC's signal into multichannel sound to distribute between the speakers. But before you spend loads of money on speakers, bear in mind that the sound quality is limited by the capabilities of your sound card (see p.46).

If you're planning on buying a new PC, and cinema-style sound is important, looking into the Windows Media Center option (see p.12).

Gaming devices

If you want to get into gaming and you don't fancy hammering away with just a keyboard and mouse, you'll need some kind of gaming device. These come in a variety of shapes and sizes – some discreet, others outlandish. The best-known device is the **joystick**, but there are countless other devices out there, from **gamepads** (commonly associated with consoles like the Sony PlayStation) to **steering wheels** for driving games.

Whatever type you fancy, look out for **Force Feedback** features, which deliver vibrations and jolts. And take note of the number of buttons and special functions: pricier joysticks, for example, may have throttle levers, pointer buttons for panoramic views and so on, while gamepads may have **gravity sensors**, which are good for flight simulation games.

Also, factor in how solid the different models are: gaming devices take a lot of punishment and inexpensive models don't always last too long.

MP3 Players

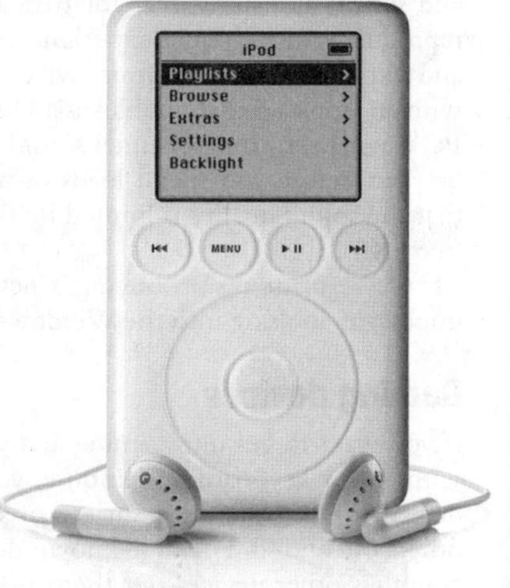

Today, more and more personal computers are functioning as music libraries and players for MP3 and other music files downloaded from the Internet or "ripped" from CD. With high-capacity hard drives now widely available, it's now possible to build up a huge collection of digital music while leaving plenty of room for all your applications and other files.

For home use, you can easily play music through your PC (hooking it up to a hi-fi if required), but if you want to take your digitized music out and about, you'll need an **MP3 player** – the digital-era equivalent of a Walkman. MP3 players fall into two categories: small and inexpensive devices which store up to a few hours of music on a memory chip; and larger more expensive devices which hold tens of thousands of songs on an integral hard drive. The best-known device in the latter category is Apple's **iPod**, recent versions of which are fully compatible with PCs.

When buying any kind of MP3 player, the main considerations are capacity, weight and battery life. Also useful (and now pretty standard) is the ability to hold non-music files, which allows chip-based players to double up as Flash drives (see p.71) and hard-drive-based players to function as external hard disks (see p.70).

For more on iPods and digital music in general, see *The Rough Guide to iPods, iTunes & Music Online*. Or check out the websites of the major manufacturers, such as:

Apple iTunes www.apple.com/itunes
Rio www.riohome.com
Sony www.sony.com

04

Setting up and switching on

turning on for the first time

So you've decided which machine to go for, parted with your money and carted the thing home. Now it's time to worry about setting up and switching on. In years gone by this was a complicated affair: ports and plugs required fiddly little screws, cables were unlabelled and the PC didn't so much spring to life as slowly stagger to its feet as you fed it a bewildering platter of floppy boot disks and cryptic commands. These days things are usually very easy to plug in and machines generally come with their operating systems pre-installed, so all you need to do is find somewhere to put your new computer and turn the thing on. Still there are a few things worth knowing and problems you may encounter…

Finding your PC a home

If you've gone for a desktop system, the chances are you've already decided where you want it to live, but there are a few things worth bearing in mind when choosing a location for your new system. Most obviously, you need a stable surface away from damp walls or condensation-prone windows. It also helps to be near an electrical power point and phone line for connecting to the Internet, though in both cases a standard extension cable can be used.

A surprising number of computers get damaged by electrical surges, which can be caused by anything from dodgy wiring in the home to a bolt of lightning. To protect your machine it's worth getting a **surge protector** – these prevent spikes in the electrical flow reaching your kit, and can be bought from most computer stores built into a **4-way plug** especially suited to PC usage.

If your PC has been delivered on a particularly cold day, give it some time to reach room temperature before switching on. And whatever the weather, make sure the vents and fans on your PC's case aren't covered: your machine will generate a lot of heat when running and even a few sheets of paper left over an air vent can cause a potentially damaging rise in temperature inside the case.

Plugging everything in

Plugging the monitor, keyboard, mouse and any other peripherals into a PC is very simple. Many of the sockets are labelled with little pictures and colour-coded to help you match the correct devices to the correct ports. And even if you don't have icons or coloured ports, connecting everything properly shouldn't be too tricky: most PCs come with an instruction manual containing a labelled diagram of what goes where. If yours didn't, don't worry – with a bit of common sense and the diagram on p.56, you should be able to work it all out. When inserting plugs into sockets, make sure they're correctly aligned, so the pins in the plugs fit into the holes in the sockets. Some require a firm push, but you should never force a computer connection as the pins are quite delicate.

Booting up for the first time

On the front of your machine you will see a couple of buttons: usually a small **reset button** and a larger **power button**. But before you switch on, turn on your monitor so that you can watch the startup sequence on-screen and be sure that your PC is getting out of bed on the right side. And check that your floppy drive is empty before lift-off, as a disk in the drive will confuse the PC when it tries to start up.

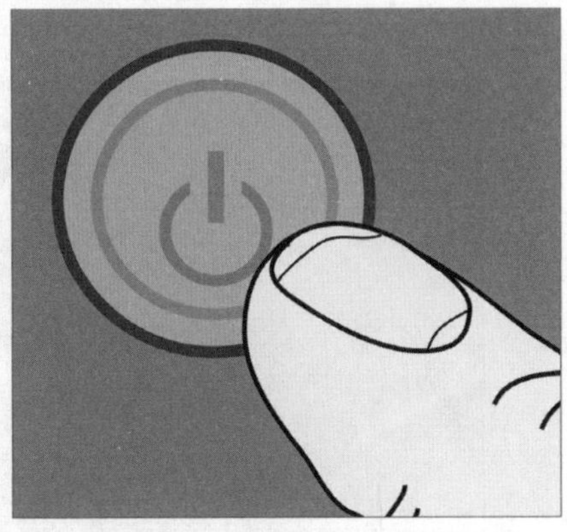

When you push the power button, you'll hear beeps and clicks and a whirring sound as the hard drive starts to do its thing. The cooling fans will be up and running, producing a continuous hum, little lights will be blinking and you'll see figures and specifications scroll by on-screen as your PC checks that all its components are present and correct. If no power appears to be getting through, check on the back of the case to see if the **master power switch** is turned off.

What you see next depends on whether or not you have Windows pre-installed. If you don't, all you'll see is some white text on a black background and you'll have to install the operating system yourself. Your computer should have come with instructions on how to do this, but if not, turn to p.243.

If Windows is present, you'll see a welcome screen inviting you to follow a series of simple self-explanatory instructions to get your machine going for the first time. At some point you'll be asked to enter your name, and the names of any other people you want to register as "users" (you can always add more later). Type in the name you want the computer to know you by: it could be John, John Smith, King

Arthur – it's not a legal document. You'll also be given the option of entering a password. If you do enter one you'll have to type it in every time you turn on your machine, but if you're not worried about other people in your home accessing your files you may choose not to bother (and don't worry, all this can be changed later, see p.146).

After a couple more simple steps, you might also get a little tune and a box prompting you to "take a tour" – click **OK** if you want to and **Cancel** if you don't. Finally, you'll be presented with the basic Windows screen, which will look something like this:

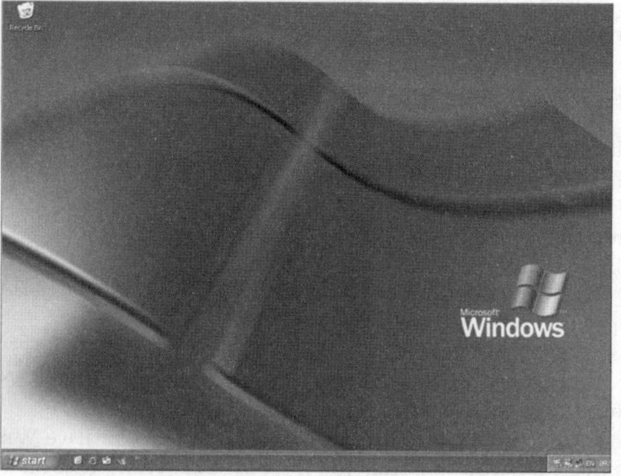

If you've got to this stage, then it's time to start exploring a brave new world of boxes, menus and icons – all of which is explained in Chapter 6 (p.95). But first, here's a couple of things you should know:

▶ **Shutting down** In the same way that your system needs to unpack itself when you turn it on, it also needs a few seconds to put everything away before the power is switched off. This is why your PC should be turned off via the Start menu (see p.105), and not simply by using the power button or mains socket.

▶ **Activating Windows XP** If you've installed Windows yourself, you will be required to "Activate" the software within fourteen days of switching your machine on – otherwise it will stop working until you do. You may also need to do this if you have bought a PC with Windows pre-installed, but usually not. Activation is a Microsoft anti-piracy initiative to stop copies of XP being used by more than one person. It doesn't require you to provide Microsoft with any personal information – not even your name – though during the activation process you can choose to register your details in order to receive updates and the like. To activate Windows XP, go to the **Start menu**, select **Programs** and click **Windows Activation**. If you have a phone line connected to your modem, you can just follow the wizard, and the in-built dialling program will connect to Microsoft and make the activation. If you don't have a phone line connected to your PC, click the **Telephone** option and you'll be given a phone number to call, allowing you to activate your copy with a real human being.

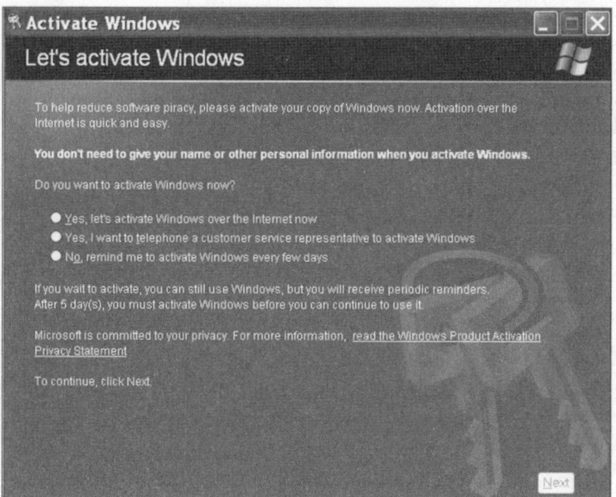

▶ **It's stopped working!** Personal computers, especially those running Microsoft software, can be rather temperamental, and sometimes they **crash** – temporarily freeze up and refuse to do anything at all. This can be very annoying, but don't worry: all PCs crash every so often and usually it's not the result of anything serious.

Occasionally these problems can be resolved by pressing the **Esc** button on your keyboard, but usually you'll have to use the so-called **three-fingered salute**: press the **Ctrl**, **Alt** and **Delete** keys simultaneously. This brings up a box with a list of all the things your PC is currently doing; if you've crashed, one of the items in the list will probably have **Not Responding** written next to it. Click on this entry, and then hit the **End Task** button at the bottom of the box. Usually this will close the application you were using last; you may lose any unsaved work, but your machine will be back in action.

Sometimes, though, this technique won't work, and you'll have to **reboot**, or reset, your PC – start up from scratch. This can be done either with the reset button on the front of the machine, or by pressing the magic **Ctrl+Alt+Delete** combination twice in quick succession. If neither of these work, holding down the main power button for five seconds usually does the trick.

If you crash regularly, it could be that you have insufficient memory for the programs you're running. You could add some more RAM (see p.315), but there are also a few other tricks you can try first. See the chapter on Troubleshooting (p.293) for more information.

working with Windows

05

Know your tools

exploiting the mouse and keyboard

The mouse and keyboard, which fall into the category of **input devices**, form the bridge between you and the PC. They're both extremely easy pieces of equipment to get used to, but you'll only get the most from them if you know how to tweak their settings, use them for shortcut manoeuvres, and, in the case of the keyboard, understand those various keys that serve no obvious function. So, before diving further into the the world of Windows, the following pages provide a rundown on getting the most from these key tools. For more on mice and keyboards, including buying advice and information about alternatives to the traditional designs, see p.58 and p.59.

The mouse

Whether it's a basic two-button rodent or a sportier creature with a scroll wheel and extra buttons, all mice have the same basic function: to move a little arrow, or **pointer**, around the screen, and make selections using various types of **click**...

Left button

The most common move you will make with your mouse is the straightforward click – point to an item, like the Recycle Bin icon which should be on your screen, and press and release the mouse's left button. The icon changes colour to show that it has been selected. Be careful not to move the mouse as you click, or you might select the wrong thing or accidentally move something.

Now try a **double-click**. This is two clicks performed in quick succession, and generally makes an item spring into life. If you double-click the Recycle Bin icon, for example, it will expand to become an active window (to close it again, click on the small "**x**" in the window's top-right corner).

The left button is also used to **drag-and-drop** stuff. Point to an item on-screen, press and hold down the left mouse button and the object will stick to your pointer, allowing you to move it around. When you release the button, the pointer loses its stickiness and the object is released. Try dragging the Recycle Bin icon into the centre.

Right button

Now turn to the right button. The basic **right-click**, as if you hadn't guessed already, is a single click of your mouse's right button. Doing this almost always brings up a small menu of options, called a **mouse menu** (also known as a "shortcut" or "context" menu) relevant to the icon or place where you clicked. Right-clicking the Recycle Bin icon, for example, will yield a menu of options including **Open**, **Explore**

Tips & Tricks

Managing the mouse

You can change the way your mouse pointer looks and behaves in the Mouse Properties box, which you can access via the Control Panel (see p.153). You can alter everything from the size and style of the pointer to the speed required for a double-click. You can even reverse the right and left buttons – useful if you're left-handed. Don't be scared to experiment.

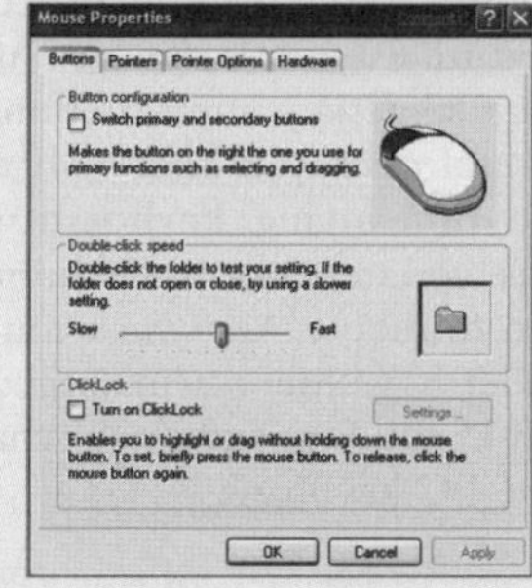

and **Search**. You can either choose something from the menu by pointing to it and clicking the right or left button, or you can get rid of it by left-clicking anywhere else on the screen.

You can also perform a **right-drag**: this is similar to a regular left-drag, but when you release your finger a mouse menu will appear asking you what you want to do with the object you've moved: **Copy Here**, **Move Here** and so on.

Scroll wheels and extra buttons

Most modern mice have a **scroll wheel** protruding from their tops, between the left and right buttons. This can be rolled and clicked to scroll down through the contents of a window, which is especially useful for webpages – hence they're often called "Web wheels". However, wheels can also be fantastically useful when combined with certains keys (see the tip on p.184).

Some mice also have **extra buttons** on their right and left sides. These can be set to do various things, such as cut and paste (see p.191) or moving back and forward in a Web browser (see p.204). However, they all work in different ways: refer to the instructions that came with your mouse to learn about the various options.

The keyboard

It's worth taking the time to acquaint yourself properly with your PC's keyboard. Even if you've been using computers for years, it's likely that at least some keys mean nothing to you, but they can nearly all come in useful once you know what they do. Just as important is learning some time-saving **keyboard shortcuts** (key combinations). These enable you to perform all manner of tasks, without swapping from keyboard to mouse. And, once you're used to using them, you'll probably wonder how you ever managed before. The most useful shortcuts are listed in the Tips and Tricks chapter (p.183). For now, let's take a tour of the PC keyboard.

▶ **1. Esc** (Escape) Backs you out of whatever task you are currently performing. This is your first line of defence if your PC appears to have frozen or crashed.

▶ **2. F keys** (Function Keys) These perform different shortcuts in different programs. **F1** usually opens built-in "help" pages.

▶ **3. Prt Sc SysRq** (known as the Print Screen button) Sends an image of whatever's on the screen to the Windows Clipboard (see p.191), which can then be pasted into a document or email.

▶ **4. Scroll Lock** Turns Scroll Lock on and off. In certain programs, such as Microsoft Excel, if it's on it means that the arrow keys will move the whole page around. As with **Caps Lock**, there's usually a little light above the number pad to let you know whether it's currently turned on or off.

▶ **5. Pause Break** This key was designed for programming use and has no function in most applications. All you need to know is that when clicked along with the **Windows key** it will open Windows' System Properties panel.

▶ **6. Delete** and **Backspace** When dealing with text, **Delete** banishes the character to the right of your "insertion point" (the vertical flashing line that shows you where you are in a document), while **Backspace** deletes the previous character in a line of text. **Delete** can also be used to send selected files and folders to the Recycle Bin in Windows.

▶ **7. Insert** This key determines what happens when you type within an existing line of text. When "on", new text is inserted at the cursor location, pushing existing text to the right. When off, new text overwrites the text to the right of the cursor. It can also be used with the **Ctrl** and **Shift** keys to copy and paste respectively (see p.191).

Notebook keyboards

Space is saved on notebooks by having a small keyboard, and by doubling up the functions of certain keys. The numeric keypad, for example, is usually found among the regular alphanumeric keys rather than having its own distinct section. Normally, you hold down the **Fn** (Function) key if you want to use these numbers rather than the letters. Notebook keyboards can be rather fiddly to use, and many people find the touchpad even more annoying. For this reason, keyboard shortcuts (see p.184) can be are especially useful for notebook users. Adding an external keyboard for when you're at home is another option (see p.59).

▶ **8. Home** and **End** Moves you to the beginning or the end of a line of text – very useful when word processing. In many programs, these keys can be combined with **Ctrl** to jump to the start or end of a document.

▶ **9. PgUp (Page Up)** and **PgDn (Page Down)** Lets you skip up and down a document in chunks, often page by page.

▶ **10. Numeric Keypad** A calculator-like section useful for dealing with numbers. It behaves like the cursor key section when Num Lock is off.

▶ **11. Num Lock** (Number Lock) When "off" the Numeric Keypad section becomes a set of cursor and navigation keys. Usually there's a little light to tell you whether Num Lock is currently on.

▶ **12. Tab** As well as "tabbing" text to the right, this key allows you to jump from one field or option to the next in dialog boxes and online forms. In conjunction with the **Alt** key it can also be used to open Windows and applications.

▶ **13. Enter** or **Return** Opens a selected item; selects the highlighted button in a dialog box; and moves your insertion point down to start a new line of text.

Tips & Tricks

Keyboard settings

As with mice, keyboards have their own dialogue box in which you can make a few settings (such as the speed with which a keystroke is repeated if you hold down a key) and the keyboard layout – if this is set wrong, or your keyboard is from another country, some symbols may be associated with the wrong keys (@ and " for example). You can access these setting via the Control Panel, see p.153).

▶ **14. Caps Lock** Turns Caps Lock on and off; when on, all letters will come out as capitals. There's usually a little light either on the key or above the number pad to show you whether Caps Lock is currently on.

▶ **15. Shift** When the shift key is held down, any letter key will yield a capital letter, while a number or symbol key will result in whatever symbol is on the top half of the key.

▶ **16. Ctrl (Control)** Used in conjunction with other keys, Control can trigger more shortcuts than you can shake a stick at. **Ctrl+A**, for example, selects all items or text in a window. See p.184 for more.

▶ **17. Windows Key** Found on most modern keyboards, this key launches the Windows Start menu. It can also be combined with other keys to trigger a bunch of system-wide shortcuts (see p.184).

▶ **18. Alt (Alternative)** Allows you to access nearly all commands by pressing letter keys (see p.186). Also combined with other keys in many shortcuts.

▶ **19. Alt Gr** Useful for some shortcut combinations, this key does the same job as pressing down **Ctrl** and **Alt** simultaneously.

▶ **20. Mouse Menu Key** Does the same thing as right-clicking with the mouse, yielding a floating mouse menu (or "shortcut menu") for any object or word that your pointer is hovering over at the time.

▶ **21. Cursors** These "arrow keys" allow you to navigate through menus, text, lists, tables, etc.

06 The Windows environment

the Desktop and beyond

So there it lies before you: the Windows work environment. If you're new to it, it may look unhelpful or intimidating, but once you get your head around a few simple principles everything becomes straightforward. This chapter introduces the basics, from the Desktop to dialog boxes.

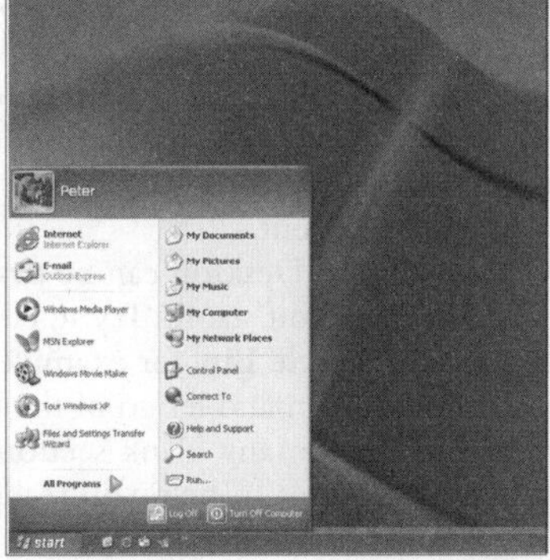

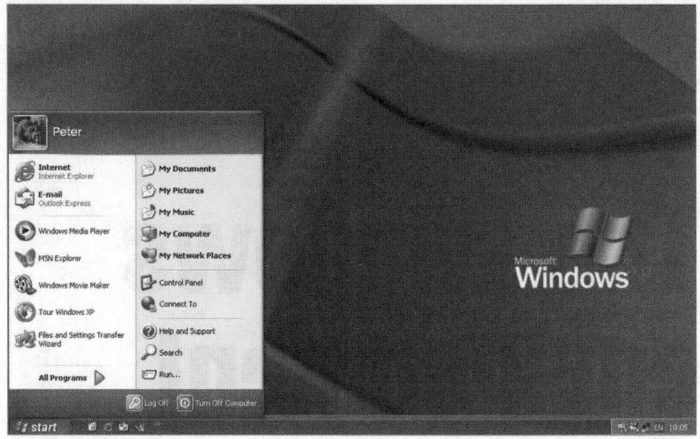

The Desktop

The "background" of the screen is called the **Desktop**. Depending on which version of Windows you are running, it will either be a big blank space or a colourful image (to learn how to change the image, see p.128). The Desktop on a PC isn't that different from a real desktop: it's an open space, with tools nearby, on which you can spread out your work. And just like in the real world, some people have very tidy Desktops, while others' are cluttered and messy. On your Desktop there will be one or more **labelled pictures** called **icons**. These are like ignition buttons that, when double-clicked, start a program or open a document.

Icons on the Desktop can be **dragged-and-dropped:** moved around the screen as you see fit. Try it: click and hold your left mouse button over the Recycle Bin, for example, move it to a blank area in the centre of the screen and let go of the button. Should things get too messy, a right-click on any blank section of the Desktop will yield a mouse menu of options to help you realign and arrange your scattered flock.

Tech Info

What is the Desktop?

Though it seems integral to the whole Windows workspace, the Desktop is **actually just a folder** (see p.112), much like any other, except that whatever gets put in this folder appears on the background (the "Desktop") of the screen. If you're so inclined, you can locate the Desktop folder within your hard drive (in Windows XP, look in your user folder within **Documents and Settings** in the **C:** drive). Drop a file in there and it will automatically appear on the Desktop.

The Taskbar

The most important part of the Windows environment is the grey or blue strip known as the **Taskbar**, which runs along the bottom of the screen. At its left end is the **Start button** – click this to open the **Start menu**, which contains icons for all your programs and more. At the right end of the Taskbar is the **Notification area** (or **System tray**), where you'll see a **clock** and some more icons. Between the two you'll see areas for **Quick Launch** icons and **window buttons** (one for each open window). Let's look at these elements in turn.

The Start button and Start menu

The Start button is, as you might imagine, a good place to start. Click on it and up pops the all-powerful **Start menu**, which is full of icons for programs, document folders and so on. You simply move your mouse pointer to the item you want and click to select it. If you hover over an item with an arrow to its right, you will be offered a further submenu of choices – and so on, until you run out of arrows.

The Start menu is different in Windows XP from all other versions of Windows. In XP (overleaf left), programs are dealt with in a white

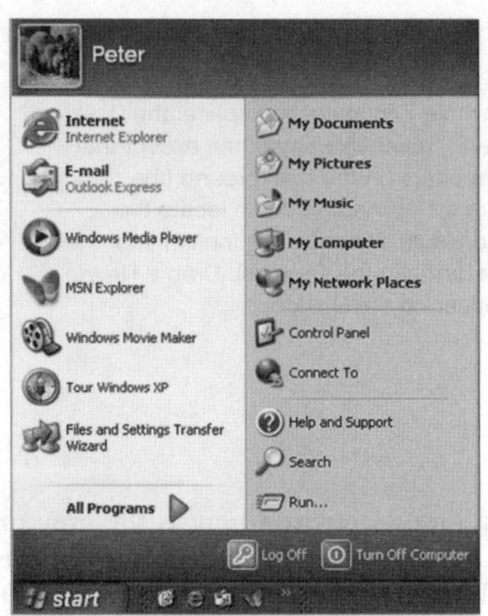

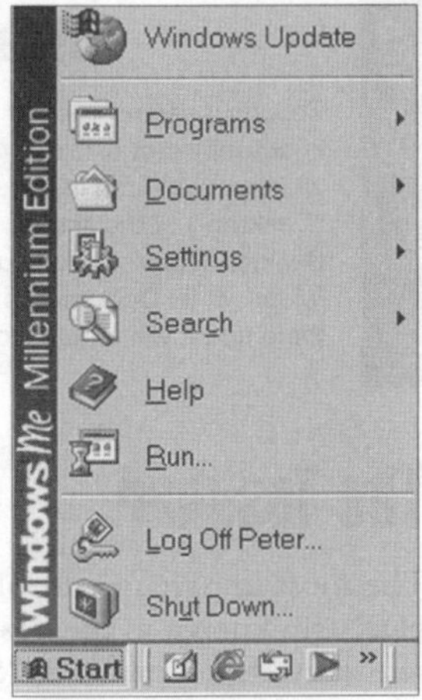

column on the left, which includes **Internet** and **email** applications, a list of your **most recently used programs** and the **All Programs** menu, which expands when you point to it. To the right, a light-blue column contains a bunch of icons for browsing through your files and changing your PC's settings. And at the top of the menu there's a strip, which identifies the current user (see p.145).

In earlier versions of Windows the Start menu is narrower (above right) – with only a single column – but it contains most of the same items and works in basically the same way. As well as an expanding menu containing all your programs, you'll find three others, including **Documents**, which houses icons for the files you most recently worked on.

Quick Launch

Next along the Taskbar, you'll see the **Quick Launch area**. Because the Taskbar is always visible – unlike the Desktop, which can become obscured by open windows – it makes sense to use a section of it to

Tips & Tricks

Hiding the Taskbar

Right-click any blank area of the Taskbar and select **Properties** from the mouse menu. Check the **Auto-hide** option and click the **OK** button. The Taskbar will now only be visible when you move your pointer to the bottom of the screen. For more Taskbar tricks, turn to p.134.

store icons for your most commonly used programs or files. Some program shortcuts are here by default, but you can add and remove items at will (see p.135). When you open Windows for the first time you will most likely see the following items in the Quick Launch area: a blue-cornered square, which usefully minimizes all the windows currently open to let you view the Desktop; a blue letter "e" that launches Microsoft's standard web browser, **Internet Explorer** (see p.200); and a little envelope graphic that starts the **Outlook Express** email program (see p.218). You may also find a colourful butterfly that launches Microsoft's **MSN Explorer browser** (see p.215).

Open window buttons

Any window that you have running will be assigned a corresponding button on the Taskbar. This is what the Taskbar is all about, really: letting you see what tasks, windows or programs are currently running. Try opening **My Computer** from the Start menu or Desktop. Not only does a window spring open, but a button appears on the Taskbar. Now summon another window by opening **My Documents** from the Start menu or Desktop – and another button will appear on the Taskbar. The My Documents window will probably obscure some or all of the My Computer window, and its button on the Taskbar will be indented to show that it's the **active window**, ready to receive instructions. Here's where the Taskbar comes into its own. To bring the My Computer back into view simply click on its Taskbar button: it will rise to the surface and become the active (or "foreground") window.

In Windows XP, when the Taskbar becomes full of window buttons they are automatically **grouped together by type**. For example, if you're surfing the Internet and you have lots of webpage windows open, you may suddenly find that they are all represented by just one button on the Taskbar. Click it and a little menu will pop up containing a list of all the separate windows – select one to bring it to the front.

Notification area

The final stop on our tour of the Taskbar is the **Notification area** – traditionally referred to as the **System tray**. This section contains a **clock** and a selection of icons (in XP you'll need to click the little button with the double arrow to see them all). Many of the icons represent system utilities, such as a virus checker, and they let you know that – while you can't see them running like normal programs – they're doing valuable work somewhere in the background. Usually you can interact with the items in the notification area by single-, double- or right-clicking the icons.

What does this do?

If you do fancy investigating a mysterious icon on the Taskbar – or almost anywhere in the Windows environment – just let the mouse hover over it and a small message, called a **Tool Tip**, will pop up. In the case of an icon you'll be given its name, while other objects deliver either a clue to their purpose or some other handy snippet of information – hover over the clock, for example, and the date will appear. Also try right-clicking an item you're not sure about. This will bring up a menu of choices, generally with one highlighted in bold type. This is called the **default** choice, and tells you what will happen if you double-click on the item.

The window

Whenever you open a document or start a new piece of work, your PC presents you with a framed rectangular space – a window – that fills either part or all of the screen. As in the real world, it offers you a view: of a document, a photo, a webpage, and so on. Once a window is open there are all sorts of things you can do to it.

Try opening **My Documents**, for example. A window will appear with "My Documents" written on the **Title bar** – the strip at the top.

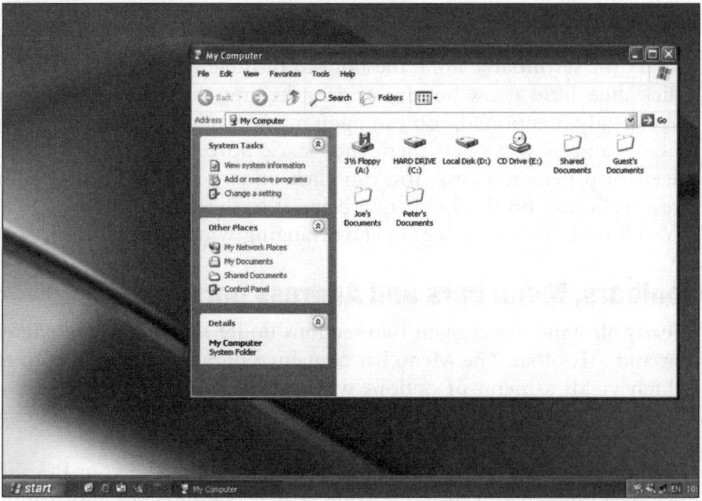

You can move your window around the screen by **dragging**: move your mouse pointer over the Title bar, press and hold the left mouse button, and off you go. And try pointing to one of the window's corners or edges: your pointer will become double-headed, allowing you to resize and reshape the frame.

In the top right-hand corner of your window you'll see three little buttons. The left one **minimizes** – press it and the window will vanish, but its button on the Taskbar will remain. Though you can't see it, the window hasn't actually closed, it's just been hidden, and a single click of the Taskbar button will bring it back into view. The middle button **maximizes** the window to fill the screen, and then becomes a **restore** button that will return the window to its previous size and shape when clicked. You can also maximize, or restore, a window by double-clicking its Title bar. The final button – the one with the "**x**" on it – **closes** the window.

If a window isn't big enough to display all its contents, you will see **sliders** (or **scrollbars**) along the bottom or down the right-hand side. Click their little arrow buttons or drag the grey sliders to reveal more.

As already mentioned, you can open many windows on the screen at once – and as you open them they stack up on your Desktop like sheets of paper on a desk. You can click on any part of a window, or press its button on the Taskbar, to bring it to the top of the pile.

You'll find tips for managing and arranging windows on p.188.

Toolbars, Menu bars and Address bars

Nearly all windows contain two sections under the Title bar: a **Menu bar** and a **Toolbar**. The Menu bar contains a number of words, each of which yields a menu of options when clicked. The Toolbar contains buttons and icons for performing various tasks relevant to the contents of the window.

Windows for navigating the Internet or the contents of your PC also include a third "bar", called the **Address bar**. This provides information about the location of whatever the window contains: an **Internet address** if you're viewing a webpage, and a **name** or **pathname** (see p.115) if you're viewing the contents of a folder or disk drive.

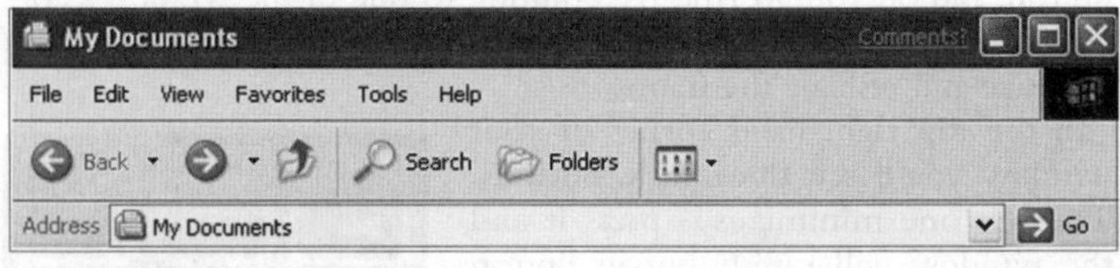

Basic elements

Now you understand the basic architecture of the Windows work area, let's take a look at some of the items you'll come across on the Start menu and Desktop.

▶ **My Computer** This essential item, which resides on the Start menu in Windows XP and on the Desktop in older Windows versions, opens a window displaying an icon for each of your computer's disk drives, allowing you to browse through all the files on your system. As well as offering links to internal hard drives, it also features icons for external storage devices attached to your machine, and any removable media such as CDs or floppy disks. For more on browsing files using My Computer, see p.113.

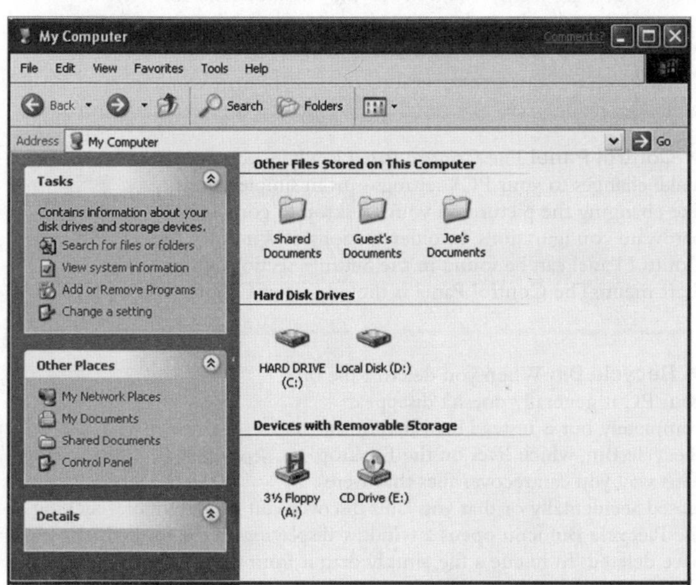

▶ **My Documents** My Documents is the suggested folder for your filing system – a place where you can organize and keep tabs on all your work, pictures, letters, music or anything else. Though you can choose to store your files anywhere you like, My Documents has certain advantages: it's very easy to access and you can instantly "send" any file there using the right mouse button (see p.122).

▶ **My Music** and **My Pictures** These folders live within My Documents, but because they're likely to be frequently accessed, icons for them also appear on the Start menu in Windows XP and Me, allowing quicker access. Again, you can store music and picture files wherever you like, but these folders are handy – and in XP they include links for various relevant tasks such as playing music files, shopping for music online and sending digital photos away to be printed.

▶ **Control Panel** The Control Panel is where you go to make changes to your PC's settings – from simple things like changing the picture on your Desktop to complex hardware configurations. In older versions of Windows, the Control Panel can be found in the Settings section of the Start menu. The Control Panel is the subject of Chapter 10 (see p.153).

▶ **Recycle Bin** When you delete a file on your PC it generally doesn't disappear completely, but is instead banished to the Recycle Bin, which lives on the Desktop. This way, you can recover files that were erased accidentally or that you later discover you need. Double-clicking the Recycle Bin icon opens a window displaying all the files which you have deleted. To rescue a file, simply drag it from the window to the Desktop or somewhere else. Alternatively, the Restore function lets you move some or all of the files back to wherever they were when you

deleted them. You'll find this option by right-clicking a file.

If you find that you are running out of room on your hard drive, emptying the Recycle Bin might free up some space. To do this, open the Recycle Bin window and select Empty Recycle Bin from the file menu or link on the left. You can also right-click the bin's icon on the Desktop and select Empty Recycle Bin from the mouse menu, though this way you don't get a last chance to check which files you're deleting forever.

When the bin contains files its icon is full of rubbish, and when it's empty so is the icon.

▶ **Turn off** and **Shut Down** At the bottom of the Start menu is "Turn off computer", or Shut Down as it's called in older versions of Windows. This is where you go to switch your computer off, giving Windows a chance to pack everything neatly away – turning off your machine by any other method is a bad idea. Click this button and you'll be presented with a few choices. As well as choosing to Turn off, you can select **Restart** (which turns off, then restarts your computer) or **Stand By**, which puts your PC into an energy-saving mode until you press any key or move the mouse.

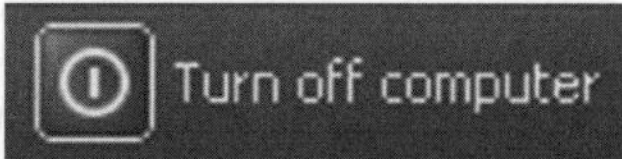

Depending on which version of Windows you're running, you may also see options for **hibernating** (see box), and to **Restart in MS-DOS mode** – an old-school techie option that yields a black screen with a command prompt awaiting your instructions.

Tips & Tricks

Hibernating

Hibernating is a shut-down option that turns off your system but retains a memory of all the programs and windows you were using, so that next time you switch on you can pick up where you left off – a bit like a Stand By for long-term use. In Windows Me, you'll find this option when you click Shut Down. In most Windows XP systems, however, you'll only find the Hibernate button by pressing "Turn off computer" and then holding down shift.

▶ **Log off** If more than one user is set up to use your system (see p.146), clicking here lets you close or hide your tasks and settings to allow another user to log on. In XP this process is pretty quick thanks to the **Fast User Switching** feature (see p.148), but in earlier Windows versions the machine basically has to shut down and restart before offering a new user the chance to log on.

▶ **Help and Support** This feature – just called Help in earlier versions of Windows – launches the Windows help pages, which you can browse or search for information about using and troubleshooting Windows. Hit the **Set search options** link to specify the parameters of your searches through the help files.

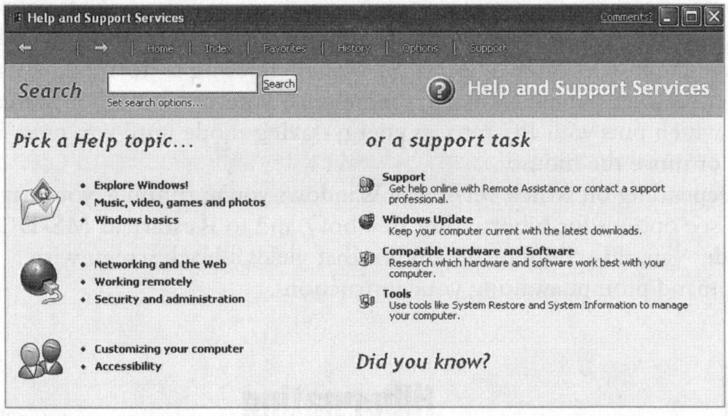

▶ **Search** This option – called **Find** in some earlier versions of Windows – helps you find files and folders on your computer (see p.118). Hitting the F key while holding down the Windows key (see p.184) has the same effect. You can also use this option to search the Web, though it's not the best way to go about it (see p.203).

▶ **Connect to** This XP icon takes you directly to the section of the Control Panel that deals with network and Internet connections. For more on this area, see Get Yourself Connected (p.195).

▶ **My Network Places** If you have home network set up, use this icon to browse the other computers. For more on setting up a network, see Chapter 15 (p.227).

▶ **Run** Found on the Start menu, Run opens a box in which you can start programs and open files by either typing their address on the computer or in some cases by typing their name (try entering "notepad" followed by Enter, for example). You can even enter a website address this way. Though you're unlikely to use Run very often, it can be useful for accessing certain system utilities and kick-starting uncooperative disk drives. It can be summoned at any time by pressing R with the Windows key (see p.184) held down.

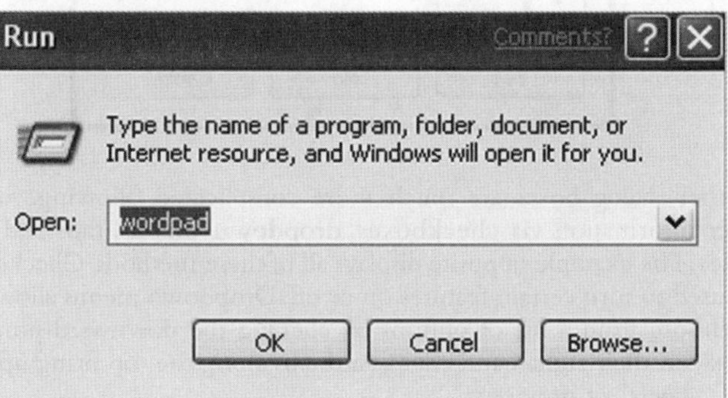

Dialog boxes

Computers, being essentially pretty stupid, can't figure out too much without your help, so they often need to ask questions: "Are you sure you want to do that?", "Do you want to save your work before turning off your computer?", "Where do you want to save the file?" And so on. But computers aren't very good at having verbal conversations – yet – so Windows uses another method to talk to us: the **dialog box**.

The most basic dialog boxes simply pass on information. They pop up, tell you something, and all you have to do is click **OK**. Most, however, are **question dialog boxes**, like the one shown here. These present you with a question and a number of answers, such as **Yes, No** and **OK**. Many also have a **Cancel** button; this closes the box and takes you back to where you were before it appeared.

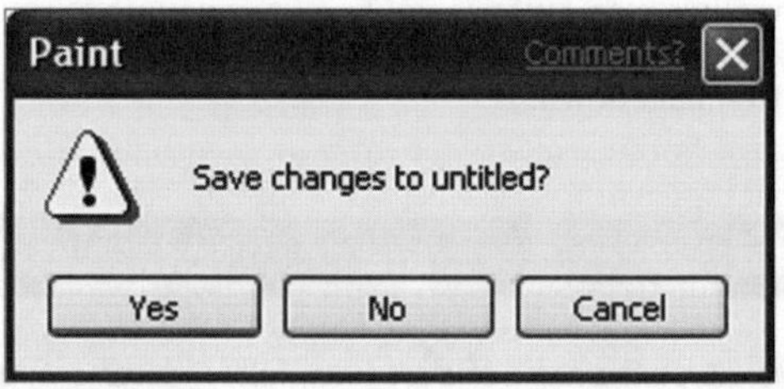

Other dialog boxes are much more complicated, allowing you to enter information via **checkboxes, dropdown menus, tabs** and **text boxes**. The example opposite displays all of these methods. Checkboxes are used to turn certain features on or off. Dropdown menus allow you to choose from a list of options by clicking the downward-pointing arrow on their right-hand edges. And tabs along the top bring up various "sheets" of options.

Many dialog boxes also have two buttons in their top-right corner. The one marked with an "**x**" closes the box (just like in a regular window), while the "?" button will add a question mark to your mouse

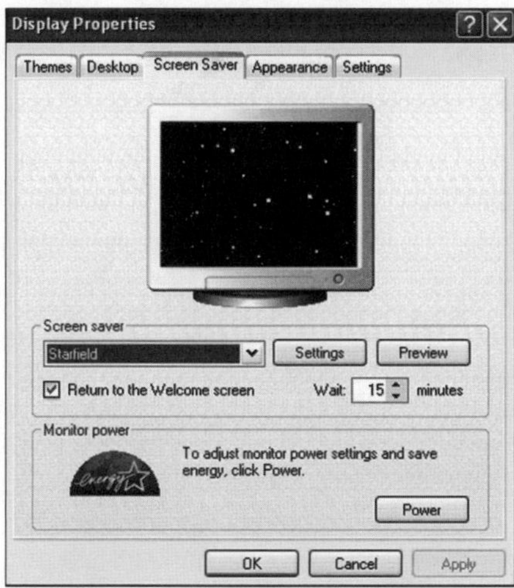

pointer which can be used to get extra help with any element of a dialog box that's puzzling you. Just click on the thing you're not sure about and a frame containing an explanation will appear.

Finally, many dialog boxes also feature an **Apply** button, which sets in motion any changes that you've made in the box without actually closing it. This is very useful if you want to try out various selections before making a final decision.

Tips & Tricks

Answering with keys

In any dialog box, one of the option buttons is highlighted – either by a little dotted line or a dark edge. Hitting **Enter** on the keyboard is the same as clicking the highlighted option. You can highlight the other option buttons in turn by repeatedly pressing the **Tab** key. If you hold **Shift** while you press Tab, you'll cycle through the options in the reverse order.

pointer which can be used to get extra help with any element of a dialog box that's puzzling you. Just click on the ? then on the item you're not clear about and a brief explanation will appear.

Finally, many dialog boxes also feature an Apply button, which lets you see any changes that you've made to the box without actually closing it. This is very useful if you want to try out various selections before making a final decision.

Navigating with keys

In any dialog box, one of the buttons is highlighted, either by a dotted line or a dark outline. Hitting Enter on the keyboard is the same as clicking the highlighted option. You can highlight the other buttons in turn by repeatedly pressing the Tab key. If you hold Shift when you press Tab, you'll cycle through the options in the reverse order.

07

Files and folders

managing your documents

Whenever you save a piece of work that you've created on a PC, you save it as a **file** – more specifically, a **document file**. Software is also stored in files, called **program files**, but a single program may consist of many separate files. If you listed all the program and document files on a PC, there would be literally thousands – so, to keep everything tidy, files are organized into **folders**. This chapter provides tips and advice on working with files and folders: how to browse, find, open, save, move, copy, arrange and delete them. With this knowledge your PC will be a tidier, more efficient and much less confusing place.

Folders

Most folders, or **directories**, are represented by icons that look like plain yellow paper folders, but some have little pictures on them or look completely different. Double-clicking on any folder icon displays its contents in a window.

The folder that you will probably have the most contact with is **My Documents** – a convenient place to keep all your document files. This folder can be accessed via the Start menu or the Desktop, depending on your version of Windows.

Files

The icons of files often look like pieces of paper with folded corners, but they come in all sorts of colours and styles.

When you double-click a file, Windows attempts to open it, and to do so requires the help of a program: if you try to open a music file, for example, Windows will need to open a suitable music application to play it back (and, if its program of choice isn't to your taste, you can set

File extensions

Tech Info

Every file has a special identification tag as part of its name – like a surname – called a **file extension**, though in Windows they're frequently hidden to keep things tidy. Images, for example, may be bitmaps (see p.73), identified by the extension **.bmp**. So if you save a digital photo as "Picture of George", your computer will actually save it as "Picture of George.bmp". You can choose to unhide extensions in the **View** tab of **Folder Options**, which you'll find in the Control Panel (or under **Settings** in Windows 98's **Start** menu). This dialog box also has a **File Types** tab; click here and you can change the default program you want Windows to use when opening different types of files.

a new default application for that file type in Folder Options (see box).

A file icon's appearance gives you a good clue about the type of file you're dealing with and which program Windows will try to open it with. But if you want to know exactly what type of file you're looking at, right-click it and select **Properties** from the mouse menu. (If you're looking at a list of files in a window, selecting **Details** from the **View** menu will also display the file types.) Some types of file are very common and are recognized by many applications, while others will open only in the program that created them.

Anonymous files

If you try and open a type of file that isn't associated with a particular program you'll probably be presented with the **Open with** dialog box, which asks you to select a program for Windows to try opening the file with, or to use an online servive to try and make a decison for you. If you know the file contains an image, try a couple of image programs from the list – but you might not get very far. One possible solution is to drag the file onto an open Web browser window such as Internet Explorer (you don't have to be online to do this). You won't be able to edit anything, but you may be able to view any text or images in the document.

Exploring your computer

Among the most important elements in Windows are the special **Explorer** windows, which, in their various guises, can be used to browse the contents of your computer. Every window that displays files, folders or disk drives is in fact an Explorer window – for example, the windows you get by opening My Computer, My Documents or the Recycle Bin.

To get used to Explorer windows, open **My Computer** from the Start menu (or the Desktop in older versions of Windows). A window will pop up containing icons that represent all the disk drives on your PC and possibly some folders too. The number and type of drives listed depends on your system, but you'll most likely see a floppy drive labelled **A:**, a hard drive labelled **C:**, and a CD drive labelled **D:**.

In Windows XP you'll also see a section on the left of the window that contains links to other places on your computer – such as My Documents and the Control Panel – and various pieces of information and "tasks" relating to any item selected in the window's main frame.

Double-clicking any one of the drive icons or folders will display its contents. Try double-clicking **C:** to view the contents of your hard drive, which is also known as your **Local Disk** (if XP questions your selection, click **Show the contents of this drive** from the blue **System Tasks** menu on the left). You'll probably see a number of folders, including **Program Files** and **Windows**. Again, if you click on these folders, their contents will be displayed in the window.

To "back out" of a folder – go up one level in the tree – go to the toolbar and click the **Up** button, the one that looks like a folder with an upward-pointing arrow on it. You can also click the **Back** and **Forward** buttons to move between windows you've already looked in (just like when using a Web browser – see p.200).

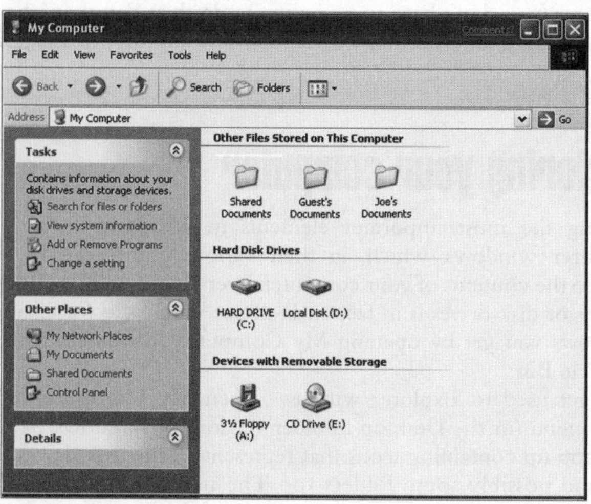

Different views

When you're looking at a list of files or drives, various options are available to change how they are displayed. From the toolbar click the last button on the right (the one with the little coloured square on it), and a menu of options will drop down offering such items as **Icons**, **List**, **Details**, **Tiles** and **Thumbnails**. Try clicking the various options to see which you prefer.

The folder tree

In any Explorer window you can choose to view another column down the left-hand side of the window. Called the **Explorer Bar**, this column can perform various tasks, the most useful of which is displaying the folder tree (or "directory tree"), which provides an overview of everything on your system. To view the folder tree, click the **Folders** icon on the toolbar – or in earlier versions of Windows click the **View** menu and select **Explorer Bar** then **Folders**.

The folder tree is a graphic representation of your folders and drives,

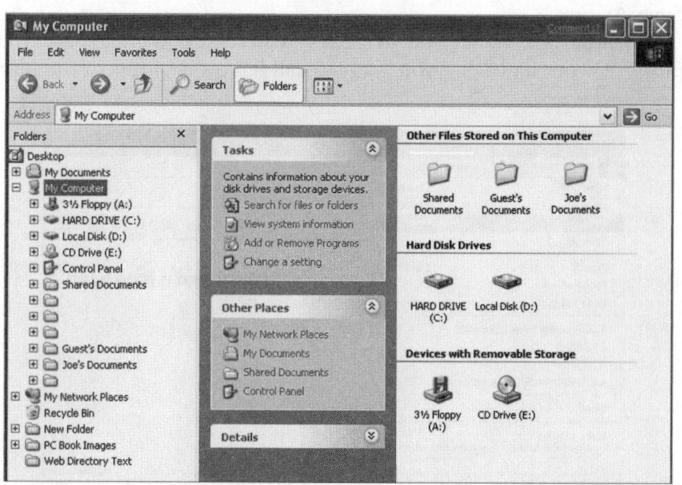

and it works a little like a family tree. Any folder or drive that contains other folders is known as a **parent folder**, and will have a little plus sign (+) next to it. Clicking on the plus sign "opens up" the folder or drive so that you can see its contents; once open, the plus sign turns into a minus symbol (–) which can be clicked to "collapse" the folder. If you click any folder in the folder tree, its contents will appear in the main section of the window. And if you click the Desktop icon that resides at the top of the tree you'll see all the items on your Desktop.

The folder tree is great for seeing the bigger picture, and it's also very handy for moving files around (see p.121).

Saving files

When you open a program and start working on a new document, it doesn't actually become a file until you **save** it. In practically all Windows applications you can save a new document by clicking **Save** in the dropdown **File** menu on the Menu bar. This will bring up a **Save As** box.

This little box allows you to choose where you want to save your piece of work and what you want to call it. You navigate to the place

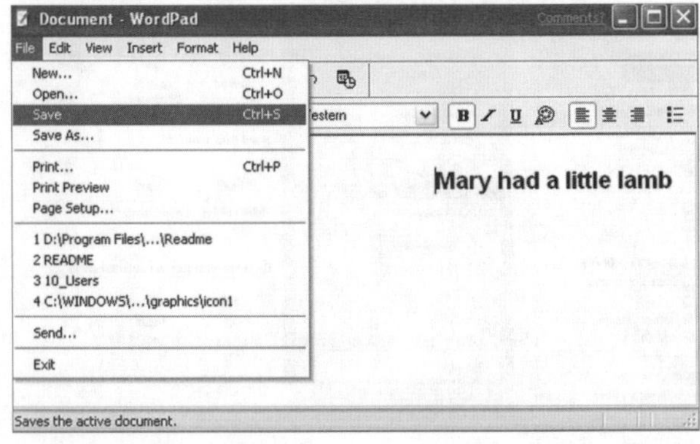

Try This

Create and save a document

If you're totally new to computer and confused by the whole idea of saving and creating files, click the **Start** button, then **Programs** then **Accessories** and selec **WordPad**. This will open the simple word processor that is built into Windows. Type yourself a message and then select **Save** from the **File** menu. From the **Save in** dropdown menu, select **Desktop**, type "Trial Document" as the **File name** and then press the **Save** button. Close the program, and you should find your Trial Document sitting on the Desktop. Double-click it and the document should open again.

where you want to save in the same way that you browse through files in Explorer windows – double-clicking on folders and using the **Up** button – or by using the **Save in** dropdown menu. Once you've found the place where you want to save your document, give it a name by typing in the **File name box** and click the **Save** button.

In the Save As window you'll also usually see a **Save as type** dropdown menu, which allows you to choose a file format from a list of the file types supported by the program you're using. You won't need to use this menu for most saves, but it sometimes comes in very handy. For example, if you write a document in a modern word processor and include some pictures, you could choose **Text Only** from the **Save as type** menu. This would lose the pictures, but the document could then be opened on any computer – including one without a decent word processing program.

Save vs Save As

If you open a file that you saved earlier and make some changes to it, you'll have two saving options – **Save** or **Save As** – both of which you'll find in the **File** menu. If you click **Save** you'll overwrite the old version with the new version. But if you want to save the altered document without replacing the older version, click **Save As**. This will open the Save As box, and you can save the new version with a new name or a different file type.

Searching for files

Sometimes you may want to open a file but have no idea where it is – if you saved a document as "Letter to Sue", for example, but you can't remember where you put it. Don't worry: you can get Windows to search for it, albeit quite slowly. To open the Windows search utility, open the **Start** menu and click **Search** (or **Search** then **Files or Folders** in Windows Me; **Find** then **Files or Folders** in Windows 98). Alternatively click the Search icon on the toolbar in Windows Explorer – it looks like a little magnifying glass hovering over a globe.

The search utility looks different in the various versions of Windows, but they work in a roughly similar way – you enter information about the file, usually its name, and click the **Search** (or **Find**) button. If you can't remember what the file you're searching for was called, explore the various other search options. You could use the **Containing text** option to search for a word or phrase contained in the document itself

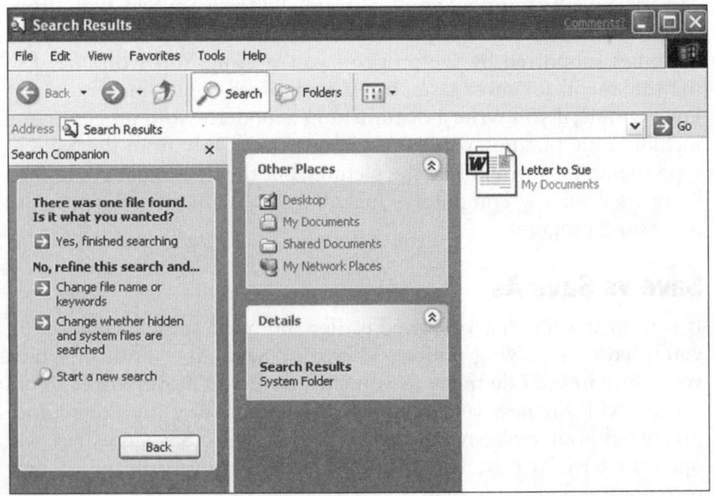

Tech Info

File locations

Though you usually select a file by clicking on icons until you reach it, you may sometimes be asked for the **pathname** of a file – its exact "address". For example, when you use Windows to search for a file, the location of each item found will be displayed in a format similar to this:

C:\Important Work\Letters\Letter to Sue.doc

The letter at the beginning tells you the drive where the file is located, and each backslash refers to a folder. In full, then, the above address tells you that the file named **Letter to Sue.doc** is in the folder **Letters**, which is in the folder called **Important work**, which is on the **C:** drive (the hard drive).

(be warned, though, that this takes ages), the **date** the file was created or modified, or look for its **type** or **size**.

Windows will start trawling through your files, displaying each one that matches any part of the name you typed, along with its location – expressed as a **pathname** (see box). If the locations don't appear, select **Details** from the **View** menu.

If the file you're seeking is found, you can double-click it to open it from there, though you may want to make a note of its location so you can find it more easily next time or move it to a more sensible place.

Doing a full search of your hard drive can take quite a while, but if you have some idea where your lost file is, you can speed things up by limiting the search to a particular folder or drive. To do this, use the **Look in** dropdown menu (sometimes part of the **advanced** options in Windows XP).

Organizing files

Just because a file is saved in one place, it doesn't mean it's stuck there for ever. You can easily delete files, move them around, rename them, duplicate them or create new folders to put them in.

Renaming files

To change the name of a file or folder, simply right-click it and select **Rename** from the mouse menu. Type in the new name, hit **Enter** and the job's done. Alternatively, single-click the icon, click its name and you're ready to type straight over the existing label.

Deleting files

As discussed in the previous chapter, when you delete a file you don't usually get rid of it completely but instead send it to the **Recycle Bin** – which is where it will remain until you either decide to retrieve it or "empty" the bin, erasing the files within (see p.104). There are four main ways to send a file to the Recycle Bin: you can drag it there using your mouse; right-click on it and select **Delete** from the mouse menu; select it with a single-click and then press the **Delete** key on your keyboard; or select it and press the **Delete** button on a window toolbar. Either way, you will be presented with a dialog box asking you to confirm the action.

Tips & Tricks

Bypassing the bin

If for some reason you don't want to send a file to the Recycle Bin but erase it completely (for example if you're deleting a large file to reclaim some disk space), select it, hold down **Shift** and press **Delete**.

Selecting multiple files

It is often useful to select more than one file at the same time – once they're selected you can move, delete or open them all in one go. This is easily done with your mouse and the Control key on your keyboard: hold down **Control**, click on each of the files you want to select and then release the key. Another technique, useful if you're selecting lots of files that are next to each other, is to hold down the **Shift** key on your keyboard and click the first and last files that you want to select – all the ones in between will become highlighted too.

Moving files around

Moving files and folders around is almost as easy as deleting them. One technique is simply to drag a file from one place to another. This works fine, but only if you can see the file and the place you want to drag it at the same time. This is no problem using the **folder tree** view (see p.115): you can view the file you want to move in the right-hand section of the window and drag it over to its new location on the left.

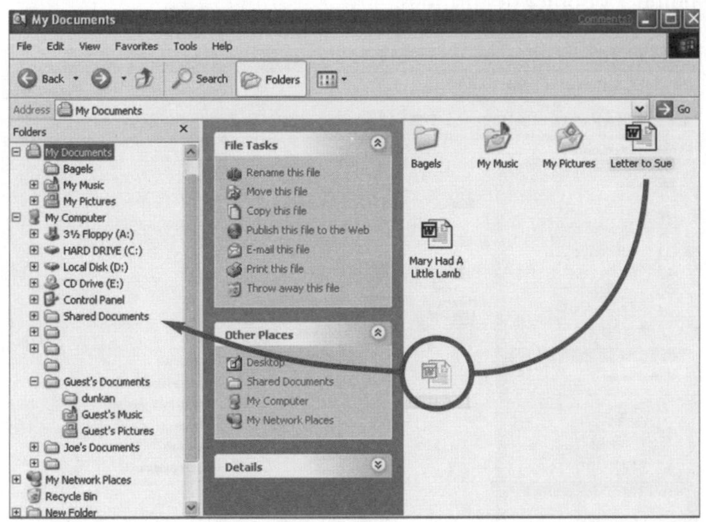

There are various other ways to move files around. In Windows XP you can select one or more files in an Explorer window and click the **Move this file** link on the left-hand side: a box will pop up in which you can navigate to the folder where you want the file to go. Alternatively, you can use the **Cut**, **Copy** and **Paste** commands, which you'll find in the **Edit** menu or toolbar of an Explorer window or in the right-click mouse menu. Select one or more files, click **Cut** and the selected file icons will become faint. Then navigate to wherever you want to put them (by double-clicking on folders and using the **Up** button) and click **Paste**. The file will appear in its new location. If you want to duplicate a file or folder, simply select it and click **Copy**. Then navigate to the point where you want the duplicate copy to appear and click **Paste**.

One last way of moving a file or folder is to right-click it and select **Send To** from the mouse menu (as shown below). From here, you can easily send a file to My Documents, a floppy or CD burner, and a number of other destinations.

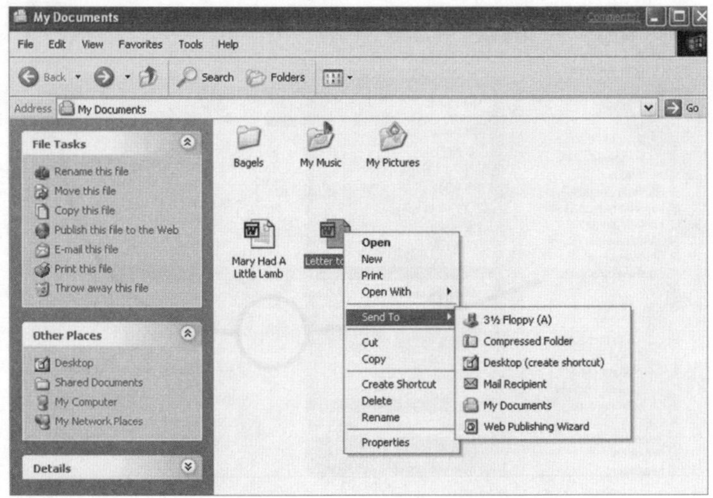

Creating folders

In order to keep all your files organized it's essential to create folders to keep them in. For example, you might create some sub-folders in My Documents to separate office work from personal work, or to keep all the files associated with one project in the same place. You can do this in a number of ways, but the easiest option is to open **My**

Documents, or wherever you want the new folder to appear, then right-click in some empty space and select **New** then **Folder** from the mouse menu. (You can also find the New command in the **File** drop-down menu on the menu bar.)

The folder will appear, its name highlighted in blue and surrounded by a box. Type in the name for the folder and press **Enter**. You can always rename it later by right-clicking it and selecting **Rename** from its mouse menu.

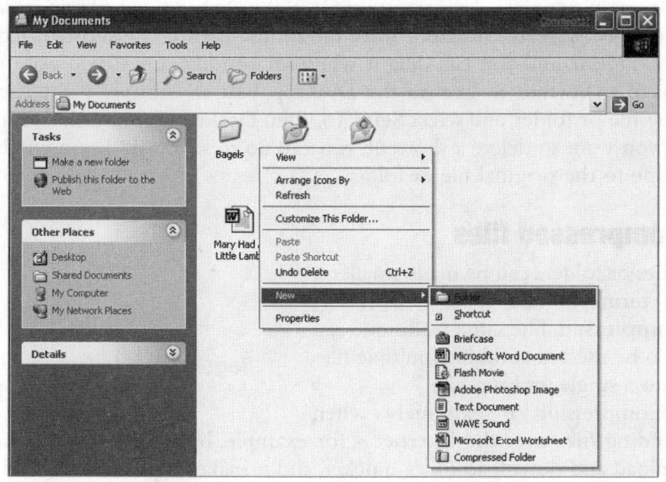

Shortcuts

A **shortcut** (or icon shortcut: not to be confused with a keyboard shortcut) is a special type of icon that acts as a link to a file, folder or program that actually lives elsewhere. This can come in very handy. Say you have a document located deep within My Documents that you use frequently but which is a trek to reach; you could create a shortcut to it on the Desktop for easy access. The same goes for programs:

if you use them regularly, create shortcuts to save you going through the Start menu every time you want to use them.

With a few special exceptions, shortcut icons look identical to the file or folder they lead to, but they have a little arrow on their bottom left corner and they are named **Shortcut to...** when created.

It's easy to create a shortcut: simply right-click on any file or folder and select **Create Shortcut** from the mouse menu. The shortcut icon will appear, and you can drag it wherever you like. Or, if you want to make a shortcut to live on the Desktop, you can simply right-click any file or folder, and select **Send To**, then **Desktop (create shortcut)**. If you want to delete a shortcut, you can do so safely: no harm will be done to the original file or folder.

Compressed files

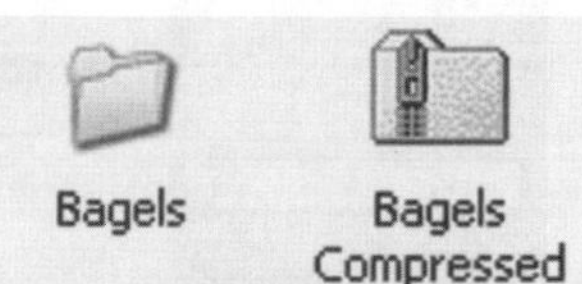

Files or folders can be made smaller – in terms of disk space – by being **compressed**. The same technique can also be used to combine multiple files into a single **archive** file.

Compression is extremely when sending files over the Internet – for example, by email – as it makes upload and download times quicker, and it makes it possible to send a single file instead of lots. However, it's also useful at home if you want to squeeze a bunch of files onto CD or Flash drive, for example, or simply save space on your hard drive.

In Windows XP and Me you can open and create compressed files without any extra programs. Simply place the files you want to compress in a folder, right-click it and select **Send To** then **Compressed File**. A new folder will appear decorated with a zipper graphic which denotes it as the compressed version.

To decompress a zipped files, simply double-click it and the original folder or file will be restored.

If you have Windows 98 or earlier, you'll need a special program to work with compressed files. There are various options out there which can be downloaded from the Web, such as **WinZip** (www.winzip.com), and 7 **Zip** (www.7-zip.org).

Tech Info

How compression works

File compression works in various different ways, but one key principle is the use of repeating patterns. Let's say that you've saved a document containing this text:

every land, every sea and every sky: here, there and everywhere

The compression program would notice that "here", "every" and "and" occur more than once, and would draw up a "key", assigning each of these patterns to something smaller. For example:

every = !, and = *, here = ^

Then it could write the same sentence as:

! l*, ! sea * ! sky: ^, t^ * !w^

In reality, of course, it's not quite this simple, and the computer would use numbers rather than symbols, but this gives you the idea.

The bigger the document is, the more compressible it will be, though the biggest determinant of compressibility is the type of document in question and the method of compression used (some, for example, work by permanently stripping out some data, rather than just rearranging it).

08

Customizing Windows

personalizing your PC

Though Windows isn't the most customizable operating system in the world, you can easily make quite a few tweaks to how things look and work. Whether you want bigger icons, windows of a different colour, or a photograph of your pet rabbit on the Desktop, it only takes a few clicks of the mouse. The following chapter reveals all…

Customize...

Dressing up the desktop

As the big space that you see when you start up your PC, the Desktop is crying out to be customized. This is easily done in the **Display Properties** box, which you can reach either via the **Control Panel** (see p.153) or by right-clicking any empty space on the Desktop and selecting **Properties** from the mouse menu.

The thing you'll probably want to play around with first is the **wallpaper** – the image or pattern that fills some or all of your Desktop. To do this, click the **Desktop** or **Background** tab. The white box at the bottom presents you with a list of built-in patterns or pictures – select one and you'll get a preview on the little screen

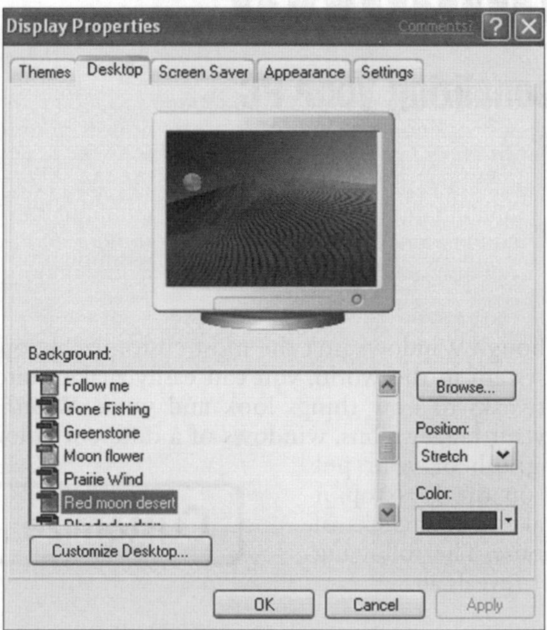

at the top. Alternatively, click **Browse** to select any other image file on your computer (a photo from a digital camera, for example). There is also a little dropdown menu called **Position** or **Display**, where you can choose whether you want the picture to be in the middle of the screen, stretched to fill it, or to be tiled across it (repeated over and over).

Bringing the Web to your Desktop

Assuming you have an Internet connection (see p.198), you can download webpages and place them straight onto your Desktop – this is when the so-called **Active Desktop** gets active. The content you choose will sit on your Desktop even when you're offline, but if you use a webpage that is continually updated, such as a stock teller or sports results service (see box overleaf), you can set Windows to refresh the content as frequently or infrequently as you like.

To add Web content to the Desktop, right-click it and choose **Properties**. Select the **Desktop** tab (click the **Web** tab if you use Windows 98 or Me), click **Customize Desktop**, and choose the **Web** tab. Press the **New** button and type in the address of the page you want (you'll also be invited to visit the Microsoft Content Gallery, where

suggested pages are available). If you have a website or HTML page saved on your hard disk, you can press the **Browse** button to locate and select it. Give it a try.

Once a webpage is on your Desktop, click on its top edge: you can resize or close it just like a normal window. And you can have as many pages as you want in view at any one time – though it can all get a little messy if you're not careful.

All the content currently available for use on your Desktop is listed in the white box in the Web tab – you can display or hide each item by clicking its checkbox. And, if you select an item and then click the **Properties** button, you'll be presented with further options including **Make Available Offline**. This is where you get to download the page (complete with all its links) and tell your PC to refresh the content online at a certain time every hour, day or week.

For more on the Internet, see Chapter 13, p.197.

News tickers and search bars

Another great way to bring the Web to your Desktop is by downloading a **search bar**, which gives you an always-available field for searching your favoured Internet search engine (see p.203). Such programs either integrate into the toolbars of Windows Explorer or sit snugly on the Taskbar. Try one of these freebies:

Google Toolbar http://toolbar.google.com
Groowe Toolbar www.groowe.com
Dave's Quick Search Taskbar www.dqsd.net

News tickers place a thin ticker-tape-like strip along the top or bottom of the Desktop (or as a floating panel). Depending on the ticker you choose, it will display a continuous trickle of headlines, share prices, weather reports, etc. More often than not they are downloadable from, and updated by, a particular site, such as the BBC's, but there are also news aggregating tickers available which draw from multiple news sources. Either way, they're generally free.

BBC News Ticker http://news.bbc.co.uk ("Ticker" link at bottom of page)
CoolTick (stock ticker) www.cooltick.com
Weather tickers http://weather.about.com/cs/weathertools
Freeware tickers www.newfreeware.com/internet/tickers

Windows, icons and the rest

If you don't like the way that the windows on your PC look, right-click the Desktop and select **Properties**. Then select the **Appearance** tab: you'll be presented with various dropdown menus for altering how the whole environment or individual components look.

If none of these options take your fancy, you could try adopting a Windows **theme**, which will change the way in which your entire work area looks and sounds – but expect some extremely tacky and ugly results. In Windows XP, right-click the Desktop, select **Properties** and click the **Themes** tab to see what's available (in earlier versions of Windows select **Desktop Themes** from the **Control Panel**). You can

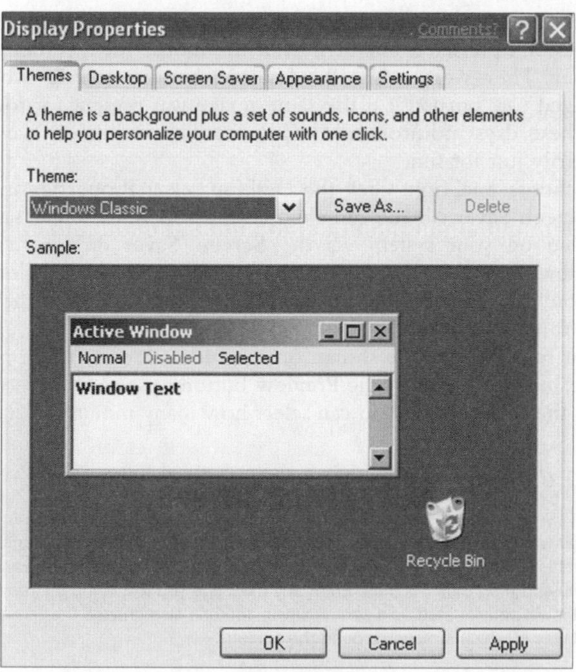

then choose from various themes, including "Science", "Nature" or "Sport" – and others are downloadable from the Web. Should you select "Nature" in Windows 98, for example, you'll see a selection of stones and leaves as your Desktop wallpaper, a butterfly for My Computer, a log fire for the Recycle Bin and stone-coloured windows. You'll also hear the sound of a wind blowing when you turn on your machine, and your screen saver will crawl with hairy caterpillars.

You can go for a partial theme by unchecking some of the options on the right of the box, or return to your previous settings in the Theme dropdown menu.

Screen savers

Screen savers are the animations that appear on your monitor when you haven't pressed a key or moved the mouse for a certain period of time. They were originally designed because screens would be damaged (or "burned") if the same image was present for too long, but these days monitors are a little hardier and screen savers are primarily just for fun.

To choose one, right-click the Desktop, select **Properties** and click the **Screen Saver** tab. You can choose from whichever screen savers are installed on your system via the **Screen Saver** dropdown menu. Windows comes with a selection built in and you can download others from the Internet. You can also choose **none** to disable the screen saver function entirely.

Your selection will be shown on the little screen at the top of the frame, but you can press the **Preview** button to see a full-size version. With the **Wait** option you can select how many minutes of inactivity

Text screen savers

Try This

If you want to create a unique screen saver (or leave a surprise message on a friend's machine), try selecting 3D text in the Screen Saver dropdown menu and then click Settings. Enter any message you like in the text box and it will be animated as a screen saver. You can also change the speed and way in which it moves around the screen.

will result in the computer turning on the screen saver, and a click of the **Settings** button gives you even more options. If you're worried about others having access to your PC when you're away from your machine, select the checkbox. This way, the computer will ask for a password every time someone tries to reactivate the PC when a screen saver is running. In Windows XP, the screen saver password will be the same as your Windows password; in earlier editions, click the **Change** button to choose one.

Screen area and colour depth

The screen resolution is the number of pixels your screen image is made up of. With a high setting, you can squeeze a lot of information onto your screen, but everything will appear very small; with a low setting everything will be bigger, but less will fit. It's worth experimenting with various settings to get the best balance. Right-click the Desktop, select **Properties**, and click the **Settings** tab. Then use the **Screen resolution** slider (labelled **Screen area** in earlier versions of Windows) to change the settings. The maximum available resolution depends on the capabilities of your monitor and video card.

Also in this tab you'll see a **Colors** dropdown menu, which determines the maximum number of colours you can see on the screen at any one time. A high setting such as **True Color (32 Bit)** or **High Color (16 Bit)** is preferable, assuming your video card and monitor are up to it.

It's worth noting that these two settings are dependent on each other – if you select a very high resolution, your maximum number of colours may drop, and vice versa.

Tweaking the Taskbar

You can make numerous modifications to the way the Taskbar looks and works. The first thing to experiment with is where you want the Taskbar to live – instead of being stuck at the bottom of the screen, you can place it on either side or at the top. Click and hold the left mouse button over a blank space on the Taskbar and drag the whole bar to one of the other screen edges. Give it a go; you can always move it back again.

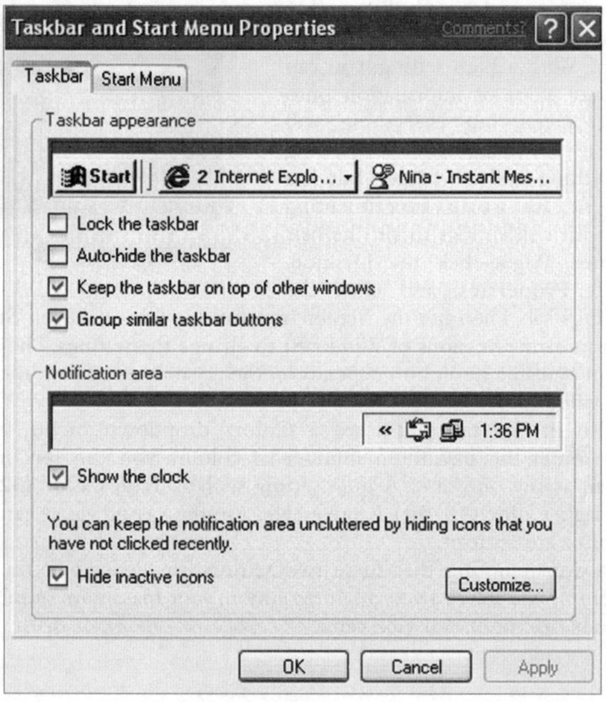

The second thing to decide is whether you always want the Taskbar in view. After all, if you want to maximize your screen area for a particular task, it can get in the way. Go to the edge where the Taskbar meets the Desktop, and your mouse pointer will turn into a double-headed arrow with which you can drag the whole Taskbar to make it as small or as big as you like. To restore it to its original size, simply drag it back again.

Another, more useful, option is to have the Taskbar automatically hide itself, only appearing when your pointer drifts close to the edge of the screen where it lives – or when you hit the **Windows** button on your keyboard. To do this, right-click on any blank portion of the Taskbar and select **Properties** from the mouse menu to bring up the **Taskbar and Start Menu Properties** dialog box. Click the **Auto-hide** checkbox and then click **Apply**.

While you have this dialog box open, browse the other options. You can also choose to hide the **clock**, set it so that windows can go "on top" of the Taskbar, and so on.

Notification area icons

In Windows XP, unused icons in the Notification area – sometimes called **tray icons** – are automatically hidden unless you turn this option off in Taskbar and Start Menu Properties (see above). In older versions of Windows this option isn't available, but you may be able to hide some of them. Try double-clicking a few icons. Some will launch a program, while others will present you with a Properties window. Search around and you may well find a **Display tray icon** checkbox; uncheck it and off goes the icon. If you don't find this option, or if you get fazed by some techie-looking stuff, just press **Cancel**.

Quick Launch area

The chances are that next to your Start button you have a number of little icons on the Taskbar for Outlook Express, Internet Explorer and so on. As mentioned in Chapter 6, this is the **Quick Launch Toolbar**, which is designed to house shortcuts for commonly used programs. If there's an icon here for a program that you never use, simply right-click it and select **Delete** – the icons are only shortcuts (see p.123), so deleting them won't do any harm to the actual program. And it's just as easy to add a program to your Quick Launch area. Browse through the programs in your Start menu until you get to the one you want to add. Right-click it and select **Send To**, then **Desktop (create shortcut)**. A new icon labelled **Shortcut to...** will appear on the Desktop, which you can drag straight onto the Quick Launch area. You can put shortcuts to files or folders in the Quick Launch area in the same way.

If you have a little double arrow sign on the edge of the Quick Launch area, as shown below, click it and further icons will be revealed. Or you can drag the little embossed vertical line to expand the section along the Taskbar until all the icons are visible.

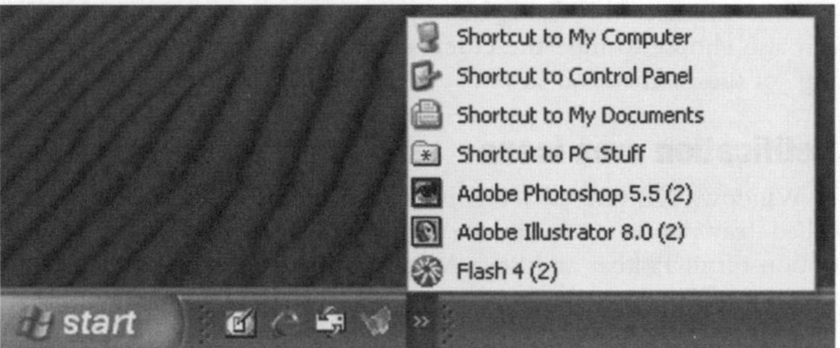

Taskbar Toolbars

The Quick Launch area is only one example of a toolbar that can reside on the Taskbar; you can create a toolbar out of any folder, and there are a number of ways to do it. Click on any blank portion of the Taskbar and select the **Toolbar** option from the mouse menu. You can either click one of the ready-to-use options (there is one, for example, that shows all the icons on the Desktop) or choose **New Toolbar** to select a folder, such as **My Documents**, **Control Panel** or one you've created specially for the job.

Tips & Tricks

Giving folders a face-lift

As well as changing how Windows looks overall, you can also customize specific folders, in a couple of different ways. One option, in Windows XP, is to select a picture or photo to appear on the folder icon when you're in thumbnail view. Open the folder, select **Customize This Folder** from the **View** menu, select **Choose Picture,** navigate to your image of choice and click **OK**.

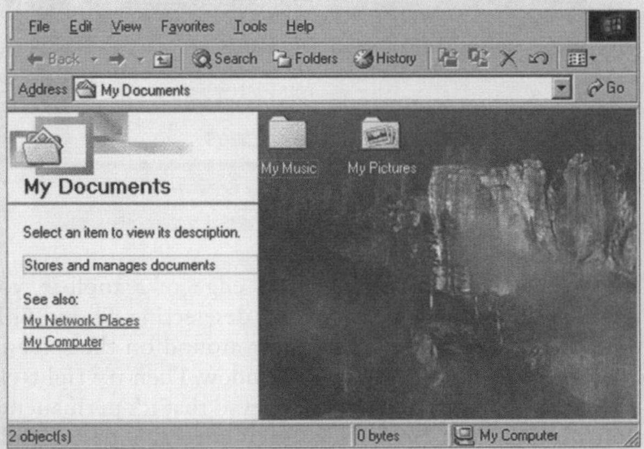

In Windows 98 or Me, you can't add pictures to folder icons but you can add a background to a folder – not that it's particulalry pretty (see above). Double-click a folder (**My Documents,** for example) and select **Customize this Folder** from the **View** menu. Then select **Choose a background picture**, click **Next** and you'll be presented with a dialog box offering you various pictures and a **Browse** button, which allow you to select any suitable picture on your computer. You may want to change the text and background colours too. Click **Next** when you're done, and your folder will be customized. To delete the new look, click **View/Customize this Folder** followed by **Remove customization** and then **Next**.

When you've made your selection, the new toolbar will appear on the Taskbar. You can rearrange the various toolbars by dragging the embossed Taskbar dividers back and forth, but they may be a bit squashed unless you drag the whole Taskbar up a bit to make enough room for an extra row of toolbars. Alternatively, drag your new toolbar as far to the right as possible and click the arrow that appears to browse its contents as a pop-up menu.

If you right-click on the left-hand edge of a toolbar, you can change how it looks by selecting or deselecting **Show Title** and **Show Text**. You can also drag a toolbar around on the screen by its left edge so that it floats like a mini-window. Then try right-clicking its Title bar and selecting **Always on top** so that it's permanently visible. To close a toolbar, right-click its left edge or Title bar and select **Close** from the mouse menu.

Spicing up the Start menu

In Windows XP you can make lots of tweaks to the Start menu to make it work exactly the way you want it to. Most of these are done via the **Taskbar and Start Menu Properties** box, which you can reach by right-clicking the **Start** button and selecting **Properties**. Then click **Customize** and you'll be offered various options about how the menu looks and works, including the size of the icons and the length of the recently used programs list. Under the **Advanced** tab, you can also make all sorts of changes to what appears on the right-hand side of the menu. And you can choose whether you want the icons to act as links that open a new window or an expanding menu (similar to the **More Programs** menu). This is especially useful for **My Documents**, allowing you to browse through your filing system and open files without opening a window.

Try This

Exploring the Start menu

If you want to move lots of things around in your Start menu or create folders to live in your Programs menu, it's easiest to use Windows Explorer. Right-click on the **Start** menu and select **Explore**. An Explorer window will open with the Start menu selected. You can then move files around and create folders as you would anywhere else.

The other XP tweaks you can make are also possible in earlier versions of Windows: you can rearrange the items in your Programs list either by dragging and dropping them or by right-clicking in the list and pressing **Sort by Name**. And you can add shortcuts to programs or files to the top section of the menu by dragging any file or folder onto the Start button.

XP's classic view

If you're a Windows XP user who pines for the bad old days, you can choose to view your Start menu with its "classic" single-column look. Right-click the **Start** button and select **Properties**. When the dialog box appears, select the **Classic Start menu** option and hit **Apply**. This will also return various icons – like My Computer and My Documents – to the Desktop, where they lived in years gone by. If you want the icons back on the Desktop but like the new XP Start menu, right-click the Desktop, select **Properties** and under the **Desktop** tab click **Customize Desktop**. In the **Desktop Items** box that appears, you can choose exactly which icons you want displayed.

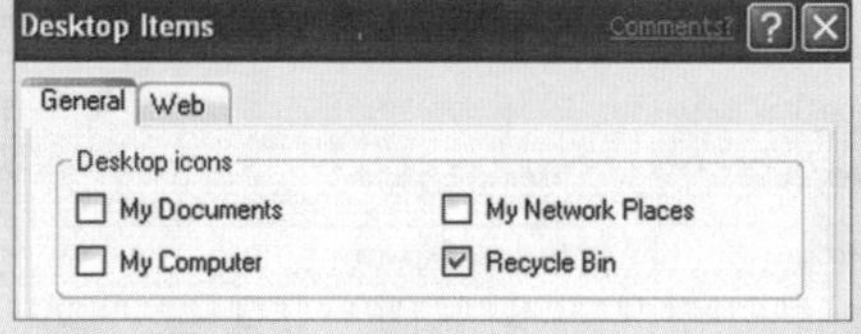

Doing away with the double-click

Part of Microsoft's strategy to make Windows look and feel more like the Internet is to give you the option of ditching the double-click so that you can browse through and select your files in the same way as you surf the Web – by single-clicking on underlined links.

If you want to try this option, open an Explorer window such as **My Documents**, select **Folder Options** from the **Tools** menu and choose **Single-click to open an item**. (In Windows 98 and Me, select **Folder Options** from the **View** menu, and select **Web style**.)

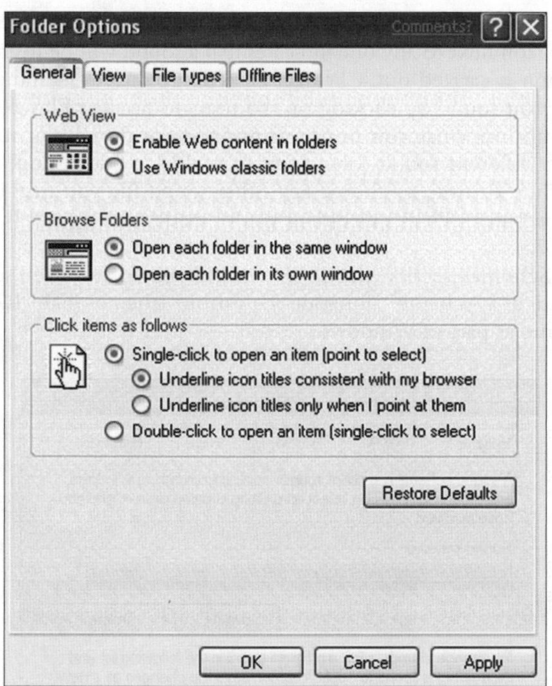

Sorting out your sounds

One final thing you might want to customize in Windows is the selection of sounds that occur when you start up, shut down, try something the system doesn't like, and so on. To change or turn off some or all of these sounds, open the **Control Panel** and select: **Sounds, Speech, and Audio Devices** followed by **Change the Sound Scheme** (in Windows XP); **Sounds and Multimedia** followed by the **Sounds** tab (Windows Me); or **Sounds** (in Windows 98).

Towards the top of the dialog box you'll see a list of actions. A little speaker icon next to any one indicates that a sound will be heard when the action is carried out. Click on an action to select it, and preview the relevant sound by clicking on the triangle-bearing **Play** button. If you don't like what you hear, you can use the dropdown menu to select a different sound (or no sound at all) for that action; alternatively, click **Browse** to choose any other sound file you may have on your computer such as a recording you've made with Sound Recorder (see p.173).

The **Schemes** section allows you to save your customized selection of sounds as a "scheme" alongside the various schemes (like "Robotz") that come as part of Windows.

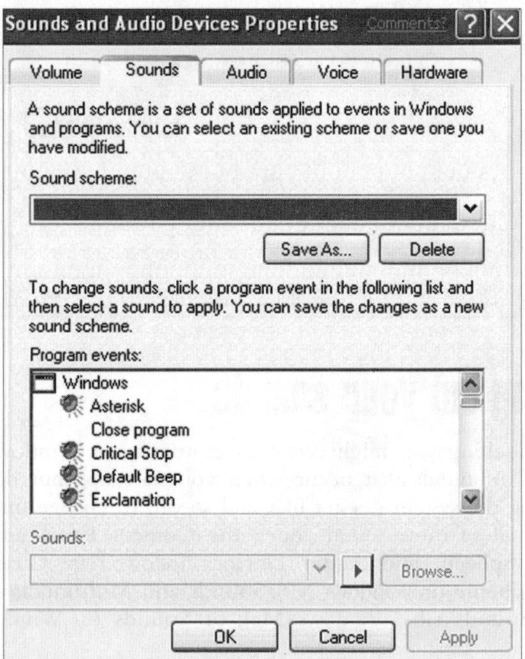

And more...

For serious customization – changing anything from the design of the Start button to the way Windows Explorer looks and works – you'll need to download some extra software. Browse the relevant sections of the software archives listed on p.406.

09 Users

sharing your computer

If your PC is used by various people within your home or office, you can configure Windows to recognize each individual as a **user**. This way, when someone sits down at the machine they'll be able to work within their own special setup – protected by a password if desired. Each user has their own My Documents folder, Web Favorites, and so on, and each can customize Windows in any way they like, from their Desktop wallpaper to their toolbar arrangements. All these individual files and settings constitute a user's **account** or profile.

Users in Windows XP

The user options in Windows Me and earlier versions are rather limited and not very secure, but can be useful nonetheless (see p.150 for more). In Windows XP, they're much more comprehensive: there are various different types of user, and each can choose to make their files private so that no one else can access them.

Either during the Windows XP installation or the first time you use your machine, you will be prompted to enter the names of the people you want to set up as users. All you need enter is a **username** for each person – it could be a first name, a full name or an imaginary moniker of your choice – and choose what type of user you'd like them to be. The primary user of the computer is the **Administrator**, while others can be registered as additional Administrators or as **Limited** users. These two types of account allows the user a different level of control within the PC:

- **Administrators** have control over all system-wide settings, they can install hardware and software, and can create, change and delete other users' accounts. They can also access all files not protected by a private password.

- **Limited users** have fewer powers, though they still maintain their own password, private files and Windows settings.

Each time you start your computer, all the users will be listed in a Windows welcome page – simply click on the appropriate username to log on. Next to each name on the Windows welcome page you'll see a little picture. Windows assigns a default image – such as a cat, flower or soccer ball – to each user when the accounts are created. But you can easily change the pictures to something more to your taste or a little more personal (such as a picture of yourself, if you have a digital camera or scanner). A user's image is also displayed at the top of the Start menu when they're logged on.

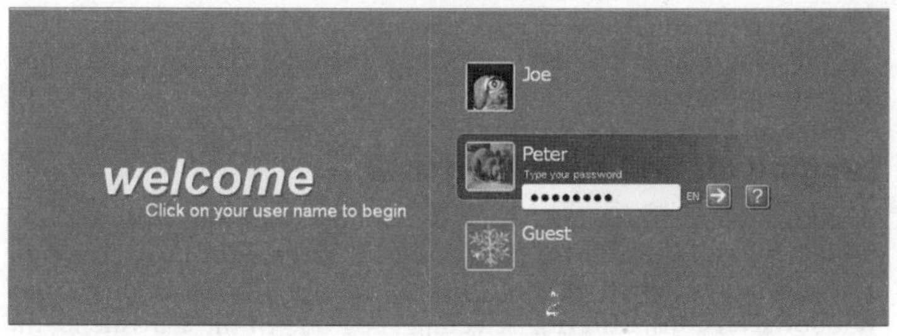

By default you won't need to enter a password to log on, but you can add a **password** to your account in the User Accounts window (see p.148). This is also where you go to add and delete users or alter individual user settings.

Guest users

If someone wants to use your machine but they're not registered as a user, they can log on as a **Guest** at the Windows welcome page. They'll be able to work within your computer, but will have no access to any user account settings or the documents of other users. If, as the Administrator, you don't want anyone accessing your machine without a personalized account, you can turn the Guest account off by going

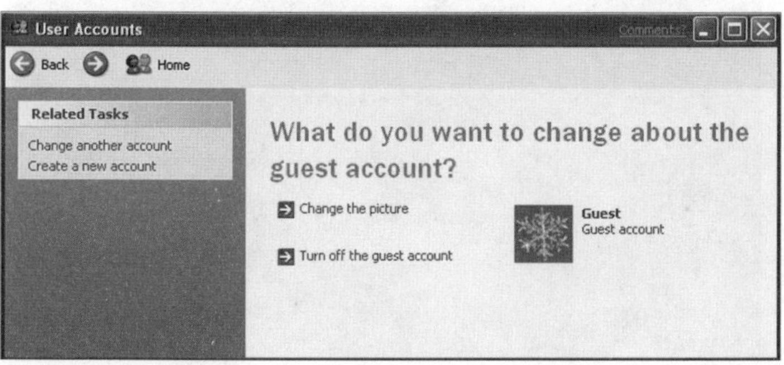

to the **Start** menu, then **Control Panel,** then **User Accounts**, clicking the **Guest** icon and then selecting **Turn off the guest account** from the list of tasks.

Logging off and switching user

Windows XP features "**fast user switching**", meaning that one user doesn't have to actually log out, closing all their documents and programs, when another wants to log in (as was the case with earlier Windows versions). Aftering selecting "Log off" in the start menu, the current user has two choices: **Log Off**, which shuts down all their settings to make way for the next user; and **Switch User**, which preserves all their settings and active programs in the background while the new user does their thing.

User Accounts window

Only an Administrator can add a new user or change the settings of the current users – Limited or Guest users are only entitled to make

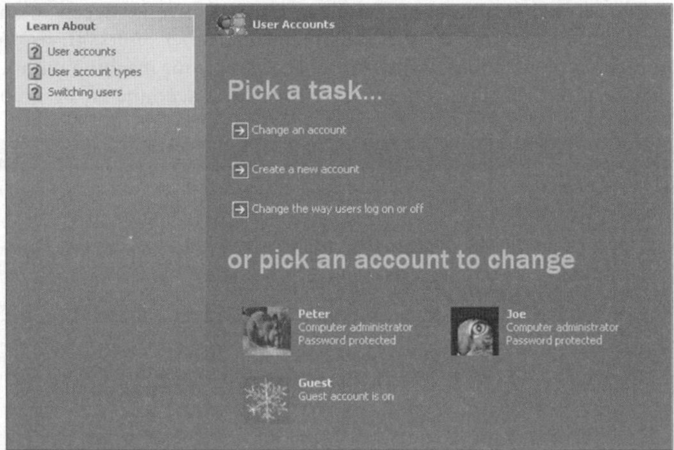

changes to their own account. Either way, all settings are dealt with in the User Accounts window, which can be opened by clicking the Start button, selecting **Control Panel** and choosing **User Accounts**. If you open the window as an Administrator, you'll see a list of all the current users. Limited or Guest users, however, will only see their own name and picture. Most of the options and tasks in these windows are self-explanatory – "Change my picture", "Change my password" – but XP does offer a couple of further options that require a little clarification.

First, you can take the opportunity to create a **Password Reset Disk**, a special floppy disk that can be used to access your account and reset your password from the Windows Welcome page if you ever forget it. Click the **Prevent a forgotten password task**, insert a blank floppy disk and launch the wizard, which will walk you through the process. This disk will not be specific to a single password, so you need only create the disk once, even if you change your password regularly.

Also on offer is the option of creating a **.NET Passport**, a special username (based on an email address) and password that lets you log on

to a family of websites run by Microsoft and certain other participating companies. The idea is that it saves you having to remember loads of different usernames and passwords – or, perhaps, it's just another Microsoft attempt at world domination.

Shared and private folders

Limited and Guest users only have access to their own folders and files, so if you want certain things to be accessible to all put the files in the **Shared Documents** folder, which you'll find in My Computer.

Administrators have a certain degree of freedom to stroll around the files and folders of the various users of the system. However, any user can make individual folders completely private – even from the prying eyes of Administrators – by right-clicking a folder, clicking **Properties**, the choosing the **Sharing** tab, and checking the box labelled **Make this folder private**.

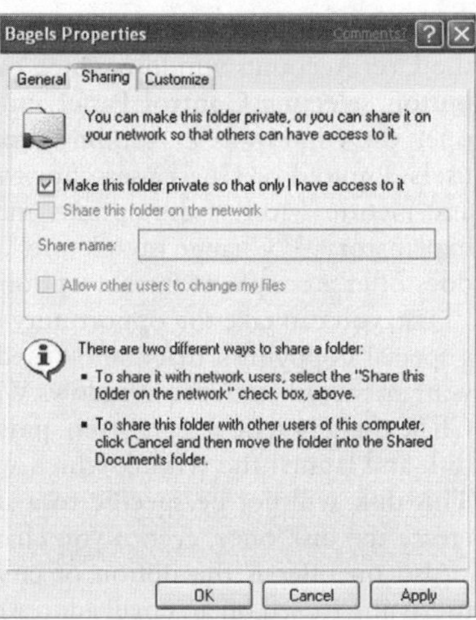

In this box you can also choose to make files available to users on other computers on your network, if you have one set up. See p.227 for more on home networking.

Users in Windows Me and 98

In pre-XP versions of Windows you can set up user profiles via the Users icon in the Control Panel. To add someone to the list, click the **New User** button and follow the steps laid down by the Add User Wizard. Be aware, though, that security is minimal: passwords can easily be discovered, and every user has access to all files and folders on the system. You can restrict people on a network from viewing your private files (see p.233), but not other users of your PC. There's also only one type of user.

You can switch between users by clicking the Start button and then selecting **Log Off**. After you've confirmed your decision, a dialog box

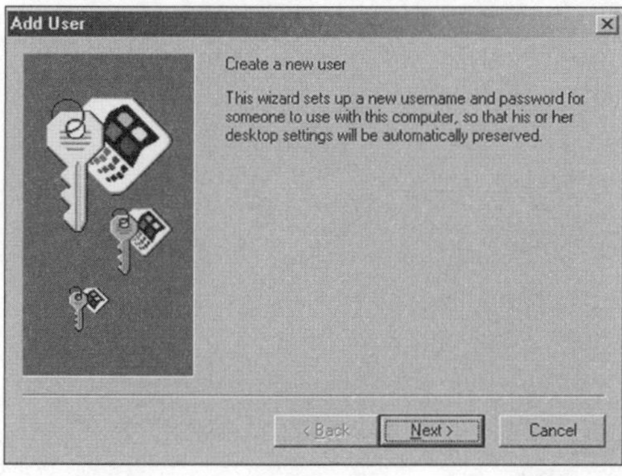

will appear so that another user can log on by entering their username and password (if they have one). However, in these older versions of Windows, switching between users takes quite a long time: the system essentially shuts down and restarts each time.

10

The Control Panel

tweaking the settings

The Control Panel is the place where you go within Windows to make all sorts of changes to your computer's settings. It houses everything from controls for pieces of hardware like your mouse and keyboard to utilities that change the appearance of your Windows work environment. You'll find the Control Panel in the Start menu (under Settings in older versions of Windows) and as a link or folder in My Computer. Many of the controls you'll never have to tamper with, but it's worth taking a few minutes to look through all the options: you'll doubtless find options you never knew existed.

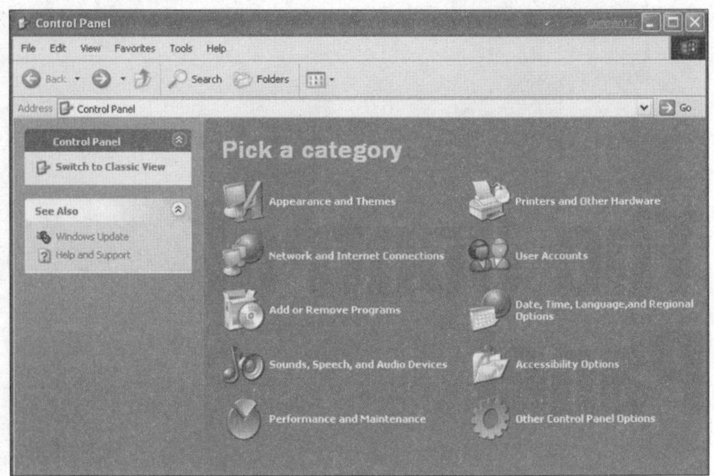

Pick a category...

The appearance of your **Control Panel** and the number of items it contains depends on two things: which version of Windows you're using and which programs you have installed on your system. In Windows XP, the Control Panel items are arranged into categories – click on one and you'll be offered a list of tasks and icons. You'll also see a list of troubleshooting options on the left of the window, which launch wizards to help you sort out any problems you might be having. Older versions of Windows, meanwhile, just display the icons in a list (in Windows Me, you'll need to click the **View all** link to see them all).

The following pages run through the items you're likely to come across. You won't find all the ones listed here in your system, and you may well have additional icons – virus scanners and other programs often add their own. Many of the options mentioned are covered in more depth in other chapters of this book, and some can be accessed from various different places in the Windows environment.

Having a browse though the many options is a good idea, but **don't change any technical settings you're not absolutely sure about.**

▶ **Accessibility Options** Contains various controls to make a PC more user-friendly for people who are hard of hearing, partially sighted or who find a standard mouse or keyboard difficult to use. By selecting the various tabs, adjusting the controls and clicking the **Apply** or **OK** button, you can: change the way your keyboard responds; set up SoundSentry and ShowSounds functions to warn you visually when your PC makes a noise; change the colour and contrast of your display to make it easier to read; adjust the speed of your mouse pointer; and enable your keyboard's number pad to move the mouse pointer. In the **General** tab you can set all these functions to switch off after the PC has sat idle for a period of time, and also enable **SerialKey devices** – special input gadgets useful for anyone who finds it difficult to operate a standard mouse or keyboard.

▶ **Add New Hardware** When you install a modern Plug and Play device (see p.52), your PC should automatically recognize and configure it. If this fails, however, or if you're adding a non-Plug and Play device to your system, run this wizard after installation to get everything going.

▶ **Add or Remove Programs** These days, most programs are so easy to install that you're more likely to use these controls for removing programs than adding them (see p.257). This is also the place where you can add and remove elements from your Windows setup (and, in Windows Me and earlier, create a Startup disk; see p.245).

▶ **Administrative Tools** Opens a window offering all sorts of techie information and options, such as graphic representations of your processor usage and hard disk fragmentation. Not for the uninitiated.

▶ **Automatic Updates** Found only in Windows Me, this option allows Windows to automatically fetch and install any updates or missing device drivers from the Microsoft Website – assuming your PC is connected to a phone socket. Click here to turn this function on or off.

▶ **Date/Time** (also accessible by double-clicking the clock on the Taskbar) This is where you go to set your clock and calendar. You can also select the time zone you are in from a dropdown list.

▶ **Desktop Themes** Lets you select how everything in the Windows environment looks and sounds according to pre-installed themes such as "Nature" or "Science". Not as good as it sounds (see p.131).

▶ **Dial-Up Networking** (in My Computer in Windows 98) Displays a list of your Internet connections: double-click on an icon to connect, or right-click it and select Properties to view its settings.

▶ **Display** Opens the Display Properties window, where you can make all sorts of tweaks to the appearance of the Windows environment. Its various options are covered in the Customizing Windows chapter (see p.127).

▶ **Folder Options** (found in the Start menu under Settings in Windows 98) Lets you change how folders look and work (see p.192) and allows you to decide which programs your computer uses to open various types of file (see p.112).

▶ **Fonts** Shows you all the fonts (typefaces) installed on your system and allows you to install new ones. Each font is represented by its own file.

▶ **Game Controllers** For setting up joysticks and other gaming devices.

▶ **Internet Options** Opens a Properties window that boasts a generous set of tabs, options and controls relating to your Internet connection and the way your Web browser behaves. It can also be opened from the Internet Explorer Tools menu. For more, see p.207.

▶ **Keyboard** Lets you change the way in which your keyboard behaves – how quickly a letter is repeated when you hold down a key, for example.

▶ **Mail** Displays and allows you to change the settings of your email accounts if you use certain email programs.

▶ **Modems** Displays information about any modems currently installed and allows you to add new ones – though most modern modems don't require you to use this function during installation.

▶ **Mouse** Lets you change your mouse settings: how the pointer looks on the screen, for example, and the speed needed for a double-click.

▶ **Network Connections** Also accessible from the Windows XP Start menu, this opens an Explorer window listing all your Internet and Network connections. Double-click an Internet connection icon to connect, or right-click it and select **Properties** to view its settings. You will also see an icon labelled **Make New Connection**, which launches a step-by-step wizard for adding a new connection.

▶ **Network** Deals with all sorts of network settings. For more on home networking, see p.227.

▶ **ODBC Data Source** Open Database Connectivity – techie stuff you don't need to know about.

▶ **Passwords** For setting up or changing Windows passwords. Ties in with **Users** (see p.145).

▶ **PC Card** Deals with PC card devices and connections (see p.8). Generally only found in the Control Panel of notebook computers.

▶ **Power Options** (labelled **Power Management** in Windows 98) Lets you choose how long your system should sit doing nothing before slipping into its power-saving standby mode.

▶ **Printers** Reveals details of any printers connected to your system. It also features the Add Printer Wizard, though thanks to Plug and Play technology (see p.52), you'll probably never need to use it.

▶ **Regional Settings** Lets you tell Windows where you are in the world and choose a format for numbers, currencies, dates and times.

▶ **Scanners and Cameras** For setting up digital cameras and scanners on your system – though most modern models will do this themselves.

▶ **Scheduled Tasks** (in My Computer in Windows 98) Allows you to schedule Windows to carry out tasks or run programs at a certain time every day, week or month. This is only really useful if you leave your computer on all the time.

▶ **Sounds and Audio Devices** This dialog box has various options for altering your Windows sounds (such as the noise the PC makes when it starts up), setting up your multimedia components and adjusting playback and recording settings.

▶ **Sounds and Multimedia** This is the Windows Me's version of Sounds and Audio Devices option (see above). In Windows 98, Sounds and Multimedia are presented as two separate items.

▶ **Speech** Lets you set your computer's default voice for reading text and dialog boxes aloud. In Windows XP you can select the kinds of information that you want to be read aloud by clicking Start and selecting Programs, Accessories, Accessibility, and then Narrator.

▶ **System** (also accessible by right-clicking **My Computer** and selecting **Properties**) Brings up a dialog box showing which version of Windows you're running and displaying various information about your system such as the processor type and the amount of RAM. There are various other tabs that provide techie information, such as a list of all your peripherals and ports. It's best not to change anything in here unless it's really necessary.

▶ **Taskbar and Start Menu** (in **Start/Settings** in Windows 98) For customizing the Taskbar and Start menu, see p.134.

▶ **Telephony** Where Windows stores information about the country you're in and your telephone area code. Why not take a moment to make sure these settings are correct?

▶ **User Accounts** (or **Users**) Lets you set up your computer so more than one user can have personalized settings. See p.145 for more.

▶ **Wireless Link** (or **Infrared**) If your PC has an infrared port – usually only notebooks do – this is where you can alter its settings.

11

Built-in programs

Windows extras

Over the years, Windows has accumulated an extensive range of built-in utilities and programs, many of which can come in very handy – from a simple calculator to utilities for tweaking and checking up on your hardware. However, unless you actually take the time to look, you might never discover just how many tools you have at your disposal. This chapter gives you a guided tour of the extras found within the Windows menus, including accessibility options – which can make things easier for people with visual or physical disabilities – and programs for dealing with music and video.

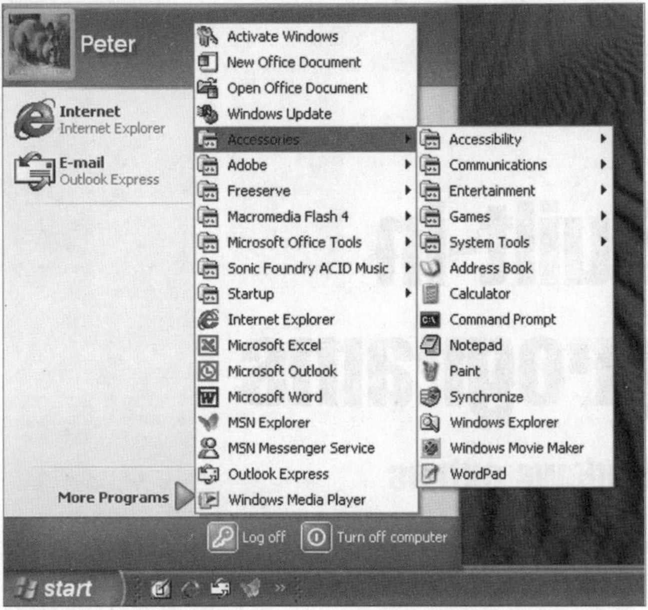

Accessories

There's a wealth of goodies to be found within an area of the Start menu called **Accessories** (see above). Click the **Start** button, select **Programs** then **Accessories**, and we'll begin. Try launching some of these handy tools:

▶ **Address Book** is pretty much what you'd expect: a computerized address book system with fields for various sorts of information and personal details. It's mainly useful when used alongside an email program such as Outlook Express (see p.219). Open it up and click New then Contact to make your first addition. All the data you enter is saved as a Windows Address Book (.wab) file, which can be exported via the program's File menu for use with other applications, or backed up.

▶ **Calculator** Select this item and you're presented with a standard and fairly boring calculator that you can operate either with your mouse pointer or keyboard. But don't fall asleep yet: from the **View** menu select **Scientific** – you've now got a powerful mathematics tool at your disposal. Use of the calculator can be speeded up with keyboard shortcuts – hitting "P", for example, inserts the value of Pi. If you really don't like this utility, there are plenty of alternative number crunchers to be found online, such as **Beautiful Calculator** (see www.rayslab.com/calculator).

▶ **Imaging** Introduced with Windows Me, this is a photo previewing and editing tool. Though it's not especially intuitive to use and is very limited when compared to some other graphics packages (see p.266), it does cover the basics: rotating, scaling, zooming and so on.

▶ **Command Prompt** (or **MS-DOS Prompt**) offers you a potentially scary glimpse of MS-DOS, the pre-Windows Microsoft operating system. If you click the icon you'll get a window housing a page which appears blank apart from a single line of coded text (such as **C:\WINDOWS>**), urging you to enter a command. This is only really for the initiated, so proceed with caution. In some versions of Windows you'll find this icon elsewhere.

▶ **Notepad** is a very basic text program for writing and editing documents that don't require any formatting (special information about the font, spacing and so on). Anything you write in Notepad is saved in the ASCII, or "simple text", format and a single document can be no bigger than 64 kilobytes, which is around 15,000 words.

▶ **WordPad** is a step up from Notepad: it's a word processor that can handle various fonts, paragraph styles and even embedded pictures. It won't provide you with anything like the variety of tools found in a full-blown word processing package (see p.262), but it does handle all the basics and can save your work in various file formats, including simple text, rich text format (RTF) and Word. If you're new to word processing, trying opening WordPad and playing around with different paragraph alignments and text styles – such as **bold**, *italic*, underline and ~~strikethrough~~.

Try This

Painting a picture

Windows Paint is a very limited program, but if you're entirely new to working with computer images it does provide an introduction to some pretty universal tools. Try opening the program, and experimenting with the various options of the toolbar. It's like an artist's toolbox, with a selection of pencils, paintbrushes and so on. To select a tool, click it once and the button will become indented.

When you've finished, if you're really pleased with your masterpiece you could save it as your Desktop Wallpaper (look in the File menu). Or you could download a decent graphics package and try out some more advanced tools – see p.266.

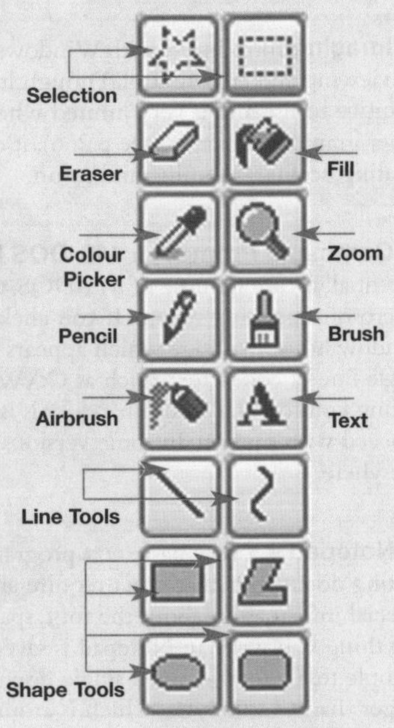

▶ **Paint** is a illustration application. As with Imaging, it's extremely limited and clunky when compared to serious graphics packages, but it's easy to use and gives you an introduction to some common digital imaging tools (see box).

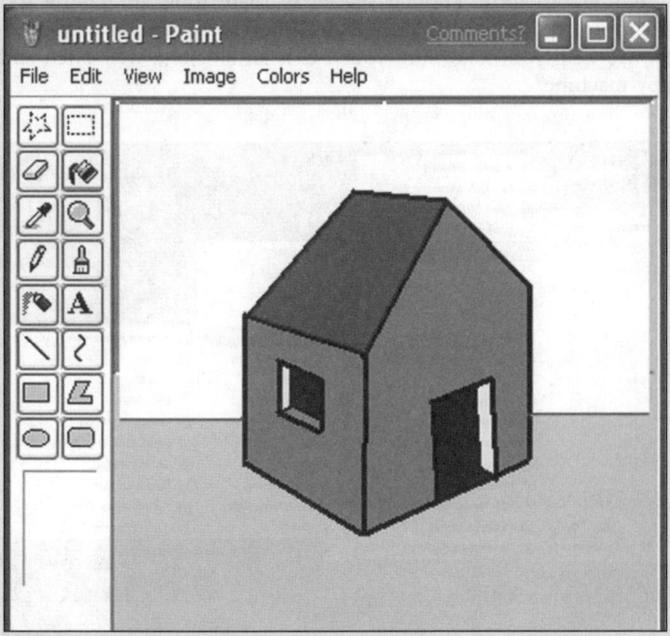

▶ **Web Publishing Wizard** This utility walks you through the process of getting your work onto the Web – from finding the files on your system to uploading files to a Web server. Though it doesn't offer all the utilities of a specialized FTP (File Transfer Protocol) program, it's a useable-enough basic tool. In XP, you'll find the Wizard in Windows Explorer: select any file and a "Publish this file on the Web" link will appear on the left. In Windows 98 right-click a file and select Web Publishing Wizard from the mouse menu. Alternatively, download a stand-alone FTP program from one of the software archives listed on p.406.

System tools

If you click the **Start** button and select **Programs**, **Accessories** then **System Tools**, you'll see a selection of utilities and programs that make up your PC toolbox. Though several of these tools are a little too techie to warrant much attention here, others are worth introducing – they will help you make sure your PC is an efficient, well-oiled and happy machine.

▶ **Disk Cleanup** Useful if you're running short of disk space, Disk Cleanup deletes **temporary files** and other redundant stuff from your system, and prompts you to remove unused programs and empty your **Recycle Bin** (see p.104).

▶ **Disk Defragmenter** reorganizes the contents of your hard drive so that the read-write heads don't have to work so hard (see box overleaf). Once you've launched it, select the drive that you want to defragment (usually C:) and let the program do its stuff. Depending on the drive's size and how fragmented it is, the process can take a good few hours, so choose a convenient time to set the ball rolling.

▶ **ScanDisk** checks the surface of disk drives for faulty clusters. It often launches automatically after you've crashed, but you can also summon it at any time if you suspect there may be a problem on your hard drive (or even a floppy).

▶ **Maintenance Wizard** Featuring in Windows Me and 98 (but not XP) this program is for setting up a Windows maintenance schedule so that your system is automatically defragged, scanned and tweaked on a regular basis. You might, for example, create a schedule that carries out these tasks every Sunday night when you're tucked up in bed. But you'll have to remember to leave your PC on before you go to sleep.

▶ **System Restore** This feature, which you won't have if you're running Windows 98 or earlier, lets you turn back the clock and reinstate your Windows settings as they were at an earlier date and time: a very useful way to clear up problems relating to bad software installations or mischievous hardware drivers scrambling your setup. This function only relates to core system settings, so it won't affect your document files – and if it doesn't solve the problem, the restore can easily be undone. When you launch the System Restore program you enter a step-by-step process

Doctor, doctor – my hard disk's fragmented

Hard disks are made up of thousands of tiny little sections, called clusters, that hold individual portions of data. Whenever you delete a file, the relevant clusters become available, and then get refilled by more data when you save something new. The problem is that, as time goes by, more and more deletions and additions can result in files being split between multiple locations on the disk, which means that when you come to retrieve a file your hard drive's read-write heads have to work ludicrously hard, darting back and forth collecting all the individual fragments of data that make up the file you're after. Though this will usually only result in things slowing down by a fraction of a second, it can make all the difference when carrying out real-time, or "streaming", tasks like recording live audio or playing back video. It will also shorten the life of your hard drive.

To get the best from your hard drive in terms of function and longevity, you should get into the habit of defragging every month or two, and also prior to saving any particularly large audio or video files to your drive. Go to Start menu, Programs, Accessories, System Tools, to set the defragger rolling.

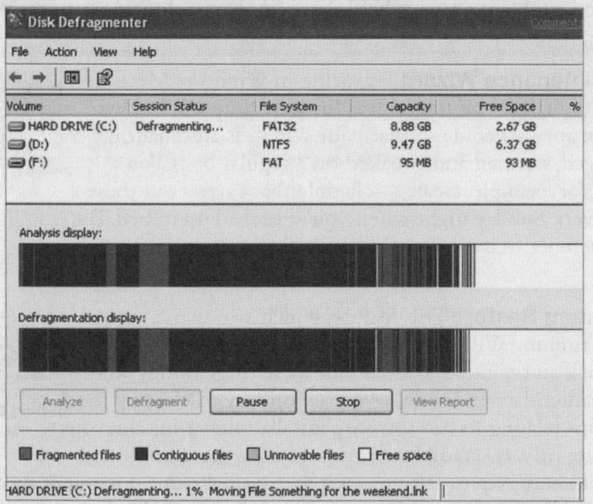

that prompts you to either record the current settings as a **restore point** (also called a **system checkpoint**) or return your computer to a previous restore point. Once you have done this for the first time, you will also have the option to undo your last system restoration. If you do opt to choose an old checkpoint you will see a new frame with a calendar on it. All the days shown in bold feature restore points – click one, and then select a checkpoint from the list relating to your chosen day.

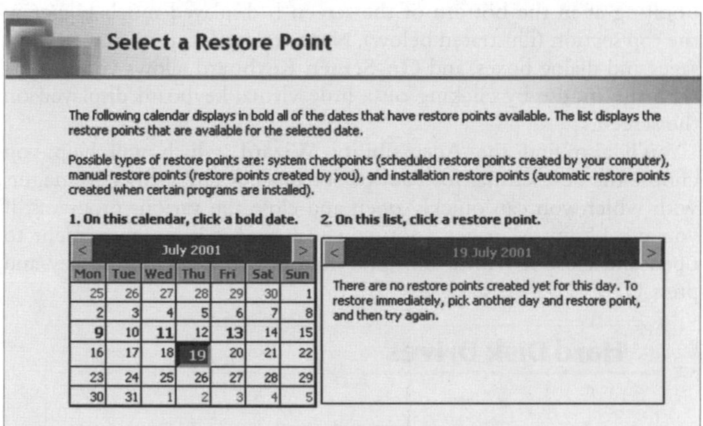

Tips & Tricks

Checkpoint Charlie

As well as the restore points you create yourself, Windows automatically creates them at regular intervals. It stores a record of those created in the previous few weeks, but you can increase the amount of hard disk space available for old checkpoints by enlarging your checkpoint history, hence allowing you to backtrack further into the past if anything goes wrong. Right-click **My Computer** and select **Properties** to bring up the **System Properties** dialog box; click the System Restore or **Performance** tab and then the Settings or **File System** button. You'll see a slider that assigns disk space to System Restore.

Accessibility programs

In recent versions of Windows, if you click the Start button and select Programs then Accessories, you'll find a folder called Accessibility. This contains a few little programs to make a PC easier to use for people with sight, hearing or mobility difficulties.

Magnifier splits the screen into two parts; whatever your mouse is pointing at in the bottom of the screen is displayed much bigger in the top section (illustrated below). **Narrator** reads out on-screen messages and dialog boxes, and **On-Screen Keyboard** allows you to type with the mouse by clicking on a little virtual keyboard displayed on the screen.

You'll also find the **Accessibility Wizard**, which will help you choose the best settings for your personal needs, and **Utility Manager**, with which you can quickly open and close the various programs. If you use Utility Manager a lot, you may find it more convenient to open and close it with a shortcut: hold down the Windows key and press U.

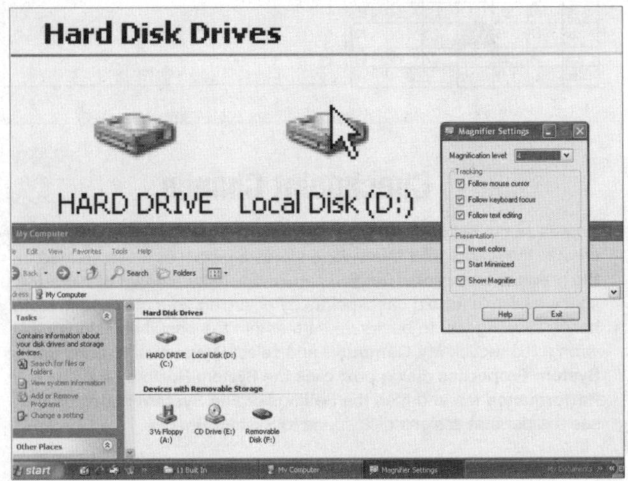

My Briefcase

This tool, which you may find on your Desktop, depending on which version of Windows you're running, is a special document folder designed for people who use some files in two locations – at home and in the office, for example. If you make changes to files at home, you can move them into the briefcase and then copy the whole briefcase onto a floppy, CD or external drive to be transported to a PC at work, where the briefcase will update the equivalent files. My Briefcase can also be used to synchronize files between two PCs linked by a direct cable connection (see p.231).

Windows music and video

Recent versions of Windows have been tailored with multimedia applications in mind – reflecting the fact that ever more people are using their PCs for a whole lot more than writing letters and balancing accounts. Whether you want to play audio CDs, mess around with home movies or build a library of MP3 tracks for use with a portable device, Windows probably has a built-in tool to do the job. But there are also thousands of alternatives out there ready to download, and many of them are better than the Windows versions, so it's well worth exploring the software archives listed on p.406.

Try This

Choose your speakers

To get the best sound out of whatever speaker system you have connected to your PC, take a trip to the **Control Panel**. First, switch to the **Classic View** if you're in Windows XP, then select **Sounds and Audio Devices**. In the **Speaker settings** section at the bottom of the panel, hit the **Advanced** button and then choose from the dropdown menu the configuration that best matches your own.

Volume controls

The Volume Control dialog box can be called up either by double-clicking the small speaker icon next to the clock on the Taskbar or by single-clicking the **Start** button and selecting **Programs, Accessories, Entertainment** and then **Volume Control**. By tweaking the sliders with your mouse pointer you can change the volume of any device on your PC that generates sounds, such as a CD drive or an integrated synthesizer. The first slider in the panel is the master control – if this is turned down you will hear nothing from any of your PC's devices – while the rest refer to individual devices. They all give you the option to adjust the balance (how a device splits its sound between a pair of stereo speakers) and a **Mute** checkbox.

If you don't see the controls for a particular device, select **Properties** from the **Options** menu, look in the bottom half of the dialog box that appears and make sure the device's checkbox is selected. In this dialog box you can also choose to view the volume settings for **recording sounds** onto your computer from microphones, CD players and the like.

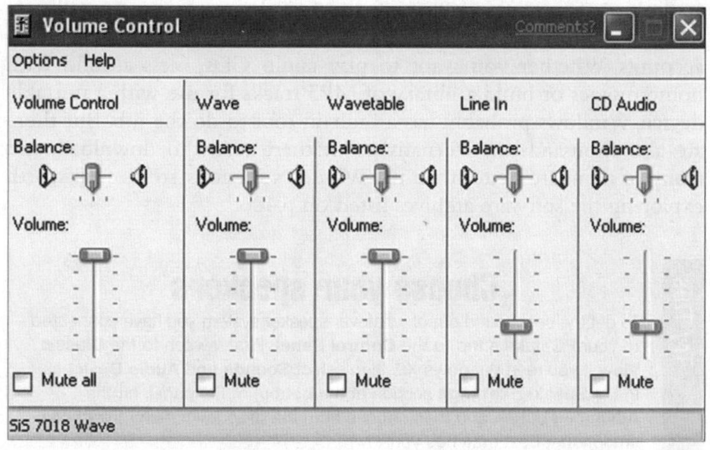

Sound Recorder

Though there are infinitely more sophisticated programs available for recording sound using a PC (see p.272), the built-in Windows utility – **Sound Recorder** – is fine if you just want to record a few seconds of sound via your PC's microphone, for example. You can open it by travelling through Start, Programs, Accessories and then Entertainment.

It's a very simple program. Click the record button (the one with the red dot) to begin recording sound from whichever source you have selected in the Record Settings view of the Volume Control window (see opposite). When you click the stop button you're left with a recording that can be played back, made louder, speeded up and saved as a **wave file** (a digital sound file).

Windows Media Player

Recent versions of Windows come bundled with Windows Media Player. If you haven't already got a copy on your system or you're yearning for the very latest version, you can download it for free from **www.microsoft.com/windows/windowsmedia**

More than just a CD player for your computer, Media Player can play back audio and video clips, help you organize an Internet-supported library of music files, encode tracks from CDs to your hard disk, tune in to radio stations via the Internet and – if you've got a CD burner – prepare selections from your files to make a compilation album.

When you open Media Player, on the lower edge of the window you'll see a selection of control buttons similar to those on a regular CD player: the big one is **Play/Pause**, the one with the square is **Stop**, the little slider is a volume control and the selection of triangles are for **Rewind/Fast Forward** and skipping between tracks. You'll also see a long slider that can be used to move to any point within the current track or video.

On the left of the screen you'll see several glossy-looking tabs. These select various modes, the first of which is **Now Playing**. When this is

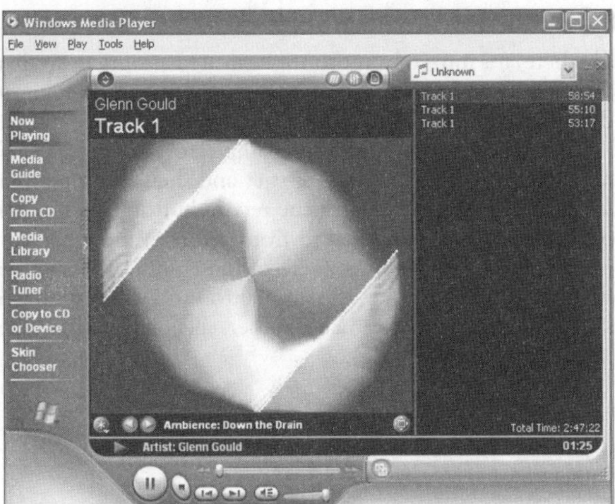

selected you'll be looking at the part of Media Player where you can watch video clips and find out which track you're on when playing music from a CD. Try inserting an audio CD into your computer's CD drive and Media Player should automatically start playing it (if it doesn't, click the **Play** button). As the sound kicks in, you'll see a psychedelic graphic – a **visualization –** in the middle of the screen, moving in time to the music. You can browse through various types of pattern using the little arrows underneath the visualization, or you can turn it off by clicking the **View** menu, selecting **Now Playing Tools** and choosing **Show Visualization**. In this section of the View menu, you can also select various tools such as a graphic equalizer (you have to select **Show Equalizer and Settings** first).

Copying music onto your hard drive

Instead of inserting a CD into your PC every time you want to listen to it, why not copy it onto your hard drive and start building a permanent library of all your favourite sounds? A hefty hard drive comes

Compressed music files

When you copy ("rip") the music on a CD onto your hard drive, Media Player and other equivalent programs massively reduce the amount of data (and hence disk space) that each track takes up. A track might be 50 MB on the CD and only 5 MB on the hard drive. This works by using "compression" algorithms that remove those bits of the sound we don't usually notice.

Some compression will not yield any noticeable difference in the sound, but if you're a hi-fi buff with a PC connected to your stereo you may want higher-than-default quality, and if you're short on disk space and copying something that doesn't require the highest fidelity (such as a voice recording), you can set the level of compression accordingly.

In Media Player, from the **Tools** menu, select **Options**, and then click the **Copy Music** (or **CD Audio**) tab. Here you will see a slider that sets encoding quality, measured in **kilobits per second (Kbps)**. Most people go with 128 Kbps, but 96 Kbps or lower is OK for small PC speakers and voice recordings, while 164 Kbps or higher is desirable for use through a proper stereo.

The most common compressed music file is **MP3**, but Media Player also uses its own **WMA** format as a default. In newer versions of Media Player you can choose to copy in the MP3 format, but you may have to get a plug-in to rip MP3s with older versions of the program.

in very useful here – music files are large and an audio library will quickly munch into your storage space (work on the basis of 1 MB per minute of music). To view all the media files already on your PC, click the **Media Library** button on the left of the player. This brings up a split screen with a folder tree on the left which looks and works just like Explorer with the folder view open. The first time you click here, you may be asked whether you want to search your PC for media files (this can save time, but you might end up with a lot of non-music sound files from games, etc).

Before copying a new CD to your library you'll need to decide where you want to store all your music files: Windows XP comes with a special **My Music** folder, which can be found on the **Start Menu**; Media Player will use this as a default location, but if you have other ideas you can choose a new location by selecting **Options** from the **Tools** menu, clicking the **Copy Music** (or **CD Audio**) tab and then selecting the **Change** button to choose a different folder.

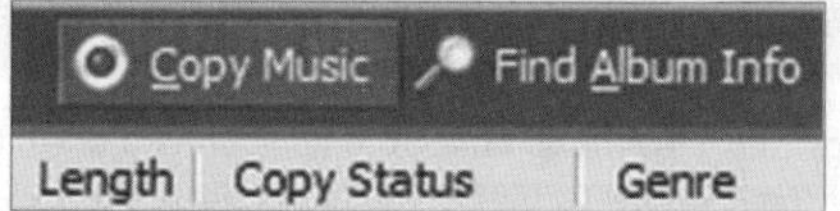

To start the copying process, click the **CD Audio** or **Copy from CD** button on the left of the Media Player window – you'll see a list of the tracks on the CD currently in your drive and a red **Copy Music** button. Click this button and Media Player will start to encode your CD and save its contents to your hard drive. As this happens, the Copy Status of each song will change from "Pending" to "Copied To Library". If you don't want to copy all the tracks from a CD, you can deselect the check-box for each track you don't want before you start copying.

Naming the tracks

Once you've copied a CD to your hard drive, you can choose to enter the tracklist so that you'll be able to tell what's playing at any time very easily. Do this by right-clicking any track and selecting **Edit** to rename it. Alternatively, if your PC is connected to the Internet, you

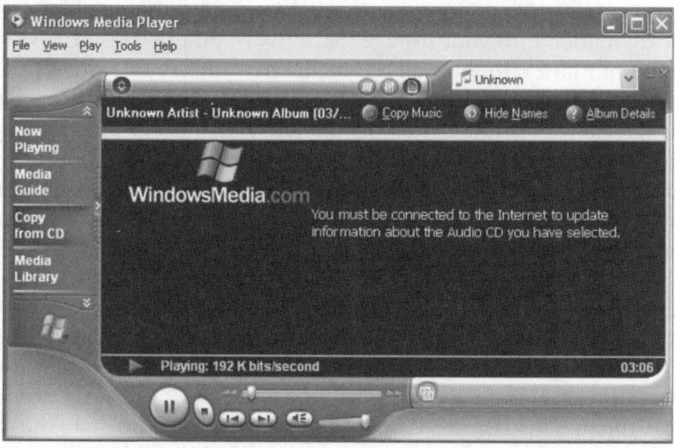

can press the **Get Names** button (at the top in the **CD Audio** section). Media Player then accesses an online database. With any luck this should result in a full tracklist for your CD and also, if you click the **Album Details** button, the chance to read some blurb about the artist and recording.

The first time you go online with Media Player you will also be prompted to download various **updates and plug-ins** (useful little extras) that have recently been made available. They are free, and easy to install once downloaded. You can check for updates whenever you like in the **Help** menu.

Playlists and Auto Playlists

A playlist is just what you'd expect: a list of tracks (not the tracks themselves) stored on your computer for Media Player to play back to you. Select **Media Library** and click **New Playlist** in the dropdown from the **Playlists** button. You will be asked to give the new list a name – do so and click **OK** – and your new playlist will appear in the **Media Library** folder tree in the left-hand pane.

Near the top of the folder tree will be an icon labelled **All Audio**: click it and a list of all the available audio files on your system will appear in the right-hand pane. Selections from here can be moved to your new playlist in various ways: you can select a song and then click the **Add To Playlist** button to get a menu of available playlists; you can simply drag a track from one pane to the other; or you can right-click a track and select **Add To Playlist** from the mouse menu.

Once your music collection starts to get really big, browsing for tracks to build Playlists can be a bit of a drag. That's where **Auto Playlists** (which first appeared in Media Player 9) come into their own. These playlists are dynamic, rather than static, automatically including every track on your machine that fulfils certain criteria. For example, you might have an Auto Playlist which includes all "top-rated songs" or songs tagged as being "hip-hop". If you added more top-rated tunes to your library, or more hip-hop tracks, they will automatically be added to the playlist in question.

To create an Auto Playlist, select **New Auto Playlist** from the **Playlists** button's dropdown. A dialogue box appears where you name

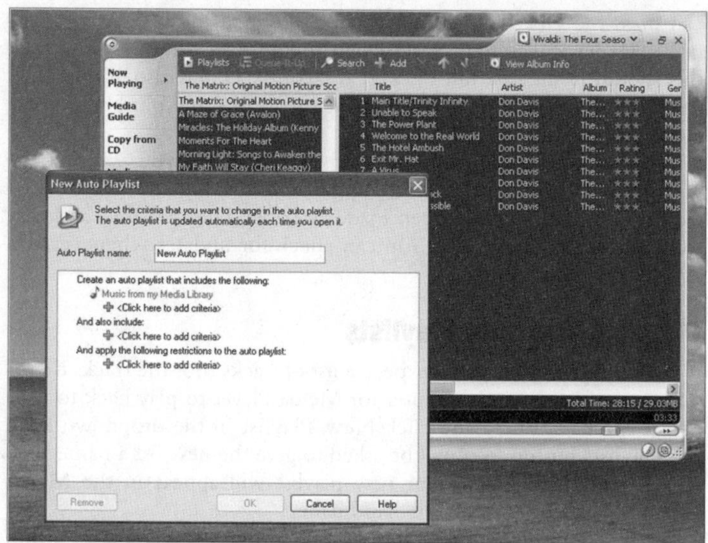

the new list and add parameters: you can make the formula as complex or as simple as you like.

If at any time an Auto Playlist comes up with a combination of tunes that you want to preserve, right-click it and select from the dropdown the option to convert the Auto Playlist to a regular playlist.

There are various freeware and shareware plug-ins to be found online that can help you generate and manage Auto Playlists. A good place to start looking is...

wmplugins www.wmplugins.com

Burning CDs

If you have a CD burner and a recent version of Media Player, you can create a playlist and write it onto a CD to make a compilation album. Just put a blank disc in your burner and select **Copy to CD or Device**

Try This

Give Media Player a makeover

If you find the standard Media Player window a bit cumbersome, you can opt to view the **Compact Mode**. This makes the window a bit smaller but doesn't allow you to get at all the tools. You can switch between the compact and normal modes by clicking the diagonal arrow icon in the bottom right of the window (this icon sometimes appears in its own little **anchor window**). The newer versions of the player also feature a **Mini-player** mode which comfortably slots your controls onto the Taskbar.

You can also change the style of the Media Player look by selecting the **Skin Chooser** button (on the left of the screen in the normal mode). Try it and preview some of the options: they're a little strange but you might find one that takes your fancy.

For more Media Player skins, get online and visit:

http://theskinsfactory.com
www.skinz.org
www.wincustomize.com
www.howard.edu/SkinsGallery

from the File menu (or the equivalent button elsewhere). Media Player will ask you which playlist you want to put on the CD. Select one (choosing **Automatic Volume Levelling** if you want tracks from different sources to play back at an even "normalized" level on your CD) and the CD writer should get straight to work.

Copying music to an MP3 player

You can also use Windows Media Player to manage songs stored on an MP3 player, if your model is supported (many, including the Apple iPod, aren't). Simply connect the device, hit **Copy to CD or Device**, select the playlists or tracks that you want to move, and the device you want to move them to.

Alternative media players

If you find Windows Media Player ugly and generally hard to get on with, try one of the many alternatives that can be downloaded from the Net. These include:

iTunes www.apple.com/itunes
J River Media Center www.musicex.com/mediacenter
JetAudio www.jetaudio.com
MediaMonkey www.mediamonkey.com
Virtuosa www.virtuosa.com

For many more, browse the software archives listed on p.406.

Windows Movie Maker

Windows Movie Maker, a simple and easy-to-use video editing program, first appeared in Windows Me, so if you're running 98 or earlier you won't have it. Windows Me and XP users will find it by clicking the **Start button**, selecting **Programs**, **Accessories** then **Windows Movie Maker**.

A full description of how to use Movie Maker is beyond the scope of this book, but the basic principle is simple. Digital video footage is imported from a video camera, DVD or elsewhere, and broken into manageable chunks called **clips**. These appear on the left-hand side of the window and can be dragged down to the **Storyboard** – shortened, repeated, overlaid or rearranged as necessary – to form a continuous movie. A soundtrack or narration can be added, and the whole movie can be previewed at any time on the screen on the right. Once your edit is complete, you can either leave the movie on your PC, burn it to DVD, or save it for Web use (via the **Send** menu).

Windows Movie Maker is perfectly adequate for messing around with home movies, but if you get seriously into digital video, you may want to investigate more serious alternatives (see p.271).

12 Tips and tricks

hotkeys and other life enhancements

It's perfectly possible to use a PC without them, but if you have the time and inclination you can greatly enhance your computing efficiency by learning some hotkeys and other tricks. Once you're used to opening applications, jumping between windows and navigating menus without even touching your mouse, you'll get things done more quickly and smoothly, and you won't want to take an axe to your computer quite as often. Indeed, you'll probably wonder how you ever previously coped. This chapter introduces the most useful and important hotkeys, as well as other tricks to ensure that Windows is your obliging servant – not the other way around.

Speeding up with shortcut keys

The best single way to slip into the PC fast lane is to use shortcut keys. The mouse isn't very efficient for many tasks – why go through a series of menus with your mouse pointer to reach a dialog box that could be opened instantaneously with a key combination?

One of the most useful shortcuts is **Alt+Tab**, which allows you to move between open windows. Try it: open a few windows in various programs, press and hold **Alt**, and tap **Tab** (while still holding down Alt). A little panel will pop up showing icons representing the windows currently open; keep pressing Tab and you'll move between them. When you get to the window you want, let go – the little panel will vanish and your selected window will move to the foreground. To move between your windows in the opposite direction hold down **Alt+Shift** whilst pressing Tab.

Another useful Alt shortcut is **Alt+F4**, which closes the program you're currently working in.

Windows shortcut keys

If you have a **Windows key** on your keyboard (see p.94), it can be used for all sorts of shortcuts, which will work in whatever program you're working with at the time. Try these out:

Windows	Launches the **Start menu**
Windows+D	**Minimizes** and **restores** all windows for quick access to the Desktop
Windows+E	Launches **Windows Explorer** with the folder tree showing
Windows+F	Launches a **Search** window

Winkey+Ctrl+F	Launches **Search for Computers**
Windows+F1	Launches **Windows Help**
Windows+Pause Break	Opens **System Properties**
Windows+R	Launches the **Run** command dialog box
Windows+U	Launches the **Utility Manager**
Windows+Tab	Cycles through open programs on the Taskbar
Windows+M	**Minimizes** all windows
Windows+Shift+M	**Undoes** the above minimize
Windows+L	Locks the computer (Windows XP)

Mouse magic

You can greatly add to the power of the mouse by using it in combination with the keyboard. Holding down Control, Shift or Alt whilst clicking can give you loads of different options – hold down Control, for example, to click and select multiple files in Windows. In many packages, even the scroll wheel has some hidden secrets: it can be used to zoom in and out when combined with the Control key in many programs, including Microsoft Word.

Seize control with Control

The Control key, often labelled **Ctrl** on keyboards, is the business when it comes to shortcuts – it can be combined with various other keys to carry out all manner of tasks. What each combination does depends on the program you're using, though the most useful shortcuts are near-universal:

Ctrl+A	Select all	**Ctrl+C**	Copy
Ctrl+X	Cut	**Ctrl+N**	New window/document
Ctrl+P	Print	**Ctrl+S**	Save
Ctrl+V	Paste	**Ctrl+W**	Close the current window
Ctrl+Y	Redo	**Ctrl+Z**	Undo

When combined with non-letter keys, Control generally provides a more powerful version of whatever key it is used with. In Windows and most word processors, for example, the **left** and **right cursors** (the arrow keys) move your flashing insertion point along a line of text let-

Oops!

Nearly every application – including Windows Explorer – allows you to **Undo** your most recent command, turning back the clock to before you accidentally deleted something or made some other mistake. Undo can almost always be be accessed in two ways: in the **Edit** menu, and the near-universal keyboard shortcut: **Ctrl+Z**.

Most decent programs go further, allowing you to undo multiple actions – by simply selecting undoing repeatedly – including undoing an undo using **redo**, which is usually **Ctrl+Y**. Some packages such as PhotoShop (see p.266) even provide a **History** palette, making backtracking very easy indeed.

ter by letter. Hold down Control, though, and they move the insertion point a word at a time. Equally, where a tap of the **Enter** key takes you onto a new line, **Ctrl+Enter** takes you to a new page. Likewise, the **Home** and **End** keys escort you to the beginning or end of a line; but combined with Control, they take you to the beginning or end of a whole document or webpage.

Take a look at the menus of your favourite programs and you'll probably find that next to each of the most important options a shortcut key is listed. This is a good way to find application-specific key combinations quickly.

Accelerator keys

A little-known Windows trick is to assign special shortcut keys to each of your programs, allowing you to open them at any time without having to fiddle about with the mouse or the Start menu. Choose a program that you use a lot, go to its icon in the Start menu, right-click it and select **Properties**. Click the **Shortcut** tab (it will probably be open already) and you'll see the **Shortcut key** text box near the bot-

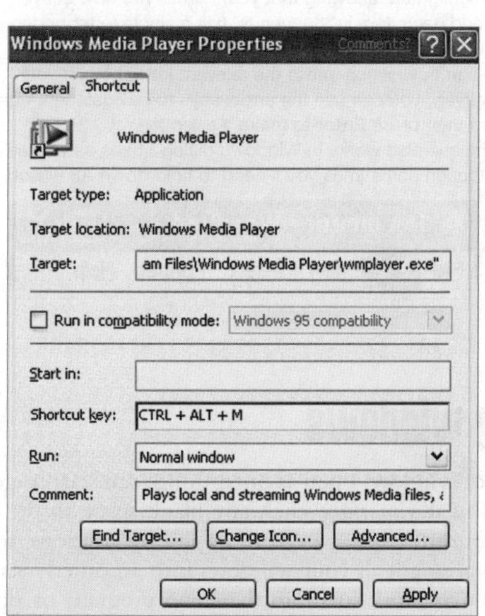

tom, displaying **None**. Click in the box and simply hit the letter on the keyboard you'd like to use as the shortcut key for the program. The first letter of the program's name makes sense – **M** for Media Player, say. The box will then show **Ctrl+Alt+M** (or whichever letter you have entered). Click **OK** to close the dialog box. Now, whenever you hold down **Ctrl+Alt** and press the letter you selected, the program will spring into life.

Try This

Why put mice on the menu?

Open **My Computer** and press the **Alt** key – the **File** menu on the Menu bar will become highlighted, showing that your menus are now active. Each menu title, and each item in the menus, has a single letter underlined: **File**, **Edit**, **Format**, etc. Instead of clicking a menu or item with your mouse, you can now simply press the relevant letter key on your keyboard. Alternatively, you can use the arrow keys to navigate left, right, up and down, and then press **Enter** to make a selection.

This useful technique also works in Windows dialog boxes as well as in most programs (though sometimes you'll need to hold down Alt whilst you press the letter or arrow keys).

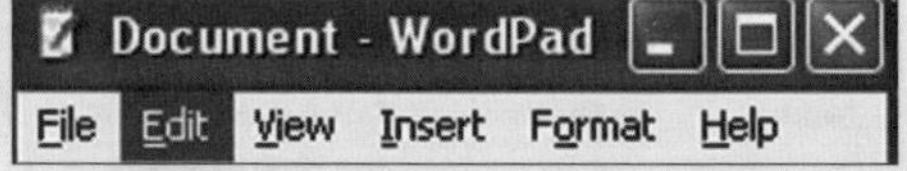

Arranging windows

If you have lots of windows open at once, things can start to get messy and confusing. But if you right-click any blank space in the Taskbar, including its bottom edge, you'll see a list of options including **Cascade**, which arranges all your windows into an orderly stack…

Or, if you want to work in more than one program or document

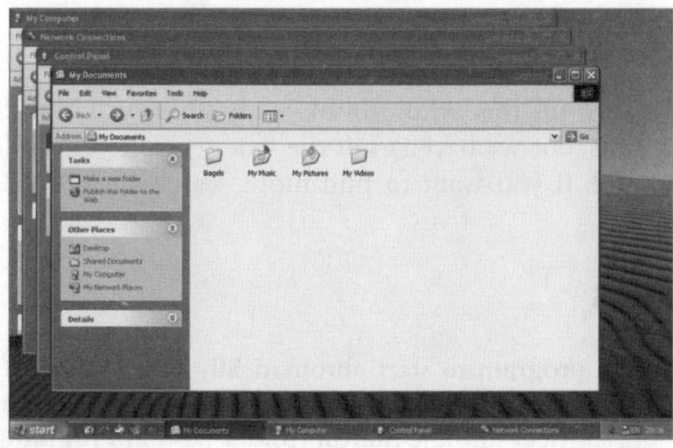

simultaneously, you can **Tile** the windows – divide the screen between them. Minimize or close any windows you don't want to see, right-click any blank area of the Taskbar and click **Tile Windows Vertically**. You can also choose to **Tile Windows Horizontally**.

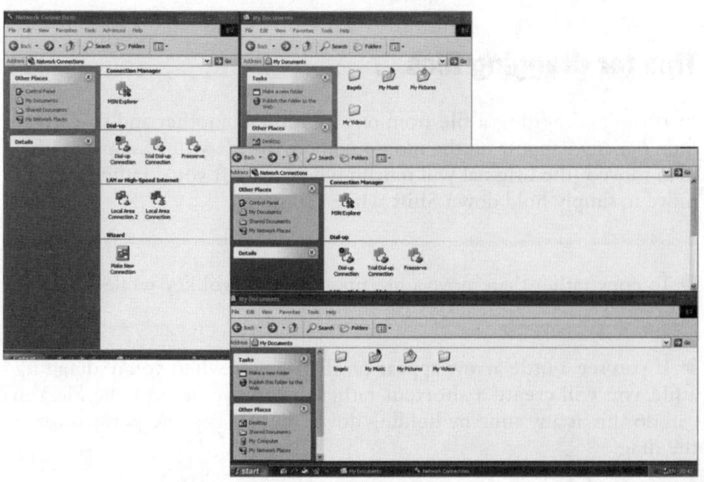

Other Windows tips

We could easily fill this whole book with additional Windows tips, cheats and hints, but we haven't got the space – so here's a selection of the most useful. If you want to find more, search on the Web or just experiment.

Startup tips

▶ If you want **a program to start automatically** when you turn on your PC, find it in the Start menu, right-click it and select **Create shortcut**. Then drag the shortcut into the **Startup folder** (also in **Programs** in the Start menu). This also works with Internet connections. If you later decide that you don't want a program or connection to start automatically, simply delete the shortcut from the Startup folder.

▶ To stop your Startup programs loading on a particular occasion, hold down the **Control** key while the Windows Startup screen is showing.

Tips for dragging files

▶ If you're **dragging a file** from one location to another and you see a little plus sign appear on the mouse pointer, the file will be copied rather than moved (the original will remain where it is). If you'd rather actually move it, simply hold down **Shift** while you drag.

▶ To copy rather than move a file, press the **Control** key while you drag.

▶ If you see a little arrow appear on the pointer when you're dragging a file, you will **create a shortcut** rather than move or copy the file. You can do this at any time by holding down the **Alt** key and performing the drag.

▶ If you want to drag a file into an Explorer window that is open but not visible, drag and hold it over the relevant window's button on the Taskbar. After a second or two the window will rise to the surface, allowing you to complete the drag.

▶ You can **abort a drag** by pressing the **Escape** key before releasing the mouse button.

The Clipboard: Copy, Cut and Paste

Cut, **Copy** and **Paste** are three of the most important and universal PC tools. Whatever you currently have selected – be it a few words of text, part of a picture, or a group of files in Windows Explorer – you can usually "copy" or "cut" it, and "paste" it elsewhere, even into a different program. Copy and Cut are the same, except that Cut removes the copied item from its original location, while Copy leaves it intact.

You can find Cut, Copy and Paste in the Edit menu of nearly all programs, and often on the toolbar, too. However, they're much quicker to access if you learn the keyboard shortcuts:

Cut = Control+X

Copy = Control+C

Paste = Control+V

Whenever you select either Cut or Copy, the selected data is temporarily stored on what's called the **Clipboard**. In turn, whenever you select **Paste,** your PC looks to the clipboard for the data it is supposed to insert (if the Paste command is greyed-out in the Edit menu of a program, this means that the Clipboard is empty). In some Windows versions you can view the contents of the Clipboard at any time by clicking the **Start** button and selecting **Programs**, then **Accessories**, then **System Tools** and finally **Clipboard Viewer**.

Generally the Clipboard can only hold one thing at a time. But some programs allow you to copy several selections to the Clipboard, which can then be pasted either separately or all together. This is sometimes called "spiking".

Tips for browsing files

▶ Windows is set by default so that when you double-click a folder or drive icon in an Explorer window, the window changes to display the contents of the folder or drive. If you hold down **Control** when you double-click, though, a new window will open to display the contents.

▶ If you'd prefer this to happen all the time, it's easy to set up. Open **My Computer** and select **Folder Options** from the **Tools** menu (or the **View** menu in Windows 98). Under the **General** tab, check the **Open each folder in a new window** box and click **OK**.

▶ Selecting **Details** from the **View** menu of an Explorer window puts the items in a list and displays columns of information about them, telling you things like a file's size, its type and the date it was last modified. If you click the grey header of each column, the items will be sorted by whatever the heading relates to: click **Name** to sort alphabetically by name, **Size** to sort numerically by file size, and so on.

▶ To set a **default folder view**, open My Computer and choose your favourite view option from the **View** menu (such as **Details** or **Large Icons**). Then click **Folder Option** in the **Tools** menu (or the **View** menu in Windows 98), select the **View** tab, and click the **Like Current Folder** button. From now on, whenever you open a folder its contents will be displayed with the view option you've chosen.

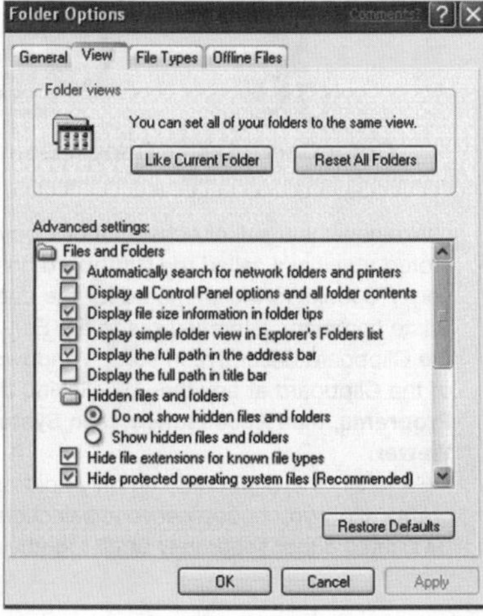

▶ You can **change the icon of a shortcut** file by right-clicking it, selecting **Properties** and then clicking **Change icon**. You can either choose from a pre-installed selection or click **Browse** and select any bitmap file on your machine.

Tips for toolbars

▶ In Explorer windows such as My Documents – as well as in most application windows – you can customize the toolbars, removing buttons you rarely use and adding new ones for commands you frequently need. Often this is done by right-clicking the relevant toolbar and selecting **Customize** from its mouse menu. You will be presented with a dialog box packed full of options and button lists. You can also generally use this dialog box to hide the text labels attached to a button and make other alterations to its appearance.

▶ Toolbars usually live up at the top of a window, but they can often be pulled around at will. Try left-clicking one, on either its edge or a blank section, and dragging it somewhere else. You'll probably discover that it can be repositioned anywhere, have its proportions changed or be anchored to any edge of the window.

Macros

Many programs allow you to record a series of commands – usually called a **macro** or **action** – which you can use to save the time and hassle of typing a string of commands in again and again. Let's say, for example, that in your word processor you regularly take a list, turn it into a table and change the text to a particular font size, colour and style. With a macro or action you can do all this with one touch of a button or by using a customized key combination.

To create a macro in Microsoft Word, for example, click **Macros** in the **Tools** menu and select **Record Macro**. After assigning a button or shortcut key, carefully make all your formatting changes and then press Stop. Next time you come to do the same formatting, simply highlight the relevant text, press the button or keys that you assigned to the macro, and hey presto. The details are different in other programs, but the basic process is the same.

Your tips and tricks

get yourself connected

13 Surfing the Web

Using Internet Explorer

For most computer newbies, getting onto the Internet is the main reason for buying a PC. And that makes sense: the Net is a truly life-changing tool, and one that is becoming ever more integral to the way in which we live. From tapping the almost infinite wealth of information on the World Wide Web to shopping online and staying in touch, it's a case of get online or get left behind. The following two chapters fill you in on using some of Windows' built-in Internet tools, including Internet Explorer for surfing the Web and Outlook Express for email. We've also provided a brief summary of how to go about getting online. But for more on everything from Web searching to newsgroups, from chat to downloading music, see this book's bestselling sister volumes, *The Rough Guide to the Internet* and *The Rough Guide Website Directory*.

Getting online (in brief)

There's a lot to say about choosing an Internet connecton and service provider. There's also lots to say about the finer points of the Web searching, email, messaging, newsgroups, chat, downloading, troubleshooting, and more – all of which is covered in *The Rough Guide to the Internet.* But, in case you aren't yet lucky enough to own a copy, here's a very brief summary of how to get online...

▶ **Dial-up or broadband?** The first question you need to answer is whether to go for a standard dial-up connection or a faster broadband connection. The advantages of a dial-up account are that they are inexpensive and they only require a standard dial-up modem, which is probably already built in to your PC. The advatages of broadband are greater speed (webpages load fast, files download more quickly, etc), a freed-up phone line (with dial-up, when you're online your phone is engaged), and the fact that they're always on (with a dial-up connection, it takes around 30 seconds to connect, but with broadband you can leave it permanently connected, or dial up automatically and almost instantly each time you switch on your computer). The disadvantages of broadband are that you need to buy a special broadband modem (though this may be included free when you sign up for an account), that it typically costs around fifty percent more than dial-up, and that it's not available in all areas.

▶ **Choose an ISP and connection** Next you need to choose an ISP (Internet service provider) and the type of package you want. Ask friends for recommendations, or pick up a local Internet magazine for reviews of the latest offers. Dial-up options usually include a flat-rate packages, with a monthly free for unlimited access (ideal if you're likely to be online for more than a few hours per week), and "pay as you go" accounts with which you only pay a local-call rate for each minute you're online (ideal for light users). If you're going for broadband, you'll need to choose between DSL and cable – there's not too much in it, if both are available (ask your local telco and cable companies) – and the speed of the package you require.

▶ **Set up the connection** Once you've chosen a specific package, there are various ways to set up the connection. With broadband, you'll need to sign up online or by phone and wait for the modem and instructions to arrive. With dial-up, you could either use the Windows built-in referral service (click the "Connect to the Internet" icon on the Desktop); phone the ISP and ask them to send a set-up CD by post; or ask for the account details and set up things manually or using the Windows Internet Connection Wizard.

▶ **Connect...** Once everything's set up, you'll find a icon for your connection either within Dial-up Networking (in My Computer or the Control Panel), on your Desktop, or, in Windows XP, in the Network Connections window (accessible via the Start menu). Double-clicking this icon should get the connection going.

▶ **...disconnect** If you're using a dial-up connection, you'll want to disconnect when you're finished using the Net, both so that your phone will be free and so, if you're paying by the minute for access, you don't incur unnecessary call charges. To disconnect, right-click the Connections icon – generally a graphic of two connected PCs – that appears when you're online in the the Notification area of your Taskbar (by the clock). From the options that appear, click Disconnect.

The Web and the Net

Though they're often used interchangeably, the **World Wide Web** ("the Web") and the **Internet** ("the Net") are not the same thing. The Internet is a giant global network of computers – including yours, when it's online. The Web, meanwhile, is one of the many features of the Net, the others including email, messaging and file transfer. The Web consists of billions of **webpages**, special documents with text, pictures and more which you view with a piece of software called a **Web browser** such as Internet Explorer.

What makes a webpage special is that can contain links (also called **hyperlinks**). When you **click on a link**, something happens. Generally, it brings up another page, but it might do something else like launch a Net radio broadcast or start a file download.

Each page on the Web has its own unique **address**, which, when written out in full, looks something like this:

http://www.mywebpage.com

Starting out with Internet Explorer

If you're running **Windows** 98 or later, **Internet Explorer** (or **IE** for short) is built into your operating system. And Microsoft's policy has been to integrate the browsing experience into the Desktop, so Windows Explorer and IE share roughly the same interface, meaning that, whether you're surfing the Web or ferreting through your hard drive, things will look and feel similar.

But just because you have IE doesn't mean you have the latest version. **It's very important to regularly update IE**, for security as well as functionality (see p.246 to read how). Equally, just because you have IE doesn't mean it's the best browser out there – many others can be downloaded for free from the Web (see p.215).

Your first time

Connect to the Internet (as described on the previous page) and launch Explorer by double-clicking the its icon – a big blue letter "e" on the Desktop, Start menu and/or the Quick Launch toolbar.

IE will probably try to access its pre-set home page, which at some stage soon you'll want to change (see box). However, for now, let it do what it wants and ignore whatever comes up. See the white bar running horizontally at the top? That's the **Address bar**. Click inside it, delete whatever is there, type **www.yahoo.com** and hit Enter (or click on the Go button at the far right of the bar).

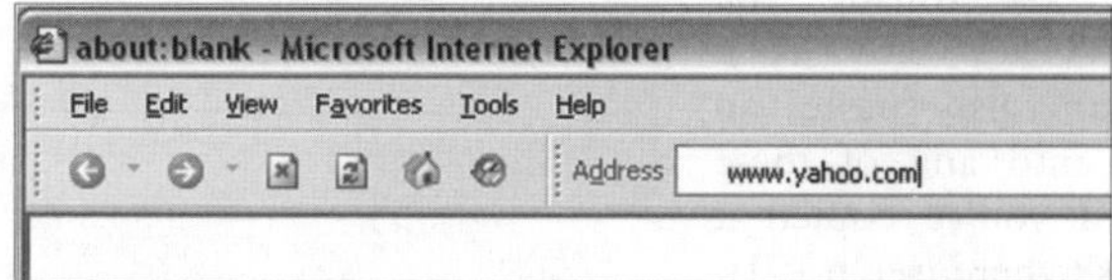

Your browser will examine the address and work out what to do next. If you've submitted a legitimate Web address, it will contact your DNS server to convert the host name into an IP address. Once it's converted, the browser will contact the website's server and request the page.

It rarely takes long to locate and load webpages. With a 56K modem, it might be five to thirty seconds, but if you've a broadband connection it can be almost instantaneous. If all works well, your browser will retrieve the page and display it on your screen. In this case, you'll arrive at **Yahoo!**, a giant site offering a massive directory and lots of other services.

Lose the homepage

Every time you go online you'll probably find that your browser automatically looks for a page that you haven't requested – usually your ISP or the person who supplied the browser. This is deeply annoying, but can easily be sorted out – all you need is to get rid of, or change, your **homepage** – or **start** page. In Internet Explorer, you'll find the solution under the General tab of Internet Options (in the Tools menu). You can change the homepage to any address you like – probably the best bet is a good **search engine**, such as www.google.com – or opt to start with a blank page. This way you don't have to wait for anything to load each time you open a window, and it won't cause problems when you open your browser while offline.

Other ways to enter an address

There are lots of other ways to enter a Web address. For example, through "Open" under the File menu of your browser; in the address bar in Windows Explorer; or through the "Run" option in the Start menu (which can be reached quickly by hitting the Windows key plus "R"). You can also paste an address into any of these places, if you've copied it from elsewhere (see p.191).

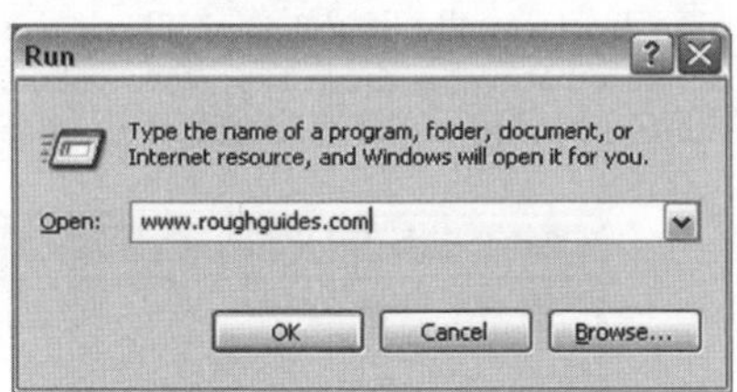

What about the http:// bit of the address?

Although the formal way to write a Web address is to start it with http:// (for example, http://www.yahoo.com) **you don't need to enter the http:// part** into your browser. For that reason, you'll often see Web addresses expressed without it – including in this book, for example.

It won't make any difference which way you enter the address; your browser will automatically add on the http:// if you omit it. This will only cause problems if the address isn't a Web address – that is, it starts with something other than: http://.

You can also usually get away without writing the www, though this doesn't always work.

Address guessing – helpful

Once you've been online for a short time you'll notice that your browser will start trying to guess the address you're entering. It will present a dropdown list of all the sites it knows that match what you've typed so far. These are supplied by your **History** (p.207). And the link that it thinks is most likely the one you're entering will appear in grey in the Address bar. Clicking Enter will go to that address; otherwise complete the address manually or use your mouse or keyboard to select one of the addresses in the list.

Address searching – not so helpful

If you enter a word or phrase rather than a properly formed address, your browser will try to guess or search for the site. However, this is more annoying than useful, so you might want to stop it happening: the various options can be set in the "Search in Address bar" section of the Advanced tab in Internet Options (in the Tools menu). If you acually want to search for something, you'd be **better off using a search engine** such as **www.google.com**

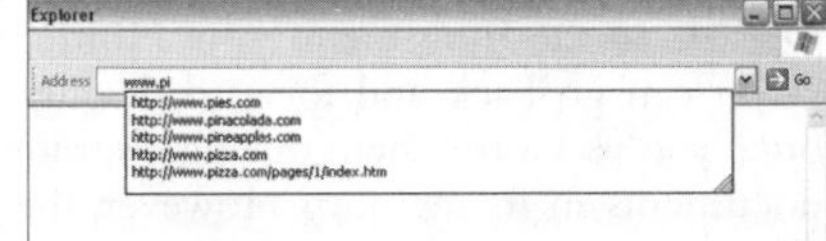

Clicking on links

You rarely have to enter addresses to get around the Web, because most of the time you'll simply be **clicking on links**. Webpages are written in **HTML** (HyperText Markup Language), which lets documents **link** to other documents. Clicking on such a link effectively turns the page. This creates a sort of third dimension.

Unless you've changed the settings, **text that contains links** to other documents – or another part of the same document – will usually be highlighted in blue and underlined (though this isn't a rule). Images and movies can also contain links, and not necessarily just one: a picture might contain various links that relate to what's in each part of the picture. For example, clicking on a country on a map might send you to a page about that country. In webspeak, this type of picture is called an **image map**.

When you pass over a link **your mouse cursor will change from an arrow to a pointing hand** and the target address should appear in a bar at the bottom of your browser. It's easy for site programmers to override this and place alternative text in the bottom bar, or make your mouse do funny things like leave trails, so don't be alarmed if it doesn't always work in the same way.

To pursue the link, simply **click on the relevant text or image**. A link is only a **one-way connection**, like a signpost. So when you get to the new page, there won't necessarily be a link back, but that's no problem as you can simply use your browser's **back button**…

The basic controls

All the main **navigation buttons** are located on the toolbar above the main browser window. Displaying them is optional, but they're hard to live without. You'll use the **Back** and **Forward** buttons most. To **go back to a page** you previously visited, click the Back button until you find it. To **return to where you were**, keep pressing Forward. And to go back to your homepage – which you can chose within Internet Options in the Tools menu – hit **Home**.

You can go back and forward through pages pretty much instantly once you've visited them during a session, as your computer stores the documents in its memory. However, the amount of material you can click through in this fashion depends on the amount of storage space allocated to **Temporary Internet Files** in your settings (see p.211).

Two other important buttons are **Stop** and **Refresh**. To **cancel a page request** – because it's taking too long to load a site or you've made a mistake – just hit Stop. Occasionally, you might have to hit Stop before Back will work. Alternatively, if a page doesn't load properly, you can hit **Refresh** to load it again. You'd also do this if a page changes regularly, and you want to load a new version rather than one that's stored in your hard drive (or on your ISP's proxy server).

Surfing shortcuts

Tips & Tricks

Especially if you're using a laptop, but also on a Desktop machine, you might sometimes find it faster and easier to use keyboard shortcuts instead of the mouse or trackpad. The basics keys are:

Back	Alt+Left Cursor
Forward	Alt+Right Cursor
Select next link or field	Tab
Previous link or field	Shift+Tab
Click on a link	Enter
Toggle between windows	Alt+Tab

Use your mouse

The next most important navigation controls are accessed with the **right mouse button**, which will yield a little menu of options when clicked. The menu will change depending upon what you click. For instance, if you click on a link, you'll have the option of opening the target page in a new window. Click on an image and you'll see the option to save it to disk. You'll also find Back, Forward, Refresh and Print in there.

Change the buttons and bars

You can customize the way the buttons and bars appear in IE, which is handy because in the default state they take up too much screen room. So once you're familiar with the buttons, choose to display them **small and without text**. To access the settings, right-click on the toolbar and choose "**Customize**", or look under "Toolbars" in the View menu.

You can also move the bars around to your liking, by dragging and dropping them using their left-hand edges. If you're running IE6.0 or later, you'll need to right-click on the toolbar and select "Unlock" first.

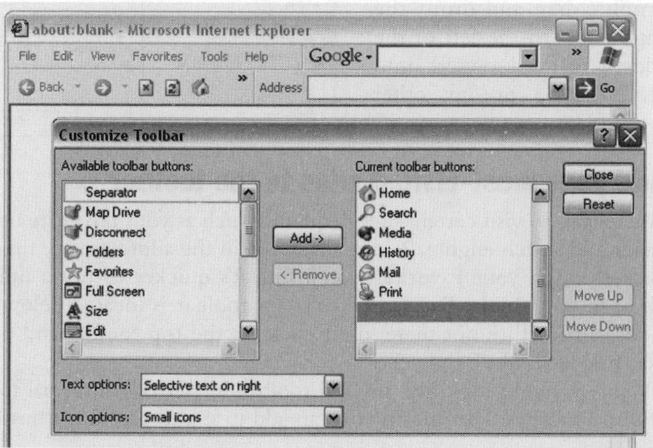

Find a page later with Favorites

Whenever you find a page that's worth another visit, add it into your **Favorites** – you'll find an option to do this in the Favorites menu. Then next time you want to visit the site, you don't have to type in the address: you can just select the name from the menu.

When you "bookmark" a site in this way, you'll be given the option of saving it directly into the menu, or into a folder – try to get into the habit of using folders to group related things together or you'll end up with a huge menu in which it's hard to find things. You can tidy up and organise your list at any time by clicking "**Organize Favorites**" from the Favorites menu.

When you add a Favorite, it will also give you the option of making it **available offline**. If you agree, it will check the page at whatever intervals you specify to see if it's changed. At the same time it can also download the page, and others linked to it, so that you can later browse the site offline (see p.211).

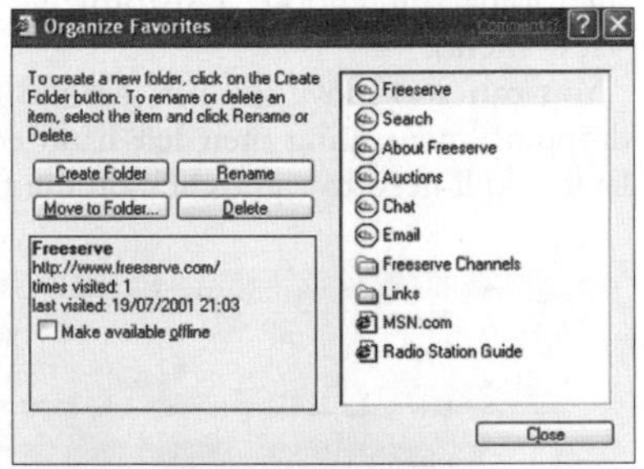

Another way to save an address for viewing later is to simply drag-and-drop the page icon (to the left of the address in the browser) onto the Desktop or any other location.

Add your most-visited sites to the toolbar

You're sure to visit certain sites frequently, such as your favourite newspaper and search engine. Rather than type in the address every time or click through your Favorites, you'll find it's quicker to put a link to them in your **Links bar**. By default, this toolbar is located below the Address bar. If it's not there, right-click on the top toolbar and put a tick beside "Links".

While it might look like any old toolbar, it's actually a special folder within Favorites. That means you can add to it and organize it just like any other Favorites folder (see opposite). You can also drag-and-drop links directly from the Address bar onto the Links bar. But before you put it to use, clear out all the junk supplied by Microsoft or whoever provided your copy of IE. And rather than stack it full of individual links, try creating a few folders.

Retrace your steps – History

Whenever you visit a site, your browser stores its name and address in a list called the **History**. To view its contents click the History button on the toolbar. You can sort the list by date, name or order of visit, or search through the contents of the pages listed. To revisit a page, simply click its entry.

In Internet Options (in the Tools menu), you can also set the length of time that sites should remain in your History. A long History folder can be useful, but in some circumstances it can also cause problems and slow things down – especially if you surf a lot – so it's wise to keep the expiry time to around twenty days. After you've been online for a month or so, try clearing your History and see if that speeds things up. If it does, reduce the time period or number of sites.

How to tell where you've been

By default, links to pages that you have already visited appear in underlined blue text, and links to pages you that you have visited appear either in black, purple or red. However, individual sites can override these settings and you can also change the default colours in the General tab of Internet Options (in the the Tools menu).

See how this works for yourself. Look at any page. Links you haven't followed should appear blue and underlined. Now click one and load the page. Next, click "Back" and return to the previous page. The link will have changed colour. What's more, **visited links will appear in the new colour wherever they crop up**, even on a completely different page that you are visiting for the first time. This can be useful if you're viewing directories and lists, as you can instantly note what you've seen before. Visited links eventually expire and revert to their old colour, depending on how long you set your History (see above).

More tricks

Download an image, movie, sound file or program

To save an image, right-click on it and choose **Save As** or **Save Image As...** from the menu.You can copy image, ready to paste it eslewhere, or even set it directly as your Desktop wallpaper (try clicking the image first to see if it links to a higher-resolution version).To save a movie or sound clip – or any other type of file – the best approach is to click on a link that leads to it and choose **Save Target As**... from the mouse menu.

If you download a lot of files with your browser, you could consider trying a special download plug-in. For example, **Mass Downloader** (www.metaproducts.com) allows you to look inside – and download selectively from – a zip archive. It will also resume broken downloads more reliably than Explorer and can scan a page and download all linked files of a specified type.

Print a page

To print a page, simply choose "**Print**" from under the File menu. Note the various layout options on the box that will pop up. To alter the margins, headers and footers, and other details, select **Page Setup**. To view how it will look on a page, select **Preview**.

Find something on a page

To search for a word or phrase within a webpage, choose "Find" under the Edit menu, or use the shortcut **Ctrl+F**.

AutoComplete

Apart from suggesting addresses from your History, modern browsers such as IE can also **suggest form entries**, such as search engine terms, user names and passwords. For this to work, you'll need to enable **AutoComplete** – you'll find various settings, and the option to delete the current data, by clicking "AutoComplete" in the Content tab in Internet Options (in the Tools menu).

Change the text size

To change the size of the text on a webpage in Internet Explorer, look in "Text Size" in the View menu. Also try holding down **Ctrl as you roll the mouse wheel.**

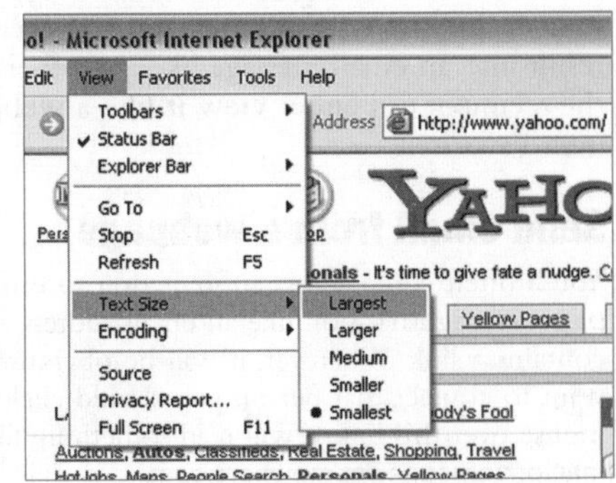

The only problem is that increasing or decreasing the text size can do strange things to a webpage's layout. If you want the text to appear bigger without this happening, you could try decreasing your **Screen resolution** (see p.133) or using a browser such as **Opera** (see p.215), which allows you to scale up the whole page instead of just the text.

Copy and paste text

To copy text from webpages, highlight the section, choose "**Copy**" from the Edit or right-click mouse menu and then switch to your word processor, text editor or mail program and select "**Paste**". Alternatively, use the standard shortcuts: hold down Control and press C for copy and V for paste.

Send addresses to a friend

One of the things you'll inevitably want to do at some point is **share an online discovery** with friends. The simplest way is to copy the site's address into a mail message, perhaps along with a note or a section copied and pasted from the page as described above. Alternatively, you can send a link or **whole page** by choosing "**Send**" from under the **File** menu. However, if you send a whole page to someone who uses a mail system that doesn't understand HTML mail, it will come through as mumbo-jumbo.

That's straightforward enough, but what if you want to **send a whole list**? You could copy and paste the addresses manually into an email, or save them to your **Favorites** in a new folder. That way you can **export** the folder (or all your Favorites) as an HTML file with the Import/Export Wizard under the File menu. Then drag-and-drop the result into an email message like any other attachment (see p.222), and the recipient can either **view it like a webpage** or **import it** into their own Favorites.

Send email from a webpage

You'll often come across an invitation to **email someone from a webpage**. It mightn't look like an email address – it might be just a name that contains a link. Whatever, it will be obvious from the context that if you want to contact that person you should click on the link. If you pass your mouse over this link it will read something like this:

mailto: someone@somewhere.com

And when you click on it, it will call up your mail program, addressing a new message to someone@somewhere.com. Just type your message and send it. Any replies will arrive through the normal channels.

If it opens the **wrong email program**, you may have the wrong program specified as your default. Look under **Programs** in **Internet Options** (in the Tools menu).

Uncover the source

If you're interested in **learning Web design**, or just understanding exactly what a webpage actually is, you'll find it informative to peek at the raw HTML coding behind the pages you like. To do so, choose **View Source** from the View menu (or the right-click mouse menu).

What's related

Internet Explorer can offer you a list of related sites courtesy of **Alexa** (www.alexa.com). Click on **Show Related Links** under the Tools menu. It looks impressive at first, but you'll usually get better value using search engines and directories (see p.203).

Browsing offline

If you're paying by the minute to be online, consider **gathering pages** rather than reading. When you use Internet Explorer, any pages you load go onto your hard drive are available for reading offline later. That means you can run back through your session after you hang up. You can prevent Internet Explorer from trying to go online by choosing **Work Offline** from the File menu.

Once in offline mode, you can **call up sites** by typing in their addresses or following links – just as if you were online – or by clicking on their entries in your History. The contents of the pages are stored temporarily in a folder called **Temporary Internet Files**. These exist partly to enable offline browsing, but primarily to speed up online browsing (if you return to a page, your browser will load the saved version rather than downloading it again from the Net).

Clear your Temporary Internet Files

The Temporary Internet Files settings are under the General tab in Internet Options (in the Tools menu). You can change their **location**, how much **disk space** to allocate and when to **check for newer versions** (every time you start Internet Explorer is usually the best choice; you can always click Refresh if you think a webpage has changed during a session).

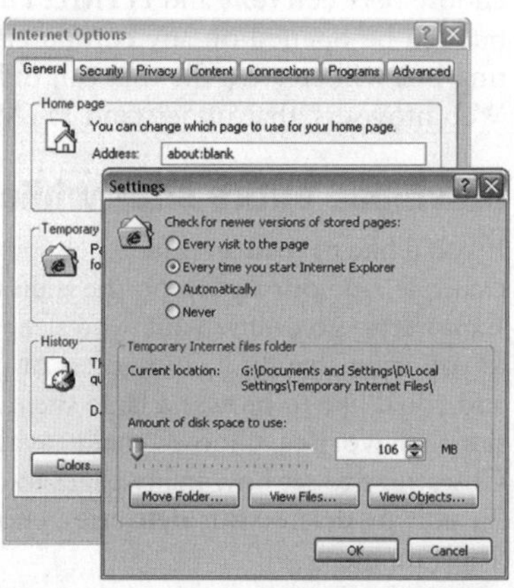

This is also the proper place to delete all the stored pages – if you try to do it manually, it will cause problems. Unless you plan to read offline, it's wise to **delete them every week or two** as, like the History folder, they can sometimes slow things down, especially on elderly machines. Indeed, if your **browser is playing up** and not loading pages properly, try clearing the files – it's often an instant fix.

Search your History

As mentioned earlier, the History folder makes it very easy to backtrack your session. But, even better, you can **search the contents of the pages stored in your Temporary Internet Files** – it's like having your own search engine. Click the History button on the toolbar to find the search box. However, these pages won't sit on your hard drive forever – they're governed by your Temporary Internet Files settings and will be overwritten next time you visit that same address. So, if you wish to archive a page permanently, save it...

Save a page

To save a webpage, choose "Save As" from the File menu. If you want the whole page – with images and all – you'll need to save as a **complete webpage** or **Web archive**. The first option automatically saves an HTML file with the images in a separate folder. The latter combines all the elements into a single file – this is much neater but it can only be viewed in IE5 or later. If you only want the text on a page, you can choose between **text** and **HTML**. The former will lose the formatting, but can be opened on any computer; the latter will retain the formatting but will create a file that can only be viewed in programs, such as Web browsers, that understand HTML.

Download entire sites while you sleep

If you'd like to read an online newspaper or other site when offline – for example, on your laptop on the train to work – you can set up Internet Explorer to go online while you sleep and download as much of the site as you want (handy if your access or phone charges are less late at night and you'd like to browse a large site during working hours). Just save the site to **Favorites**, choose "**make available offline**", and then click on Customize to set how many pages to download and when to grab them. To edit or delete your deliveries, choose **Synchronize** from under the Tools menu.

But if you're serious about ripping the contents from a site for offline use, look no further than **Offline Explorer**, an amazingly feature-packed tool designed specifically for the job. You can set it up to extract only certain types and sizes of files, and configure all manner of keyword restrictions in the server and directory names. For example, you could visit a music site before you retire for the evening, right-click on the page, choose "download page with offline explorer", set the parameters and wake up to a folder full of MP3s.

Offline Explorer www.metaproducts.com

Privacy & security

Cookies

A **cookie** is a small text file placed on your computer by a Web server as a sort of ID card. This means that next time you drop by, it will know you. Actually, it doesn't quite know it's "you", it only recognizes your individual browser. If you were to visit on another machine or with a different browser on the same machine, it would see you as a different visitor. Or, conversely, if someone else were to use your browser, it couldn't tell the difference.

Most websites routinely **log your visit**. They can tell a few things like which browser you're using and the last site you've seen. This is recorded against your IP address. However, because most Net users are issued a different IP address each time they log on, this information isn't useful for building individual profiles. If analysts can log this data against a cookie ID instead, they have a better chance of recognizing repeat visitors.

On the next level, if you **voluntarily submit further details**, they can store them in a database against your cookie and use it to do things like tailor the site to your preferences, or save you entering the same data each time you check in. This won't be stored on your computer, so other sites can't access it. And they won't know anything personal about you – not even your email address – unless you tell them.

Still, many people object to cookies, either because they feel they're an invasion of privacy or because they can leave a record of where you've been browsing (see below). If you want to, you can refuse all cookies or be prompted to accept or refuse each one individually. Go to the **Privacy** tab in Internet Options (in IE's Tools menu) and choose from the slider settings (though it's probably best left on the default, "Medium"). To delete those cookies already on your system, look in the General tab.

For more on cookies, see:

Cookie Central www.cookiecentral.com

Censor Web material from kids

Internet Explorer employs the **PICS** (Platform for Internet Content Selection) system, allowing you to **bar access to certain sites** that might be on the wrong side of educational. You can set ratings for language, nudity, sex and violence. The settings can be found under **Content Advisor** in the Content tab of Internet Options (in the Tools menu). If you **forget your password**, you'll need to delete a registry key to restore full use of the browser. For instructions, see:
www.ieinfosite.co.uk/tip_view.asp?id=16

Hide your tracks

Because your browser records all your online activities, it's easy for someone to find out where you've been spending your time. As we've seen, every site you visit is stored (for a time, at least) in your **History**. So if you open your History folder you'll instantly see where you've been. More evidence is stored under the **Address bar**. Just click the down arrow on the right-hand side of the bar to reveal a list of recent sites. The contents of those pages are stored as **Temporary Internet Files**, and it's very likely the sites deposited their own telltale **cookies** in the special cookie folder. Finally, if you've entered anything into a form such as a search engine, double-clicking in that form may reveal a list of previous entries courtesy of **AutoComplete** (Autofill on

Macs). To cover your tracks you must either delete all these files and records, or ensure they're not recorded in the first place.

You can delete Temporary Internet Files, History and Cookies under the General tab in Internet Options (in the Tools menu). Deleting History will also clear the entries from your Address bar. To clear your AutoComplete entries – or disable this feature altogether – go to the Content tab.

Other browsers

Most people stick with Internet Explorer simply because it comes bundled with Windows, but other browsers are out there, and many of them are more fully featured than IE, with useful tools such as tabbed browsing (opening many pages in a single window). Most browsers are are available to download for free, so try a few out and see if you find one you prefer.

The obvious ones to try first are **Opera**, which claims to be "the fastest browser on earth" and is very feature packed (but has an ad bar on the free version), and **Mozilla**, which is the open-source version of Explorer's traditional rival, **Netscape**. Netscape itself is still around – and pretty decent – though it looks unlikely there wil be any new versions in the future, so it's not worth getting used to. Then there's **MSN Explorer**, another Microsoft product that ships with XP (the one with the butterfly icon); it may be easy to use, but its primary function is to make the Web a Microsoft-only experience. You're better sticking with Explorer or one of the others mentioned above. For more information, see:

Mozilla www.mozilla.org
MSN Explorer http://explorer.msn.com
Netscape http://browsers.netscape.com
Opera www.opera.com

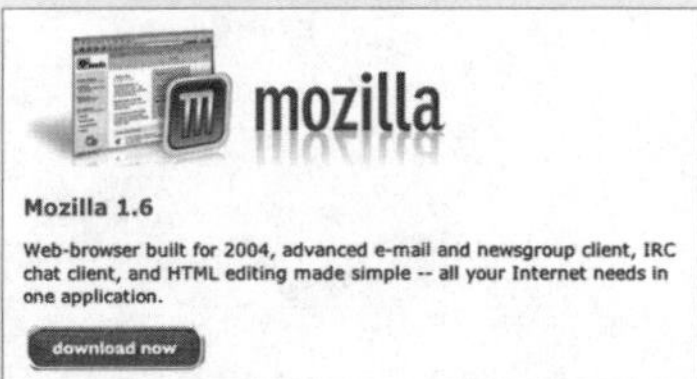

Or, for even more browsers, see:

Browser News www.upsdell.com/BrowserNews/
Download.com Browsers www.browsers.com

To **delete individual sites from your** History in Explorer, click on the History button, right-click on the entry in question and choose "Delete" from the pop-up menu. To **disable History completely**, set the "number of days to keep pages in History" to zero – but it's wiser to check the box to "**Empty Temporary Internet Files folder when browser is closed**" under the Advanced tab instead. Both these options will prevent you from browsing offline, or searching through the contents of your past sessions.

While these measures are fine for stopping the average punter seeing what you've been doing online, they're not airtight. Deleting a file doesn't actually remove all traces of it from your hard drive. To do that you need a special program such as the free **Eraser** (**www.heidi.ie/eraser**). The same folks also make a completely stand-alone browser that promises to leave no records anywhere (**www.heidi.ie/NoTrax**).

14

Email & messaging

Outlook Express and Messenger

This chapter focuses on two of the most useful and fun means of online communication and their relevant Windows programs: Outlook Express for email and Windows Messenger for instant messaging. Naturally, there's a lot more to say about email than we have space for here. And there are also many other ways to communicate via the Internet, including forums and chat rooms on the Web, Usenet newsgroups and Internet relay chat. For more on all these areas, see *The Rough Guide to the Internet*.

Email

Email – which is short for **electronic mail** – has become the standard for businesses to communicate, overseas friends and family to stay in touch, and office employees to chat to their peers instead of doing any work. For the uninitiated, it may seem like a simple, perhaps even silly, concept: you type a message on one computer and send it to another instead of simply picking up the phone and talking in person. But as anyone who uses email will tell you, it brings about a whole different mode of communication – as informal and instantaneous as a phone call but with all the benefits of good old-fashioned letter writing.

Email also lets you do lots of clever stuff: send one message to lots of people, **forward** a message you received to someone else, **attach** documents and pictures to a message so that the recipient can open them on their machine – the list goes on.

Webmail accounts

An alternative to using a POP3 account, like the one provided by your ISP, is to a Web-based email account from one of the many free online providers, such as **Gmail**, **Yahoo!** and **Hotmail**. With these accounts, you don't use an email program, but simply visit the Website of the provider, enter your username and password (which you'll be given when you open the account), then send, receive, store and manage your emails online. The main advantage of Web-based accounts is that all your mail is available wherever you are, since it's all stored on the account provider's server (computer). However, they also have some serious drawbacks. For one thing, they only provide you with a **limited amount of space** – sometimes just a couple of megabytes. A single email with a large attachment may push you over your account limit, and then you won't receive any more messages until you delete some. Secondly, you might find your account "**frozen**", and your messages deleted, if you don't log in for a certain number of weeks. Furthermore, you can't view your mail without **going online**, and everything **takes longer** – especially if you have a slow connection – as every message you open is like opening a webpage. For more on email accounts, see *The Rough Guide to the Internet*.

Accounts and addresses

To send and receive email you need an email address, which, like a real address, is what the sender adds to their message to direct it to you. An email address always looks something like this:

myname@myISPorcompany.com

There are various types of email accounts, including **Webmail**, with which you read, send and manage your email via a Web browser (see box). A better option, however, is a **POP3** account, which is almost always included when you sign up with an ISP. With POP3 mail (which, incidentally, stands for Post Office Protocol 3), you send, receive and manage your mail with a dedicated **email program**. There are plenty of these around, but a pretty good one, called **Outlook Express** – or **OE** for short – is built into Windows. You can open OE by clicking the little envelope icon in the Start menu or on the Quick Launch area of the Taskbar.

Setting up

Depending on how you signed up with your ISP, you have probably already chosen an email address, even if you haven't used it yet. And, depending on whether you used the ISP's installation CD, it may even have automatically set itself up in Outlook Express. If not, your ISP should be able to provide you with a simple set of instructions for getting things going. Usually it simply involves choosing an address and password online, and then entering this information (along with your ISP's mail server addresses) into Outlook Express's **Accounts** window (which you'll find in the Tools menu).

For more on setting up an Internet connection, contact your ISP, or see *The Rough Guide to the Internet*.

The basics: composing, sending and receiving

Using email is a breeze – there are only a few concepts to get used to and all of them are easy to grasp. The following few pages should be enough to get you going. And, though we focus on Outlook Express, other email programs all work in pretty much the same way.

Once your email account is set up, Outlook Express should look something like this:

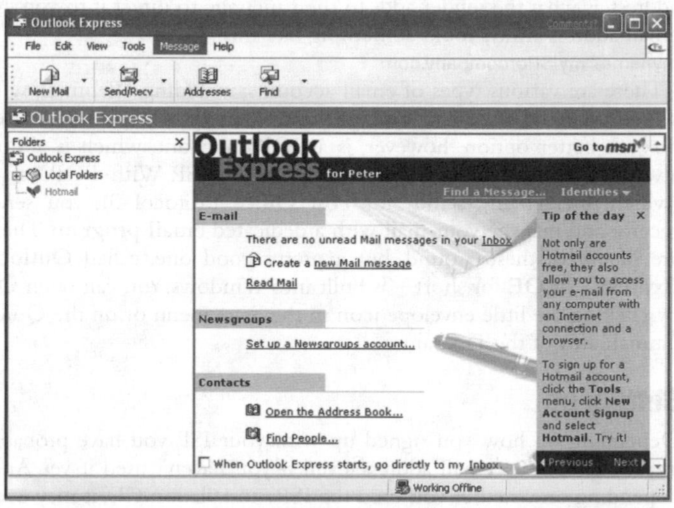

Your emails are arranged into folders, which will appear listed down the left (if they're not visible, double-click **Local Folders**). The most important folders are the **Inbox**, where messages arrive; the **Outbox**, where messages you've written are held until you click **Send/Receive**; and **Sent Mail**, where copies of your outgoing messages are stored. However, you can also create folders yourself (see box on p.222), to help keep your mail archive nice and tidy.

Click the **Inbox** and you'll see all the messages you've received so far in the top right-hand section of the screen – if you haven't given your address to anyone yet, there will probably just be a couple of nondescript welcome emails from your ISP and Outlook Express. To check if you have any new mail, simply click the **Send/Receive** button on the toolbar. Your computer will try to connect to the Internet and download any new messages.

Composing and sending a message

Click **New Message** (**Create** or **Compose** in some programs) and you'll be presented with a blank message window.

Enter the email address of the person you want to send the message to in the **To** section. As a trial, you could send something to yourself, then you'll get to send and receive something straight away.

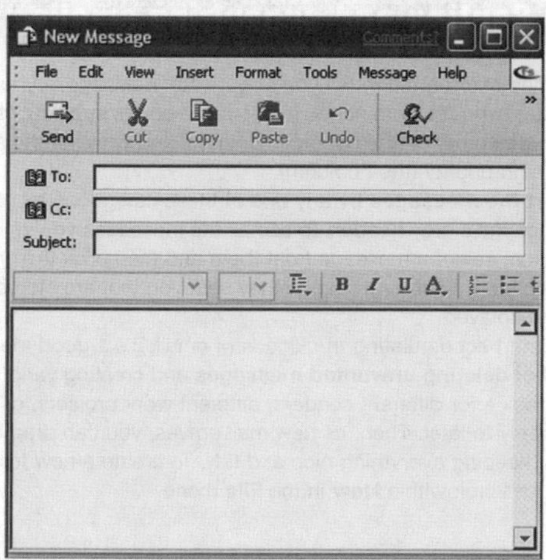

If you want to send the message to more than one person, simply write more addresses, separating them with semicolons. You can also **copy** the message to one or more people by entering their addresses in the **Cc** section (the term comes from "carbon copy"). They will receive the message but see that it was addressed primarily to someone else.

Then enter a **subject** for the message – you don't have to, but it makes it easy for the recipient to see what the message is about and to find it if they need to refer to it later. Finally, if you have more than one email account set up in Outlook Express, use the **From** dropdown menu to choose the account you want to send the message from.

Then simply write your message and click **Send**.

If you are replying to an email, it's even simpler. Click **Reply** on the toolbar and a new message window will appear with the To and Subject sections already filled in. If you've been sent a message that was addressed or copied to more than one person, you have the choice to click **Reply All**, which sends the new message to everyone who received the original.

Sorting and organizing emails

Various columns of information tell you about each message in your Inbox or any other folder: who it's from, when it was received, its subject, whether there are any attachments (the paperclip column) and whether the sender has marked it as high priority (the **!** column).

You can **sort the messages** by any one of these categories by clicking on the relevant column's grey header. To see all the messages you've received from one person, select a message from them and then click the grey header of the **From** column. All the messages they sent you that are stored in the folder will be displayed.

Before you start accumulating truckloads of email, it's a good idea to get into the habit of **deleting unwanted messages** and creating various **folders** within your Inbox – for different senders, different work projects, or emails that you need to reply to later. Then, as new mail arrives, you can drag items into these folders, keeping everything nice and tidy. To create a new folder, click on the Inbox and look within **New** in the **File** menu.

Attachments

One of the beauties of email is that you can attach any file or files to a message – a photo, a document you'd like someone to look over, a form to be filled in and returned or anything else you fancy sending. All you do is click the **Attach** button when composing a message, select the files you want to add and click **OK**. Bear in mind, though, that large files can take a long time to **upload** (send) and **download** (receive), especially with a slow connection – so if you send all your friends a 50 MB video file you may become unpopular very quickly. If you do have large files to send, consider **compressing** them to reduce their size (see p.124) and, in general, don't send anything bigger than a few megabytes without warning the recipient – unless you know they have broadband.

Address book

Try clicking the **Addresses** button on the Outlook Express toolbar to open your Windows address book (which can also be accessed via the **Accessories** section of the Start menu; see p.162). This is a useful place to keep details of all the people you correspond with. If someone's name and email address is in your address book, you can simply type their name in the **To** section of a message and Outlook will immediately insert that person's email address for you.

Working offline

When you're writing a long email, bear in mind that you can choose to **Work Offline** via the command in Outlook's **File** menu. This way you can disconnect from the Internet to free up your phoneline – and save some money if you're paying for your connection by the minute. Then, when you're ready, click **Send/Receive** and your PC will go online and send your mail. You can even set Outlook to automatically disconnect each time it finishes sending and receiving: from the **Tools** menu select **Options**, and then, under the **Connection** tab, check the **Hang up after sending and receiving** box and click **Apply**.

Instant messaging

Instant messaging (IM) allows you to "chat" – exchange typed messages in real time – with one or more friends, or "buddies" as they're called in this contexts. And, unless they've chosen to hide their presence, you can instantly tell which of your contacts are online, so you can send them a quick note and expect an immediate reply. If they're not online, you can send a note for them to receive the second they log on. You can also **trade files**, **play games** and, if your connection is up to it, talk with **sound and video**. It's not quite like being in Star Trek, but it's getting there – and it's free.

Setting up instant messaging

To use instant messaging, the first thing you need is a messaging program. Then you need to set it up with a user name and password. Anyone running Windows XP already has **Windows Messenger** pre-installed – you'll find it in the **Start** button's under **Programs**. However, there are various other programs out there that you can download, including MSN Messenger, which is more up-to-date and has more features (including video phone calls), but also disaplys ads. Other popular messaging programs are made by AOL, ICQ and Yahoo:

AOL Instant Messenger www.aim.com
ICQ www.icq.com
MSN Messenger http://messenger.msn.com
Yahoo! Messenger http://messenger.yahoo.com

Windows and MSN messengers are compatible, and so are AIM and ICQ, but other than that, these systems are incompatible. If your friends are spilt across numerous systems, you can install more than one program (you'll need a username and password for each), though it can get annoying, as having multiple programs running in the background can slow your system

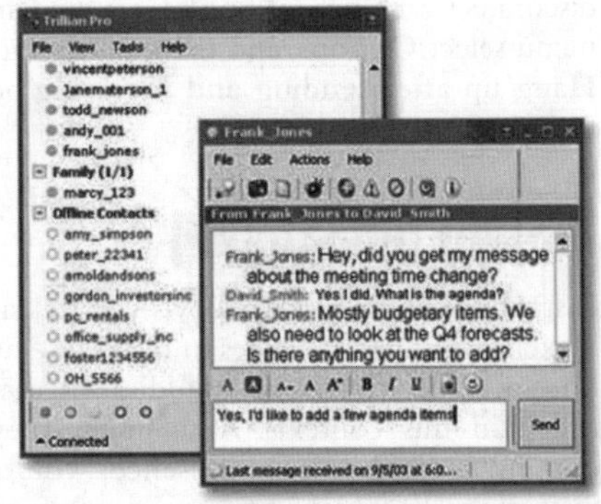

down. You might be able to improve things by using a single program that can tap into the various systems, such as **Trillian**:

Trillian www.trillian.cc

Getting started

Once you've got your IM program installed, you'll need to set up a username and password. The exact method depends on the program, but it's usually pretty self-explanitory and happens automatically when you first launch the program. In Windows Messenger, the sign up process basically involves creating a **.NET Passport**.

Once you have your username and password, you're ready to log in, and add some "buddies". If your friends are already set up, email them and ask them for their usernames (it will often be their email address, but not necessarily), which you can then add to your **buddy list** – refer to Help within your program of choice for specific instructions. From that point on, it's hard to go wrong.

Exploring the options

Once you've got instant messaging up and running, take the time to browse through the various **Options** (usually an entry in the Tools menu). For example, you can choose whether you'd like the program to start up whenever you turn on your computer, when you connect to the Net or simply when you ask it.

Also check out the options for appearing like you're offline, busy, etc – sometimes you might want to be able to see which of your friends are available, but not necessarily want them all to be able to see you. However, if you simply have someone on your buddy list who you'd rather hide from permanently, add them to your Block List (look in Options or Preferences).

Video calls

There are various special programs for making voice and video calls between two computers, but the major instant messaging programs described above – including **MSN**, **AIM** and **iChat** – have these functions built-in. Refer to their Help menus if you can't work out how to get it going.

To place a voice call through the Net, you need a **microphone** and **speakers**. Ideally you'll also have full-duplex sound capability (see p.47). For video calls – or video conferencing, as it's often called – you'll also need a **webcam** (see p.74) and preferably also a reasonably new computer. Webcams aren't expensive, though you may end up kicking yourself if you buy the very cheapest model, as the quality varies enormously.

To have decent-quality conversations – voice or video – you'll also need **broadband** (see p.198), and so will the person you're speaking to. Via a dial-up connection, voice calls sound shoddy and video looks like a tiny slide show. It's fun for a few minutes, and perhaps worth it if it means seeing live footage of a loved one across the world, but it's not a serious means of communication.

15 Networking

hooking up the home

Though the term "**network**" is commonly associated with the computer matrices of large companies, all it means is a number of computers linked together so that their users can do neighbourly things like share files, an Internet connection and printers. These days, setting up a home network is very simple and, with the advent of **Wi-Fi**, it's neither expensive nor complicated to go wireless, which allows you to get online anywhere in the home or garden. There are several different ways to set up a home network, each of which has advantages and disadvantages. But in most cases their are just two basic decisions: wired or wireless? And router or peer-to-peer?

Wires and Wi-Fi

With wires...

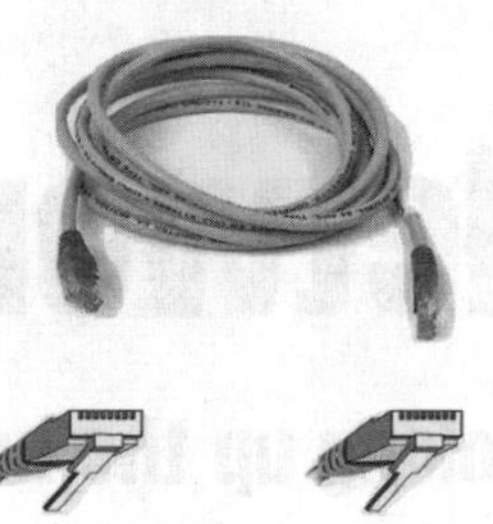

The traditional way to wire up a small computer network is **Ethernet**. Most recent PCs have an Ethernet socket built-in. If you have a computer without one, you could add the socket with an inexpensive **network interface card** (NIC). These traditionally come as PCI cards that live inside your PC's case (see p.321 for advice on installing a PCI card), but external USB models, as well as PCMCIA cards for laptops, are also available. Once each computer has an Ethernet port, all you need are one or Ethernet cables to run either directly between the computers or via router (see p.230).

The speed of the network will depend on the type of Ethernet ports and cables you have, but in most cases you'll be able to transfer data between the computers at 100 Mbps (megabits per second). Newer machines and in some cases 1 (Gbps gigabits per second).

... or without

If running a wire between your computers is impractical or too expensive – and the cable can be pricey – there are other options such as phone or powerline networking (see box on p.231). But you'll probably find it quicker, cheaper, easier and better to go wireless. With the boom in **Wi-Fi** technology (see box), this is now very easy and inexpensive. Instead of an Ethernet port, each computer needs to have Wi-Fi capability. This is built-in to many recent laptops,

Wi-Fi and other airwaves

Wi-Fi, or **IEEE 802.11x** as it's known in geekspeak, is a set of wireless standards that allow computers and PDAs to communicate with radio waves. It works through walls and other obstacles, with a range of up to a few hundred feet (depending on how much is in the way).

There are various different flavours of Wi-Fi. **IEEE 802.11b** is the most ubiquitous but it's quickly being replaced with the faster **IEEE 802.11g** (or "**54g**"), which can send and receive data at 54 Mbps instead of 11 Mbps. However, these various types all work seamlessly with each other (at least in theory). And the same is true of Wi-Fi equipment by different manufacturers: any device bearing the Wi-Fi logo will work with any other. Even Apple Mac Wi-Fi equipment, which is branded **AirPort**, is perfectly interoperable with Windows-based systems.

Another popular wireless standard is **Bluetooth**, which is slower and has a shorter range, but is very easy to use with multiple devices and is commonly built into mobile phones – good for connecting on the move. But the future really lies in wireless technologies with a much wider range, which will span whole cities or even countries. Technologies working towards this, such as **Wider-Fi** (IEEE 802.16) and **Mobile-Fi** (IEEE 802.20), already exist, but they're still a way from commercial reality.

and can be added to other computers with an inexpensive Wi-Fi adapter. These are available in various forms, either external devices that plug into a USB port (like the one pictured opposite), PCMCIA cards for laptops, or internal PCI cards.

Wi-Fi networks aren't as fast as most wired ones but they're fine for most home tasks – and certainly fast enough to get the best out of your Internet connection. With a laptop, a wireless network lets you connect throughout the home and garden, as well as at **Wi-Fi hotspots** in cafés, airports and other locations.

Peer-to-peer or router?

Regardless of whether you're going for a wired or a wireless nework, there are two main ways of setting it up.

Peer-to-peer

If you only have two computers to network, you can connect the machines together in a simple **peer-to-peer** network. In this arrangement, the two computers connect directly with one another. One of them also connects to the Internet as usual (via a dial-up or broadband modem) and "shares" the connection with the other computer.

The main advantage of a peer-to-peer network is that they are inexpensive and simple, but this arrangement isn't ideal for more than two computers, and it also means that the computer which connects to the Internet has to be switched on and connected to the Net in order for the other one to get online.

Router

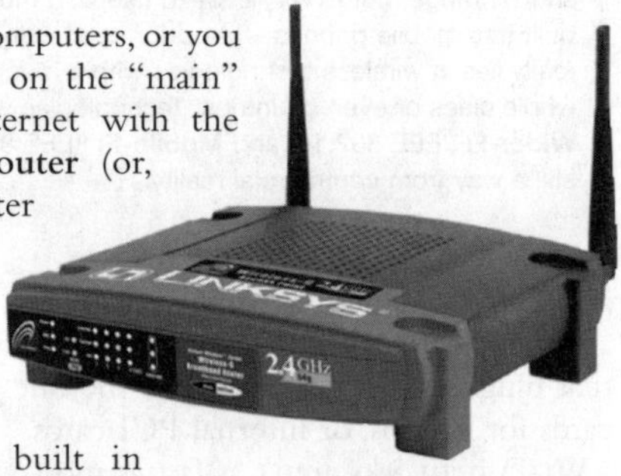

If you have more than two computers, or you don't want to have to turn on the "main" computer to access the Internet with the other one, you'll need a **router** (or, technically speaking, a router with a network hub built in, but these days that goes without saying). In this arrangement, the router attaches to the Internet (either via a separate or built in modem) and each computer connects to the router, either using Ethernet cables or, if the router has wireless capabilities, then using Wi-Fi. Note that you can mix wires and Wi-Fi on the same network: most wireless routers provide Ethernet ports as well as a Wi-Fi signal.

When choosing a router, there are many factors to consider, the most important being **speed** of the Ethernet and Wi-Fi connections; the number of Ethernet ports; and whether or not the router has a built-in ADSL or cable modem (if you already have a USB broadband modem, it won't be compatible with most routers).

Other networking options

Though Ethernet and Wi-Fi are the most popular networking options, there are a few other possibilities, including:

▶ **Telephone network** Though not as fast as Ethernet, a phone network is easy and tidy to set up: instead of running new cable around your house, you simply plug each computer into a different phone point and they communicate via the existing wires. Data is transferred between the PCs at a much higher frequency than regular phone calls, so your network will never interfere with either your voice or Internet calls. You'll need to buy a kit with the appropriate network cards.

▶ **Powerline network** This system works in the same way as a telephone network, but utilizes your home's electrical cabling, with the computers connecting directly to conventional power sockets. Though attractive in principle, this system gives a slow network connection, the wires tend to be very "noisy" (the signal may be unreliable), and there are also security issues to consider – it isn't difficult for people outside the home to intercept your data. For more info, see: www.homeplug.org

▶ **Direct cable connection** allows you to connect two PCs (one acting as the **host**, the other as a **guest**) with a cable running between their **parallel**, **serial** or **USB** ports. If you don't have Ethernet ports or Wi-Fi – and you don't want the hassle and expense of buying and installing them – this can be useful for moving files from one machine to another. All you need is the correct bi-directional cable. Bear in mind, though, that the data transfer rate is a bit sluggish and the settings can be faffy to get right. For more information, see: www.wown.com/j_helmig/dccmain.htm

Setting up

In a peer-to-peer network, once you have your Wi-Fi adapters and/or Ethernet cables in place, kickstarting your network basically means running Windows' built-in network set-up wizard. In different versions of Windows, this is variously called the **Network Setup Wizard**, the **Internet Connection Sharing Wizard**, or the **Home Networking Wizard**, but you should find it either in the Communications section of Accessories (in the Start menu's program list), or as an option with-

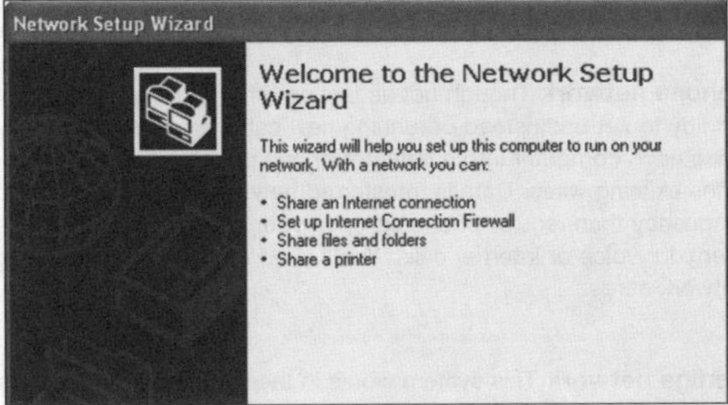

Wi-Fi and security

Because Wi-Fi can work through walls, your network won't stop at your front door. This is great news for surfing in the garden, say, or sharing an Internet connection between various apartments in a house, but it does raise security issues – passers-by with laptops can log on. Some people welcome this, and even put a sign or chalk symbol, to invite passing Web hounds to log on, check their mail or browse the Web. But if you'd rather keep your network closed to the public, be sure to enable WEP encryption – the instructions with your Wi-Fi adapters will explain how – or at least think carefully about which files and folders you want to make available on the network. Even WEP can be cracked, but unless you have a vindictive and very technically competent neighbour, this is extremely unlikely to happen.

in My Network Places (on the Desktop). In Windows 98 you might need to install it: select Add/Remove Programs in the Control Panel, click Windows Setup, then Internet Tools, select Details and check the Internet Connection Sharing box.

The Wizard is pretty straightforward, prompting you to give your computer a network name, and possibly offering you the option to create a **network setup** floppy disk for setting up older computers on the network.

If you're setting up a network with a router, things can be a little more complex, but these days it usually just involves configuring a few things via a Web browser. Follow the instructions that came with your unit, and if you get stuck look online for help (see p.234) or phone your ISP.

Using your network

Once your network is up and running, you can use any computer on the network as if it were simply an extension of your main machine. Assuming that the other PCs are switched on, you will be able to locate, browse, open or alter their "shared" files (see below) via the **My Network Places** icon on the Start menu, in My Computer, or on the

Sharing files on a network

You can choose to make files and folders on one PC accessible via the other computers on the network. In Windows XP right-click a folder that you want to share, choose Sharing and Security from the mouse menu and check the Share this folder on the network box. You can also use this dialog box to assign the folder a network name, and to prevent others from editing the file's contents, by making it read only.

In pre-XP versions of Windows right-click a file or folder, select Sharing, and you'll be presented with a dialog box with various options. You can choose between: Read Only, which allows others to look at a file but not change it; Full, which permits others to read and edit the file or folder; and Depends on Password, which allows you to give a different password for Read Only and Full access.

Desktop. And you'll be able to print via any shared printers: select **File** then **Print** in any application and select the networked printer from the dropdown menu.

For more on networking, see:

How Stuff Works www.howstuffworks.com/home-network.htm
Practically Networked www.practicallynetworked.com

Or if you're struggling to get your PC and Mac to be network friends, turn to:

MacWindows www.macwindows.com

software

16

Operating systems

the software foundations

The one piece of software that a PC can't function without is an **operating system**, or OS. This is the underlying system that bridges the gap between the hardware of a computer and the application software running on it. It also defines your user experience, determining what you see when you start up your machine and how you deal with files and programs. Modern operating systems have a GUI (graphic user interface), which allows you to communicate with your PC using icons, menus and a mouse pointer rather than having to type in encoded messages via the keyboard. But this user-friendly surface belies an amazing level of complexity.

Indeed, operating systems are incredibly complicated multitasking software setups, which take care of everything from helping a word processor save a document onto the hard drive to assigning RAM space and processor time to the various tasks the PC has been set.

Windows, Linux and other animals

The most commonly used operating systems, and the focus of this book, are the members of Microsoft's **Windows** family – such as Windows 98 and Windows XP – which between them are installed on more than 90 percent of the world's PCs. This remarkable market position is largely the result of a situation that arose in the early 1980s (see p.350). To cut a long story short, Microsoft produced **MS-DOS**, the forerunner of Windows, for the first PCs, and as PCs boomed there were so many programs written to run on the operating system that before long no alternatives could really break into the market. Today, Microsoft's domination is such that most PCs come with the latest version of Windows pre-installed, and when people claim to know how to use a PC what they really mean is that they know how to work Windows.

However, this isn't the end of the story. There are, and always have been, a number of alternatives to Microsoft's operating systems. And one of them, **Linux**, is posing an increasingly real threat to the Windows monopoly. Linux is one of the many versions of the **UNIX** family of operating systems, which is traditionally associated with large-scale computer networks but now finding its way into many home computers – not only via Linux, but also **Apple's Mac OS X**, which is also based on UNIX.

Identified by its cartoon penguin mascot, Linux is an **open source** product (see box) that started life in the early 1990s as the hobby of a young Finnish student called **Linus Torvalds**. Today there are

Open source software

Most software is distributed in a "compiled", execute-only form, meaning you can run the program but you can't actually see the **source code** – the code that the programmer wrote to make the software. Indeed, commercial source codes are preciously guarded corporate secrets. With open-source software, however, the source code is freely distributed, allowing experienced users to fix bugs and add features, catalysing the development of new and more stable versions, most of which are made available to the public at no cost.

Besides a world-class operating system – **Linux** – the open source community has created a huge range of excellent applications, including many for Windows. These include an excellent office suite called **OpenOffice** (see p.261) and a fully featured photo editor known as **GIMP** (see p.267).

many versions – **distributions** – of Linux available, most of which you can download for free, but there are also companies, such as **Red Hat**, that sell a commercial Linux package complete with technical support.

Linux is still some way from being as easy to use as Windows. But it's quickly getting there. If you fancy giving it a go, perhaps running alongside your copy of Windows on a separate partition (see box overleaf), read some more online, select a distribution and start downloading:

Linux.org www.linux.org
Woven Goods for Linux www.fokus.gmd.de/linux

Or, if you don't have broadband, pop into any decent bookshop and buy a Linux book. These usually include a copy of the OS on CD.

Windows versions

The Windows brand is now a household name – you'd have to have spent the last ten years on Mars not to have an inkling that it has something to do with computers. What many people are less familiar with are the various versions of this Microsoft operating system. Until 2001, Windows followed two distinct paths, one paved for domestic users

Partitions

A **partition** is a section of a hard drive that is treated as a discrete unit. A single drive can have many partitions, each of which will work as if it is a separate physical drive with its own letter (C, D, E, etc) and icon in My Computer. All hard drives in use have at least one partition, generally labelled as drive C, but the term is most commonly used in relation to drives with more than one partition.

Some people use partitions simply to **organize their data** – document files on C and program files on D, for example. This is a particularly good idea if you work with video or music a lot, as the read-write heads of the drive will not have to dart around so much to the large retrieve files during playback. And if you fancy trying out an **alternative operating system**, partitions again come into their own: a drive with two or more partitions can hold more than one OS – this is known as **dual booting** and lets you choose which operating system to boot each time you start up.

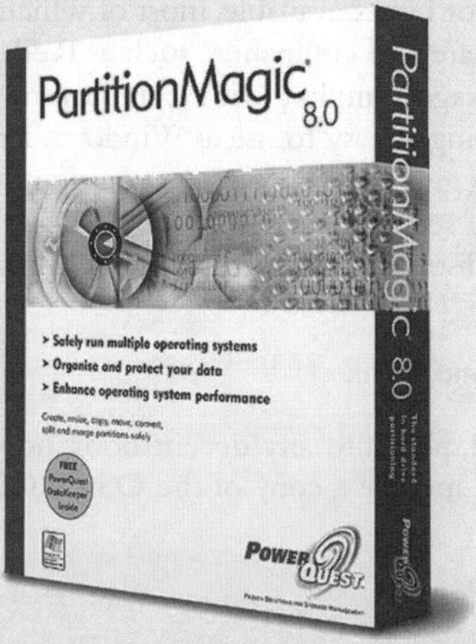

Sometimes when you install a new operating system from disc, you'll automatically be offered the chance to create a new partition as part of the installation process, though Windows versions may ask you to use the **Fdisk** utility (see p.334). However, this deletes all the information currently stored on the drive in question. If you don't want to lose the data on the drive you'll need to get hold of a program such as **PartitionMagic**, which lets you manage and alter the size and properties of your hard drive's partitions (a free trial version of Partition Magic is available from www.powerquest.com/partitionmagic).

Though it sounds simple in principle, partitioning can be quite a complicated process – so, before you dive in, do a bit of background reading on the Web.

and the other for businesses. The domestic realm was dominated by **Windows 95** and **Windows 98** – collectively known as **Windows 9x** – and **Windows Me** (Millennium Edition). This branch of the Windows family was designed with multimedia applications in mind, and each new version had a few extra features and was a bit more stable (less likely to crash) than its predecessor. Business users, on the other hand, were catered for by the various versions of **Windows NT** and **Windows 2000**. The strengths of these systems reflected business requirements – reliability, networking and security features were high priority – but they didn't support many multimedia programs.

These two strands of Windows – 9x/Me and NT/2000 – are based on two different **kernels** (the underlying codes), though they look and feel very similar. It was a long-standing intention of Microsoft to integrate them, creating a Windows platform that could satisfy both home and business users. Hence the current verion, **Windows XP**, which is built on the Windows 2000 kernel – making it pretty stable, secure and network-friendly – but also features the multimedia power of Windows Me. Distinct versions of the platform are available for home and business use, but they're basically the same, give or take a few extra features.

As was discussed in Chapter 1, there are also versions of Windows for specific types of system, such as multimedia "Media Center" setups and tablet PCs. And there's also **Windows CE**, a slimmed-down version designed to run on handheld devices.

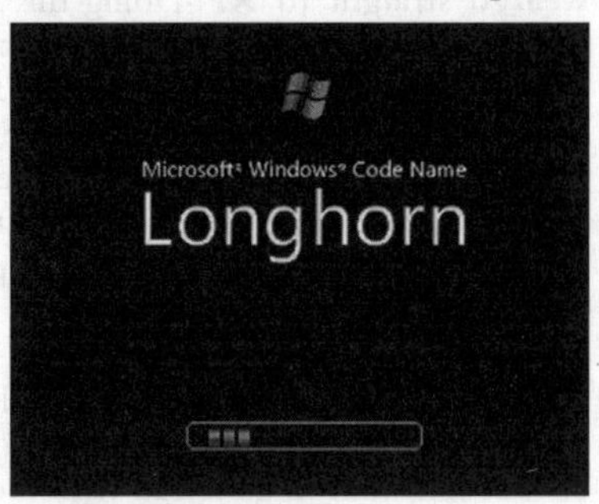

The next completely new version of Windows, code-named Longhorn at the time of writing, is expected in 2005. To keep track of the latest news and developments, look no further than:

Paul Thurrott's SuperSite for Windows: www.winsupersite.com

Upgrading Windows

If you recently purchased a new computer, you probably have the latest version of Windows. But if your PC is running an older version, you might consider upgrading. Whether or not this is possible or worthwhile depends on the age and specifications of your hardware. Each new version of Windows is bulkier and requires more system resources than the last – if you haven't got enough free hard disk space, plenty of RAM or a processor that's speedy enough, they either won't run or they'll seriously under-perform.

For XP, Microsoft's stated minimum is a Pentium 233 MHz processor, 64 MB of RAM and a 1.5 GB of hard disk space. With this, however, your PC will be running by the skin of its teeth. A 300 MHz processor, 128 MB of RAM and a few gigabytes of spare hard disk space are more realistic, and much more is preferable – you don't want to shell out for a new operating system and end up with a slower PC than you had before. If your machine hasn't got the necessary beef, you may well be able to upgrade your hardware (see Chapter 22) to make a newer operating system work smoothly; but unless your current Windows version is unreliable or poorly featured, it may not be worth the time and money.

If you decide to go for it, upgrading between Windows 95, 98 or Me is very simple – though if you have the necessary hardware, you may as well **go straight to XP**. Doing this is just as easy, though you might have to reinstall some of your applications afterwards. XP is worth considering: it is much more stable fully featured. All the extras first introduced in Me are there – built-in file compression (see p.124), System Restore (see p.167), etc – as well as better security and networking features, remote management tools and more. Though you can choose to run it with the "classic" Windows appearance, XP also boasts a new look, with different icons, a revamped Explorer and a better Start menu.

A word of warning, though: not all older hardware can be used with XP. Check whether drivers are available for all your devices – from printers to CD drives – before buying a copy. If you can't get the drivers but still want to go ahead with the installation, you can use the XP installation CD to create **multiple partitions** (see p.238). This will allow you to boot your PC with the older Windows version if you ever want to use certain devices.

Installing Windows

There are two types of Windows installation. The first is an **upgrade installation**, which involves installing a new version over an old one. The second is a **clean** or **full installation**, which means putting Windows onto a blank system.

Upgrade installations

An upgrade installation is very simple – but still be sure to back up all your documents, downloaded programs, emails and so on (see p.288) in case things go wrong. Once you've done this, insert the Windows CD into your CD drive and watch the **Setup Wizard** spring into action. This wizard will guide you through the process, asking for information along the way. When the wizard has finished doing its thing, the new version of Windows will boot for the first time – hopefully with all your old settings, files and applications intact.

Though this is the easiest option, many people recommend a full installation, especially upgrading from Windows 98 or Me or XP, as this way any problems in your current system won't persist.

Booting from CD

If your computer won't automatically boot from the CD and you don't have a Startup disk to hand, try going into your system **BIOS setup utility** (see p.337) and setting the CD drive as the primary boot device. This is done in different ways in different BIOS utilities, but generally it's quite self-explanatory and just requires you to look through the menus until you find one named something like **boot devices** or **startup priorities**. Usually the machine will be set to boot from the floppy drive, then the hard drive. Change it so that the order is the CD drive followed by the hard drive (if this isn't possible your machine probably doesn't support CD booting). Exit the BIOS utility with the Windows CD in place and the installation should begin. You may want to return the BIOS boot settings to their previous order after the installation is complete.

Full installations

With recent versions of Windows, doing a full installation is almost as easy as doing an upgrade – even if you're installing on a blank drive. Simply set your computer to boot from the CD drive (see box on previous page) and restart the system with the Windows CD in place. From there, the exact proceedure will vary with different versions of Windows, but it should be pretty self-explanatory, with the Windows Installation Wizard walking you through the process.

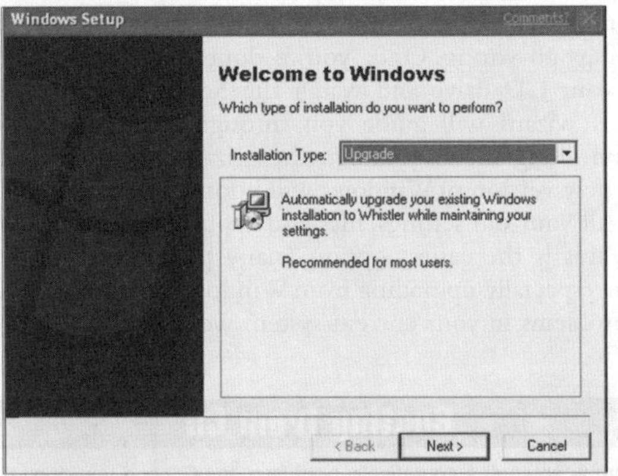

However, things won't necessarily be quite this simple. If your system won't boot from CD, you'll need to use a **Startup disk** (see box). And if you're installing Windows 98 or Me on a brand-new drive you may also need to partition it (see p.240).

But however you get there, once the wizard is doing it's thing, you can't really go wrong.

At some point you'll be asked for a **Product Key number** (which will be somewhere on the Windows packaging) and you'll have to decide where in your computer you want Windows to be installed (choose the default, **C:\WINDOWS**). You'll also probably have to choose between a **Typical** or a **Custom** install. A typical install is fine

Startup disks

A **Startup disk** or **boot disk** is a floppy disk containing enough information to allow a blank PC to navigate to the CD drive to get a Windows installation under way. When installing Windows on a new hard drive (see p.330) you might also need one of these disks to run a program called **Fdisk** (see p.334) prior to making the installation. They can also be very useful if things go wrong and your machine won't boot up normally.

Your copy of Windows Me or an earlier version may have come with a Startup disk, but if not you can create one in the Windows **Control Panel** – use a friend's computer if necessary. Double-click the **Add/Remove Programs** icon, select the **Startup Disk** tab, insert a diskette into the floppy drive and click the **Create** button.

If you have a full version of Windows XP it might have come with the necessary floppy disk – if not you can either use a Startup disk created in Windows Me or 98, or download the necessary files to make the disk from Microsoft. Links for downloading files for all Windows boot disks can be found at **Bootdisk.com**.

Bootdisk.com www.bootdisk.com

If your CD drive doesn't seem to be recognized by the floppy, it could be that the Startup disk you have doesn't feature CD-ROM support – try one listed at the link above, as they all do.

for practically all users, but if you're feeling brave and you have a knowledgeable friend to consult, a Custom install will give you more freedom to choose exactly what you do and don't want. You might also be asked if you want to visit the Microsoft website and check for updates – if you're connected to a phoneline, go for it, but if not, don't worry: it's not essential and can always be done later.

Once the installation has finished it's worth checking that all your hardware is working. And if it's Windows XP that you've just installed, don't forget to "activate" it within fourteen days (see p.83).

chapter 16

Updates and Service Packs

Like other operating systems, Windows is not a static product. Minor improvements to the code, solutions to known problems and security "patches" are frequently made available by Microsoft. They are free to download, will install themselves with little fuss and are essential if you want to make sure that your system runs smoothly and doesn't unnecessarily fall foul of viruses and other such evils (though they should not be seen as an alternative to an up-to-date virus scanner; see p.285).

To get the latest updates, either click Windows Update in your Start menu, or go straight to:

Windows Update www.windowsupdate.com

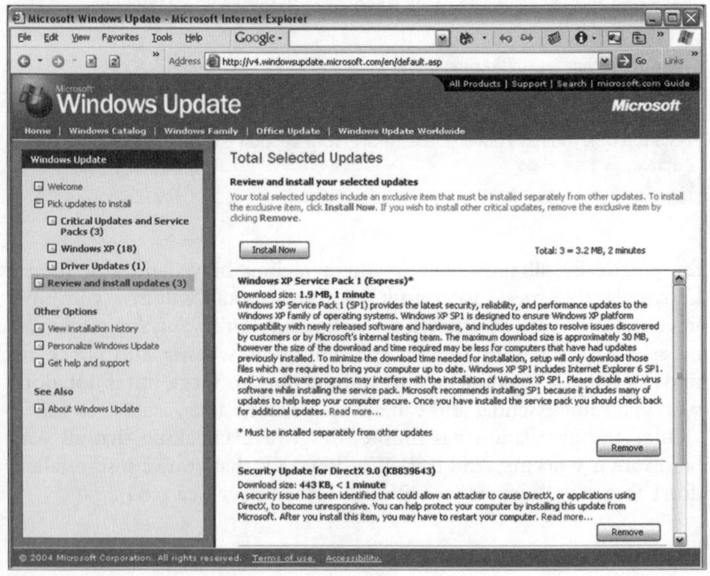

Alternatively, you can set up Windows to automatically handle these updates as and when they become available. Note that in Windows XP you'll need to be an administrator to do this (see p.146). Here's how it's done.

▶ **1** Open the **Control Panel** and click **System**.

▶ **2** Click the **Automatic Updates** tab and select **Keep my computer up to date**.

▶ **3** Use the other options under this tab to choose whether you want Windows to warn you when it is going to either download updates or install them. You can also use this dialog box to set up a schedule for when you want the updates to occur – handy if you have an always-on connection and a PC that you leave turned on over night.

Now, whenever an update is available, Windows will either simply get on with it or ask you to agree to the updates prior to them being downloaded or installed. If it is not a convenient time when these availability messages appear, click **Remind Me Later**; how soon this "later" is can also be set under the **Automatic Updates** tab in the **System** dialog box.

Service Packs

The kind of Windows updates described above tend to be small, frequent and relevant to a specific niggle, issue or security loophole. Occasionally, however, Microsoft release a major update called a **Service Pack** which might offer new utilities and major code changes as well as a bundle of all the updates that have been released since the release of the relevant version of Windows (or since the previous Service Pack, if there has been one).

Naturally, Service Packs tend to be pretty big, so Microsoft usually makes them available on CD (depending where you live you might have to pay a small charge for postage). However, they are also availble to download from the downloads section of Microsoft's website.

In September 2002, Microsoft released **Windows XP SP1** (later relaunched as **SP1a**) and at the time of writing they are preparing to launch **Windows XP SP2**, code-named "XP reloaded". It is expected that the majority of its contents will relate to security, but there may also be a few new features and surprises…

Windows XP downloads www.microsoft.com/windowsxp/downloads/default.asp
SP2 Preview www.winsupersite.com/reviews/windowsxp_sp2_preview.asp

17

Program software

buying it, downloading it, installing it

Programs or applications are special sets of coded instructions that interact with your operating system and hardware to enable you to carry out a particular set of tasks, such as touching up a digital photograph or recording and arranging music. Depending on the jobs that these pieces of software are expected to do, they can either be tiny little things (often called **applets** or **utilities**) that run in the background without your intervention, or hefty beasts that demand great chunks of your PC's resources and feature elaborate sets of on-screen palettes and toolbars. This chapter takes a look a quick look at different types of software, and how to install and uninstall it. For reviews of individual applications, see p.259.

The basics

Back in the 1980s, software would find its way onto your computer via **magnetic cassettes** or **floppy disks**. And because personal computers didn't come with a hard drive, you actually had to move a program onto your PC every time you wanted to use it, loading all the code from tape or disk into the PC's memory (RAM) before a single task could be performed. These days application programs will reach you either on **CD** or – ever more frequently – be downloaded straight from the **Internet**. You **install** them onto your hard drive, and from then on they are quickly unpacked to your RAM whenever you click the necessary icons.

Tech Info

Parlez-vous machine code?

The fundamental language spoken by all PCs is **machine code**, which consists of binary numbers – 0s and 1s. Machine code is described as the **lowest-level** computer language. It's great for computer processors, but as you can imagine it's not ideal for humans: it would be practically impossible for a computer programmer to sit down and write a program in 0s and 1s. Instead, programmers work with **higher-level** languages, which can be translated into machine code by special programs called **compilers**. The highest-level languages, such as **BASIC**, are the easiest to use: many of the instructions are very intuitive and contain standard English words such as "WRITE" and "CLOSE". Most programmers, however, use slightly less high-level languages – such as **Java** and **C** – which are better at producing faster, more compact code.

100100100100101000101001010000010(
010101010100101011100111000100010(
010111010101010111111100101001101(
111001110101011101010101011111110(
001000001010101100001010000111101(

Although installing software may be incredibly easy to do, the stuff that goes on in the background is not as straightforward as you might think. In Windows, it's rarely the case that you drag the program files onto your hard drive and plonk them wherever you fancy as you might with a document file. Nowadays applications come with their own special **installation programs** (or wizards) that need to be run in order for everything to be set up properly – so make sure you follow the instructions. Equally, when you remove a piece of software from your PC it needs to be properly **uninstalled** so that there are no loose ends left behind to confuse other applications.

Shopping for software

If you thought the choice was overwhelming when you were buying PC hardware, just wait until you start looking around for software. The range on offer is enormous, from free utilities to full commercial "suites" or packages.

If you're going for software that you have to pay for, you may be able to purchase your package of choice from a shop, website or mail-order company. However, these days the most obvious way to get hold of it is to **download it straight from the Internet**. This way the software is available 24 hours a day, 365 days a year.

The only real disadvantage of downloading software is that – in the case of big programs, at least – it can be problematic with a slow or unreliable Internet connection. Also, you don't get a paper **manual**, though you'll usually get a non-paper version in **pdf format** – which anyhow is also now the norm if you buy boxed software in a shop.

Free and almost free...

There's an amazing amount of free software around – on the Internet, of course, but also on **PC magazine cover discs** or given away free with computer hardware. It's perfectly possible, indeed, to have a powerful PC system run entirely on freebies. However, not all free software available online is legal (see box p.253), and not eveything you can install for free will work forever.

The legal stuff comes in various forms. Though the terms are sometimes used interchangeably, technically speaking:

▶ **Freeware** is any software that the author distributes for unlimited free use; however, there may be restrictions on you distributing or altering the program.

▶ **Shareware** is software that can be downloaded for free, though if you like or make use of the program you're encouraged (or sometimes required) to make a small contribution to the developers.

▶ **Donationware** is similar to shareware: you are expected to make a contribution to the developer (or sometimes a third party, such as a charity) based upon how useful you have found their software to be.

▶ **Beta versions** are basically "works in progress" that developers distribute for free in order to get feedback, so that they can improve the final version. They will often only work for a limited period and will, by their nature, contain imperfections, or "bugs".

Trial versions

If you're interested in buying a particular package, before reaching for your wallet it's worth checking out the manufacturer's website to see

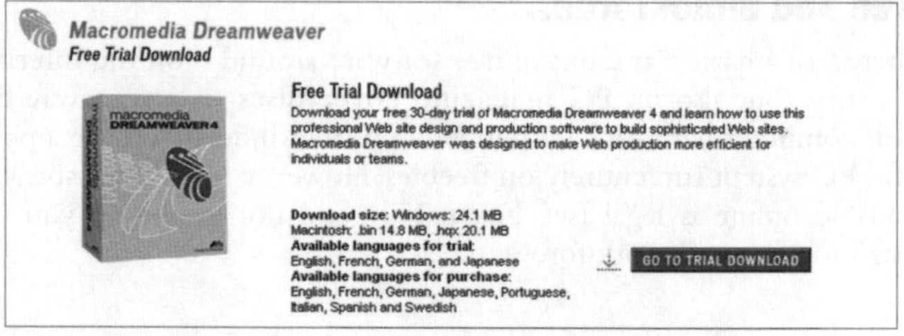

Pirates and their warez

When looking for software online, you should be aware that the Net is teeming with illegal, "pirated" or "cracked" versions of commercial software programs, collectively referred to as **warez**. The battle between software companies and crackers has been raging for years, but piracy has proved near-impossible to stop, especially with the level of anonymity offered by the Internet. Any measures designed to prevent the illegal movement of software are always quickly overcome by the pirates. For example, serial numbers and copyright protection keys are frequently published online, making it easy to activate an illegal piece of software.

It's sometimes argued that piracy is actually beneficial for the producers of industry-standard software, because their market position relies on people knowing how to use their programs – difficult if they are too expensive for educational use alone. Whatever your opinion, remember that downloading and installing such software remains very much **against the law**.

if they offer a downloadable **trial version** or possibly even a pared-back **free version**. The music hardware and software producers Digi Design, for example, offer a free, stripped-down version of their impressive Pro Tools system via their website (**www.digidesign.com**).

If you want to find out about a package but have no idea who the manufacturers are, try finding the software you want using a search engine such as **www.google.com**.

Installing software from CD

Many of the applications you'll install will be from CD. Doing this is a very easy process: turn your PC on, insert the CD into the CD drive and sit back. With any luck you'll hear the drive start to spin and the first frame of an **installation wizard** (a little application that installs the main program for you) will appear on the screen. If nothing happens

tip

Whether you're installing from a download, a CD or a floppy, the file that will set the ball rolling is most commonly titled setup or install, perhaps with the .exe on the end.

when you insert the disc, go to the **Control Panel**, select **Add/Remove Programs**, **Add New Programs** then **CD or Floppy** (or just click the **Install** button in earlier versions of Windows). Alternatively, go to the **Start** menu, select **Run**, type **d:\setup** (replace "d" with whatever letter represents the CD drive on your system) and hit **OK**.

Once the installation is under way, the wizard will do the rest. All you need do is read the contents of the various frames that appear, clicking **Next** to move through the various stages of the installation. You'll probably be asked questions about where you want the program to be installed and whether you want to do a standard or custom installation. In general, if you don't understand something, just click **Next**, as it's hard to go wrong with the default settings.

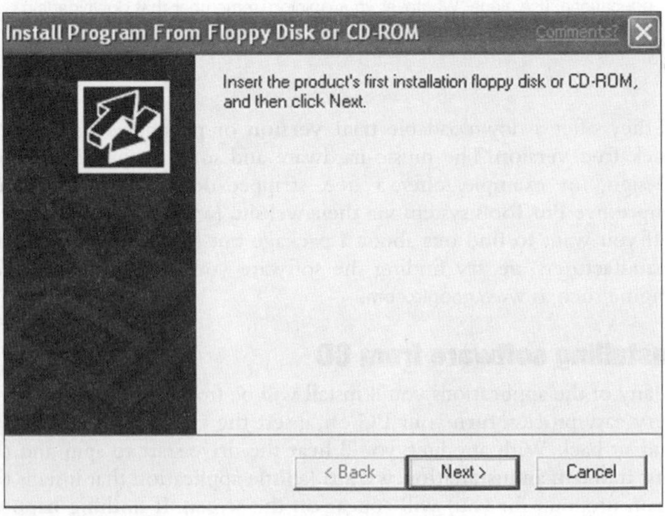

You'll usually need to enter some information, such as a **product key** or **serial number** (the security code that came with the CD, designed to stop people copying and selling software illegally) and your name.

Some application installations might also prompt you to update other applications that they depend on, such as Quicktime or Flash – usually these are supplied on the CD, though you might want to go online and grab the most recent version.

dongles

Some PC applications are supplied with a dongle: a physical device, around the size of a keyring, that needs to be connected to your PC (usually via a USB port) whenever you want to use the application. Like product keys, these are designed to prevent software piracy.

You may also be asked during the installation if you want to connect to the Internet to register your application with the manufacturer and search for any program updates. If you're connected and have a few spare minutes, by all means do so – you might find something worth having. But don't worry about this too much: if you decline now, the software will almost certainly hassle you to get online again sometime soon.

When the installation is complete you will see a final frame prompting you to click a **Finish** button. You may well be asked to restart your PC – which updates the various settings that have been altered by the presence of the new program – and you might be offered a peek at the **Readme** file that came with the software. Readmes are handy little documents that usually open into **Notepad** or **WordPad** (see p.163) and they are designed to bring you up to speed with various bits of information about the software. They tend to include an overview of the application, any last-minute tips that didn't make it into the manual and some hints on installation procedures – handy if you've encountered problems.

If you want to check what's in a Readme prior to an installation, they can usually be found by browsing the folders on the software's CD using **My Computer**.

Downloading software

There's no end of software online, both at the websites of the manufacturers, and at special **software archive** sites such as those listed on p.404. Once you've found something that takes your fancy, take a few moments to read through the manufacturer's guidelines and system requirements. If you're happy, hit the **Download** button on the site and Windows will display a special **Download dialog box**, which asks you whether you want to "open the file from its current location" or "download the file to disk". Click the latter, select where you want the file to go (you can put it anywhere, but perhaps create a folder called "downloads" on your Desktop to keep things tidy) and press **OK**.

The file will start to transfer itself to your system; you'll see a little graphic representation of files winging their way to a folder and, more importantly, an indication of how much longer the download is likely to take, though this is not an exact science as it all depends on the second-by-second speed of your connection. If you lose your Internet connection halfway through the download process you'll probably have to start again from scratch, though Internet Explorer may succeed in continuing where it left off.

Given that applications are often rather large, most downloaded pro-

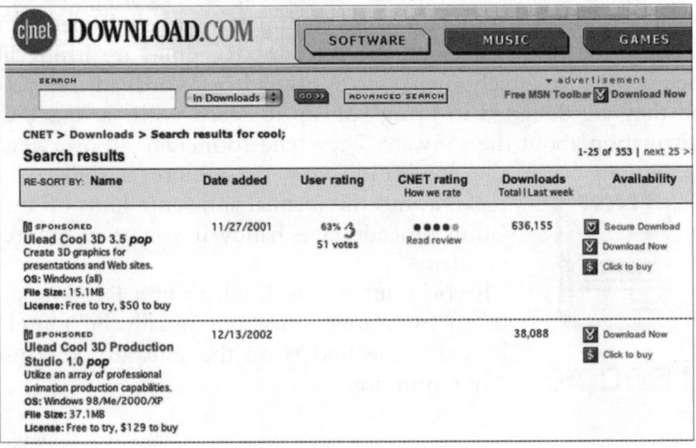

grams are compressed (see p.124) so that they can reach you faster. Some are **self-extracting**, meaning that once the file has downloaded you can simply double-click it to launch an **installation wizard**. But others are **zipped**, which requires you to extract them yourself. If you have Windows XP or Me this will simply involve double-clicking the zipped file; in older versions of Windows you'll need an extra program to "unzip" the file (such as WinZip; see p.125).

Once unzipped, the downloaded file will either reveal a folder or a self-extracting program in the form of an icon that you double-click to get started. If you get a folder, it should contain a file called either **install** or **setup** (perhaps with a **.exe** file extension), which can be double-clicked to launch the installation.

Once the installation is complete, drag the downloaded file or folder to a safe place. It's also a good idea to make a backup of it (see p.288), so that you've always got the original files to hand if you need to reinstall the software at a later date.

Uninstalling software

To uninstall a program – remove it completely from your system – turn to the **Add/Remove Programs** dialog box in the **Control Panel**. Select the program you want rid of from the list of installed applications and then click the **Remove** or **Remove/Change** button. Once you've confirmed that you wish to delete the program, Windows will

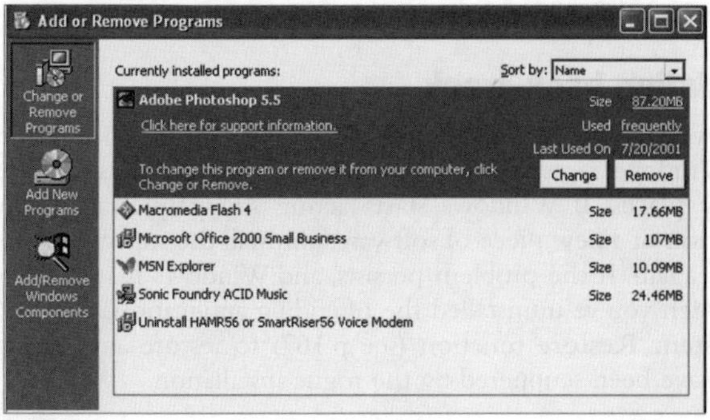

Cleaning up properly

Though Windows does a reasonable job of uninstalling software, residues do often remain. If you install and uninstall a lot of software, you might want to look into the various programs that will help remove this and other types of clutter, generally keeping your house in order. These include:

Aladdin Spring Cleaning www.aladdinsys.com
Clean Sweep www.symantecstore.com
InstaClean www.ideasoft.com
McAfee Uninstaller http://us.mcafee.com

remove all the relevant files from your PC (not including documents created with the program). You might be told along the way that certain files are **shared files**, meaning that they are used, or potentially used, by other applications. It's best to play it safe and not delete these, as their removal could stop other programs from working properly.

If the program you want to remove is not in the Add/Remove Programs dialog box, see if you can find an **Uninstall** icon for its folder in the Start menu's Programs list. If there isn't one, open My Computer, click the icon for your hard drive (usually C) and then open the **Program Files** folder. This should contain a folder for the program in question. See if this folder includes an Uninstall icon. If there isn't one, backtrack once and delete the unwanted program's folder by right-clicking it and selecting Delete. This will get rid of most of the relevant files.

Installation back-track

When you install an application it may well make changes to your main Windows registry settings, placing files and folders in all sorts of unlikely places. If Windows starts acting strangely straight after the installation of a new piece of software, uninstall the software (see above) and try again. If the problem persists, and Windows is still playing up, even when you've uninstalled the offending application, then try using the **System Restore** function (see p.167) to restore any settings that might have been scuppered by the rogue installation.

18

Application roundup

reviews and recommendations

There is so much software on the market these days that the choice can be more than a little overwhelming. Much of the best stuff is very expensive, but there's also an amazing amount of free (or nearly free) software available, some of which is just as good as the commercial alternatives. Before splashing out on Microsoft Word, for example, take a look at OpenOffice (see p.261). And before buying anything, make sure you try it out by downloading the trial version first. This chapter provides short descriptions of some of the best available applications – free and commercial – for a wide range of different purposes. For a list of online software retailers, see p.406.

Office software

Whether you're running a small business or just trying to manage your personal correspondence and accounts, you'll need some suitable software. As mentioned in Chapter 11, Windows comes bundled with WordPad (see p.164), but it doesn't take long to outgrow this very basic word processor. When it comes to extending your office tools you can either buy individual applications – such as a word processor, spreadsheet or high-end email program – or an **office suite**, which will include some or all of the standard office programs.

Office suites

When it comes to office suites, most businesses and colleges use **Microsoft Office**. This comes in various different versions – Student, Small Business, Professional, and so on – each of which contains a different selection of Microsoft's flagship office programs such as **Word**, **Excel** and **PowerPoint** (more on these below).

Microsoft Office http://office.microsoft.com

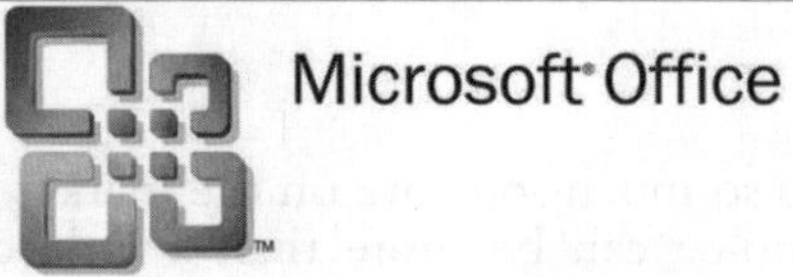

All these programs are fully featured and, because they're so popular, you'll rarely have a compatibility problem with Microsoft Office unless you happen to work somewhere that uses a different package. However, it's far from perfect – some of the features get in the way more than they help – and it's also very expensive. You can get a discount if you're a school or college student, a parent or a teacher…

Microsoft Education (UK) www.microsoft.com/uk/education
Microsoft Education (US) www.microsoft.com/education

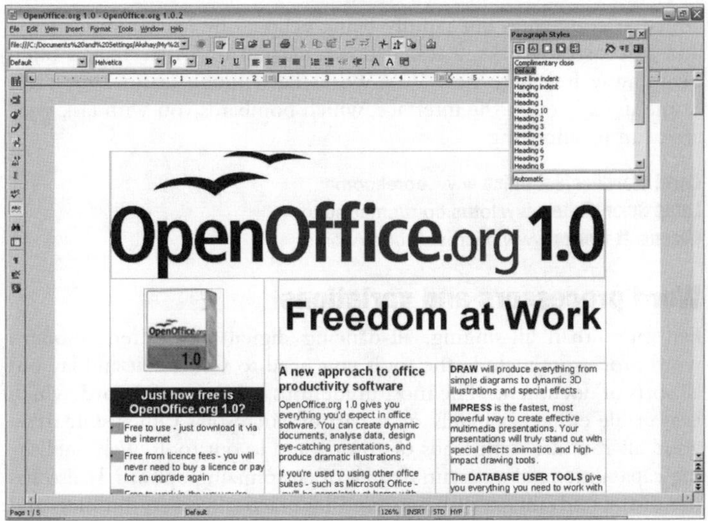

… but you should seriously consider saving your money and opting for the completely free and mostly brilliant **OpenOffice**. An open source package (see p.239), OpenOffice can do pretty much everything you could want from an office suite, including opening and saving documents in Microsoft Office formats. Download it from:

OpenOffice www.openoffice.org

If OpenOffice doesn't satisfy your needs, you could try another budget option such as the respected **Ability Office**, which is very good value for what you get (and is sometimes even given out for free on PC magazine cover discs).

Ability Office www.ability.com

Other office suites you may come across include **Lotus SmartSuite** and **Corel WordPerfect Office** – two fully featured packages that are aimed at companies but rapidly being eclipsed by Microsoft Office – and **Microsoft Works**, a scaled-down version of Office that is often given away free with new PCs. Works has enough features for most home users, though the interface, which bombards you with task wizards, can be annoying.

Corel WordPerfect Office www.corel.com
Lotus SmartSuite www.lotus.com/smartsuite
Microsoft Works www.microsoft.com/works

Word processors and variations

Far more than all-singing, all-dancing digital typewriters, modern word processors include the tools you need to write, edit and lay out all sorts of documents. The most ubiquitous is **Microsoft Word**, which is available either separately or as part of Microsoft's Office suite. It's a good all-rounder with loads of editing and layout tools, Web publishing capabilities and a certain degree of customizing options. It also has the distinct advantage of being used by practically every business and college under the sun, so you're unlikely to experience many compatibility problems. However, most people will only ever use a fraction of Word's many features, so it's worth less expensive options, such as Corel's **WordPerfect** and **OpenOffice** (p.261), both of which do a good job of opening and creating Word documents.

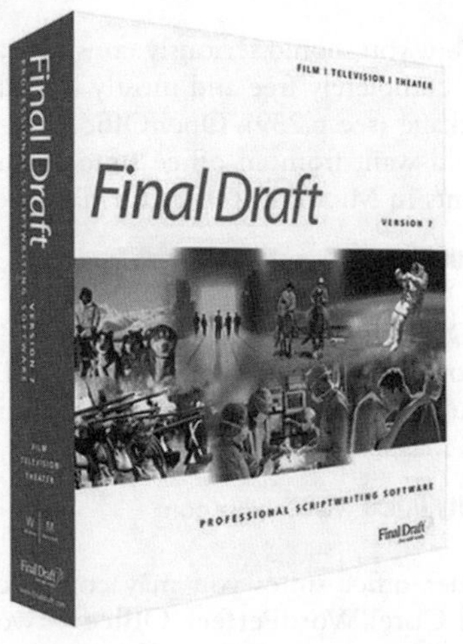

As with most categories of software, there are various specialized alternatives to the traditional word processor. One example is **Final Draft**, specifically produced for use by scriptwriters. It features various fancy editing and layout tools and will even assign voices to individual characters and read your drafts back to you.

Microsoft Word www.microsoft.com/word
Corel WordPerfect www.corel.com
Final Draft www.finaldraft.com

Got a new word processor but still can't type properly? Check out Mavis Beacon, the best-known typing tutorial software: www.mavisbeacon.com

Desktop publishing

Desktop publishing – or **DTP** – programs offer a broad range of tools for manipulating text, images and shapes to create professional-looking layouts for books, magazines, leaflets, posters and so on, ready to be submitted for professional printing.

Currently the industry-standard DTP programs are **QuarkXPress** and **Adobe InDesign**. Both are very powerful, with InDesign having the edge in terms of features and usability. It's also cheaper than QuarkXPress, though still prohibitively expensive unless you have a serious publishing project of some kind.

There are less expensive DTP applications, among them **Microsoft's Publisher**. Available alone or as part of certain versions of Office, Publisher is usable enough and comes with various ready-to-go templates for cards, pamphlets and the like, but it's pretty limited and clunky overall. If you're only producing documents to print at home, a modern version of Word (p.262) or OpenOffice (see p.261) is almost as good.

Quark XPress www.quark.com/products/xpress
Adobe InDesign www.adobe.com/products/indesign
Microsoft Publisher www.microsoft.com/publisher

Databases

These programs are primarily used to store information about large numbers of people or things: employees at a company, books in a library and so on. Though they're not really designed for home use, if you have the time and inclination you could decide to build up a database for anything from your hand-written recipe archive to your record collection.

Microsoft Access is one of the most popular database programs among business users, offering a complete and versatile array of tools and a work environment that's very similar to the other members of the Microsoft Office family. Another popular choice is **FileMaker Pro**, which is known for being user-friendly, easy to customize and good for making your database look nice.

Again, though, for simple use, your money might be better spent on an inexpensive and less complex package such as the one that comes with **Ability Office**.

Microsoft Access www.microsoft.com/access
FileMaker Pro www.filemaker.com
Ability Office www.ability.com

Spreadsheets

Spreadsheets are grid-based programs designed for the manipulation and presentation of numeric data – sorting, summarizing, comparing, graphing, and so on. They're mainly used for financial planning and budgeting, but can also, to a limited degree, be used as databases.

As ever, Microsoft's product, **Excel**, is the most widely used. And, in this case, it's probably also the best. However, unless you're a little too

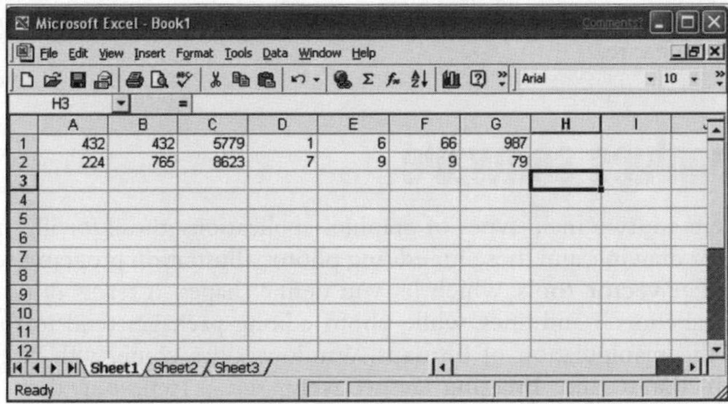

into home accounts, or you're training to be a financial planner or accountant, you'll probably never get into the nitty-gritty of its pivot tables and other advanced features. So try the less pricey spreadsheets built into **OpenOffice** or **Ability Office** (see p.261).

Microsoft Excel www.microsoft.com/excel

Presentation software

These packages are designed for producing slides, flowcharts and multimedia business presentations. **Microsoft PowerPoint** is by far the most popular and features an impressive array of tools – everything short of full-on pyrotechnics to help you impress your clients and boss. It's also very simple to use.

Microsoft PowerPoint www.microsoft.com/powerpoint

And the rest...

Modern office suites may also include anything from a set of digital reference books and home-accounts software to route planners and Web design software. Though much of it will be little more than padding added to justify the "suite" tag, you may find something handy, so have a good rummage around once you've installed your new software.

Graphics software

There are two main types of graphics applications: those for illustrating or drawing, and those for editing photos. Illustration programs tend to offer **vector tools**, which let you define shapes in terms of points (or "anchors") and lines, while photo editing packages tend to focus on the manipulation of **bitmaps**. Windows does come with one of each (**Paint** and **Imaging** respectively; see p.163), but they are extremely limited, so if you want to spread your artistic wings you'll need to look around for some alternatives.

Packages vary greatly in price and performance: there are some amazingly powerful applications out there but they're expensive and complex, so if you only want to mess around with the occasional photo you'd probably do better finding something a bit simpler. The best way to find out which graphics programs suit the work you want to do is, of course, to give them a whirl. You can usually download a trial version from a manufacturer's Website; alternatively, look out for demos bundled with PC magazines – trial versions of the best programs can be found on cover discs month after month.

Photo and image editing

The industry-standard photo editing package is **Adobe PhotoShop**. With its incredibly powerful editing, effects and layer tools, PhotoShop is ideal for the serious photographer or computer artist, but it's also expensive and takes quite a while to master. A more affordable and slightly easier to use option is **Jasc Paint Shop Pro**. It covers similar bases to PhotoShop, and recent versions also boast

a healthy set of Web and animation tools. Or, if you want a cheap and cheerful photo editor, check out **MGI Photo Suite**. This package is aimed at families, and it helps you arrange your images into albums as well as actually edit them. Though it does come with some handy tools for removing red eye and dust marks, don't expect anything too advanced.

The bargain of the bunch, however, is the **GIMP** (GNU Image Manipulation Program). Ones of the proudest achievements of the open source programming community, it's a fully featured image editor to rival PhotoShop. Unlike PhotoShop, though, it's completely free.

Adobe PhotoShop www.adobe.com/photoshop
GIMP www.gimp.org/windows
Jasc Paint Shop Pro www.jasc.com
MGI Photo Suite www.mgisoft.com/photo/photosuite

Illustration packages

One of the most popular vector illustration packages is **Adobe Illustrator** (pictured opposite), a sister program to PhotoShop. Though it's a bit pricey and can take quite a lot of getting used to, it's a fully featured package, great for printing and Web publishing, and is capable

TIFFs, GIFs and JPEGs

Tech Info

When you start working with graphics programs, you'll soon discover that there are various different types of image file format, each with different strengths and uses, and some only compatible with specific programs. One of the most common non-Web image formats is the **TIFF** (short for Tagged Image File Formats and recognizable by the **.tif** file extension). A TIFF is basically a bitmap (see p.73) that can support any size of image and any resolution. They can be black-and-white, greyscale or full colour. This format – and others such as EPS (Encapsulated PostScript Format) – is used for images destined to be printed rather than used on the Internet.

When it comes to the Web there are only two formats commonly used: the **GIF** (Graphics Interchange Format, with the **.gif** extension) and the **JPEG** (Joint Photographic Experts Group format, with the **.jpg** or **.jpeg** extensions). Both of these file types compress the information in an image so that the file is smaller and, in turn, faster to squeeze down a telephone line.

The defining feature of a GIF – besides the fact that it can be **animated** – is that it is **palette**-based, meaning it reduces the number of colours used in an image to a specified number (up to 256). As such, GIFs are particulalry good at reducing the file size of graphics with large areas of the same colours. JPEGs, on the other hand, are much better for complex images such as photos. When you create JPEGs you get to specify the amount of compression you want, allowing you to trade image quality against file size. Experiment with various degrees of compression and see if you can tell the difference.

of generating spectacular results. Other popular packages include **Corel Draw**, which can be bought as a complete but expensive graphics suite, and **Macromedia Freehand**.

Adobe Illustrator www.adobe.com/illustrator
Corel Draw www.corel.com
Macromedia Freehand www.macromedia.com/freehand

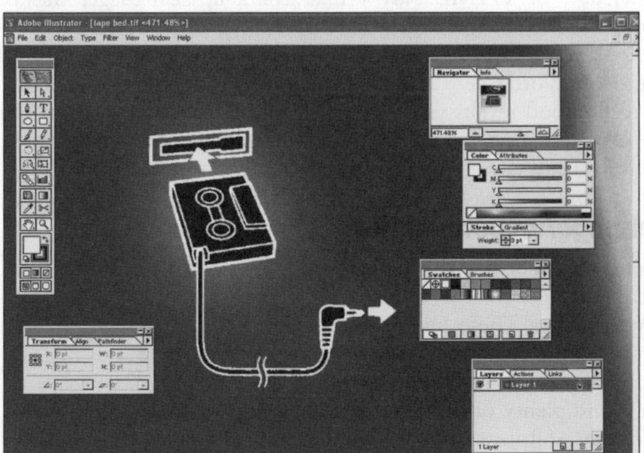

3D illustration

If you fancy branching out into the third dimension, take a look at **Ulead Cool 3D**, an inexpensive and user-friendly package that's ideal for anyone who wants to learn the basics of generating and animating 3D shape, text and logos. There are also loads of other 3D applications out there, but many are either insanely expensive or, in the shareware category, fairly limiting and corny. One of the better options is **Crystal 3D IMPACT! Pro**.

Crystal 3D IMPACT! Pro www.crystalgraphics.com
Ulead Cool 3D www.ulead.com/cool3d

Web-design software

Once you've mastered the basics of processing images, you may want to apply your new-found skills by designing your own website. This is not as hard as it sounds – the software available is intuitive to use, amazingly sophisticated and lets you construct pages without any knowledge of **HTML** (Hypertext Mark-up Language, the code behind most webpages).

You can get away with building a site using a recent version of **Microsoft Word** (see p.260), if you already have it on your system. But for really good results you'll need a dedicated **web-design program**, or – if you want a site with all the bells and whistles – a selection of applications to cover the various different parts of the process.

Webpage/website editors

There are scores of programs available for generating webpages, or whole sites. These range from simple utilities that automate the boring bits of HTML coding – you'll find plenty of these for free in online software archives (see p.399) – to professional-level tools such as the industry standard, **Macromedia Dreamweaver**. The latter is a superb piece of software, allowing you to do pretty much anything you could hope for, but it has a price tag to reflect this. In between the two extremes are a few middle-level Web design programs such as **Microsoft FrontPage**. Though it's a little less flexible than Dreamweaver, FrontPage is very easy to use, especially if you're already familiar with the Microsoft Office environment.

Macromedia Dreamweaver www.macromedia.com/dreamweaver
Microsoft Frontpage www.microsoft.com/frontpage

Web imaging and animation

If you get seriously into Web design you may want to add to your toolkit. The obvious candidates are **Macromedia Fireworks** – which provides a friendly environment for creating vector-based graphics and tweaking bitmaps for use on the Web – and the same company's **Flash**, which can be used to create interactive animations and streaming audio to inject something a bit special into your site.

If you fancy having a crack at animation without blowing loads of money on Flash, try **Swish**, a great-value package that lets you produce Flash animations quickly and easily.

Macromedia Fireworks www.macromedia.com/fireworks
Macromedia Flash www.macromedia.com/flash
Swish www.swishzone.com

Digital video editing software

Thanks to increasingly expansive hard drives, FireWire connections and a steady fall in the price of digital video hardware, creating and editing movies with your computer is becoming more and more easy and affordable. If you're just starting to experiment with video editing and you have Windows XP or Me, you might as well learn some basic skills using the built-in **Windows Movie Maker** (see p.180). But if you want to transform your raw footage into something slick and professional-looking, you'll need some better software that offers advanced editing features and effects

(such as various ways to fade between shots) and the option to save your finished masterpiece in various different file formats, such as Real, WindowsMedia and Quicktime.

Unsurprisingly, you can expect to pay a lot for the best applications, such as the powerful yet easy-to-use **Adobe Premiere** and **Sony Vegas**, which is excellent for sound editing as well as video. However, there are some excellent and much less expensive alternatives available, one good example being **Magix Movie Edit Pro**.

Adobe Premiere www.adobe.com/premiere
Sony Vegas http://mediasoftware.sonypictures.com
Magix Movie Edit Pro www.magix.com

Music applications

Ten years ago the PC was not a music-friendly machine, but these days there are a wide range of programs available that are capable of turning your computer into a **fully featured home recording studio** – as long as you have the necessary hardware (see p.48).

The most popular music-making programs are **multitrack** packages that allow you to assemble a piece of music layer by layer – instruments, sounds, vocals and so on. Most modern multitrackers can deal with both **audio** and **MIDI**. Audio describes "real" sounds that are recorded via a microphone or "sampled" from CD, tape and so on; MIDI, which stands for Musical Instrument Digital Interface, is a system that deals with synthesizer instructions, allowing your computer to communicate with electronic keyboards and other devices. MIDI enables you, for example, to record a synthesized string accompaniment or trigger pre-recorded audio samples. Working with regular audio, on the other hand, will allow you to replicate the processes of a regular recording studio.

The most popular multitrackers include everything you need to record and edit music: a virtual mixing desk, comprehensive recording facilities, a wave editor for dealing with audio, digital effects and even score-production tools (which write whatever you play on virtual manuscript paper). But there are also music programs available that focus on just one of these areas.

Multitrack packages

When if comes to all-in-one MIDI and audio multitrack recording programs, most of the major companies produce both pro-level suites and less expensive, pared-back alternatives for the home user. In the UK, the market leader is Steinberg, with their high-end **Cubase SX** and less pricey **Cubase LE.** In the US, it's Cakewalk, with the serious **Sonar** (pictured) and scaled-back **Home Studio**. Both Cubase LE and Home Studio are good choices, though many commentators think that the best combination of features and ease of use is provided by relative newcomer **Tracktion**.

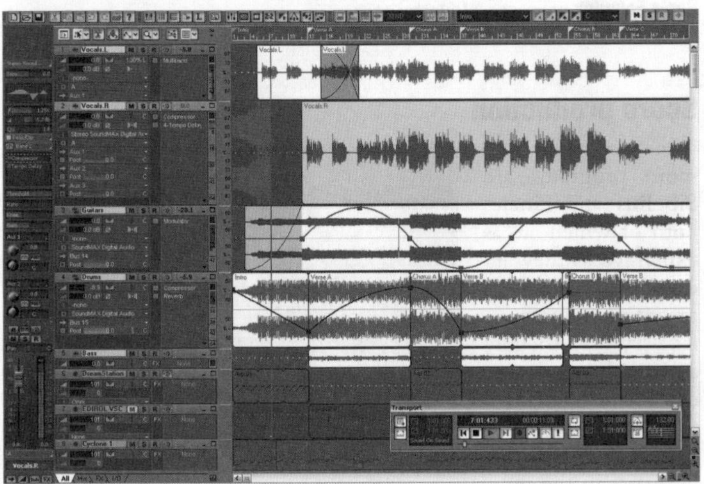

A completely different type of multitracker is Sony's inexpensive **Acid**. This incredibly intuitive program takes any wave file thrown its way and fits it to a tempo of your choice, allowing you to make impressive sample-based songs in minutes.

Acid http://mediasoftware.sonypictures.com
Cakewalk www.cakewalk.com
Steinberg www.steinberg.com
Tracktion www.mackie.com/products/tracktion

Standalone wave editors

If you want professional-standard wave editing capability, go for a stand-alone wave editor such as Sony's **Screenblast Sound Forge** or Steinberg's **WaveLab**. These programs are very powerful, but they're pricey, difficult to master and contain many tools you're unlikely to need as an amateur.

Steinberg www.steinberg.com
Sonic Foundry www.sonicfoundry.com

Score production

The two big-name score programs are **Sibelius** and **Finale**, both of which are as expensive as they are excellent. Sibelius is great for composers – it's very user-friendly and with a plug-in can even recognize scanned-in scores – but Finale is favoured by many in the publishing industry. If you don't require professional results, various programs are available for a fraction of the cost. **GenieSoft Score Writer**, for instance, is an excellent buy.

Sibelius www.sibelius.com
Finale www.codamusic.com
ScoreWriter www.geniesoft.biz

Dance music programs

There are various programs designed specifically for making convincing dance music very easily. One of the best is **Propellerhead's Rebirth**, a virtual rack of classic analogue synths. It's an addictive package that makes generating techno ludicrously easy. The same company also make the more flexible but still dance-focused **Reason**.

Rebirth and Reason http://www.propellerheads.se

CD & DVD burning software

If you have a CD or DVD burner – whether it came with your PC or was purchased separately – it will almost certainly have come with some software for creating and copying music, video and/or data discs. And as we've already seen, Windows Explorer, Windows Media Player and Windows Movie Maker all have in-built disc-burning tools. However, many people find these limiting and clumsy and opt instead for sophisticated software offering more functions, allowing you, for example, to fade music in and out, and alter the length of the gaps between tracks. Many also have layout tools for designing CD labels and jewel-case covers.

Probably the most popular choice is **Roxio Easy Media Creator**. Scaled-down versions of this package are often given away free with CD and DVD writers, but the high-end editions (which you can often upgrade to without much hassle or expense if you already have a basic version) include many more tools and options. Other options include **Nero**, which features everything from a built-in audio editor to a karaoke filter, and the serious but less user-friendly **Gear Pro**.

Before buying any CD or DVD, check that it will work with your drive, especially if you have an old or external model.

Easy CD & DVD Creator www.roxio.com
Gear Pro www.gearsoftware.com
Nero www.nero.com

Handy extras

There are various little programs that are useful to have installed on your system, most of them simply to allow you to view documents or other material that you may come across online.

The following freebies are definitely worth downloading:

Adobe Acrobat Reader www.acrobat.com
Allows you to view documents saved as PDFs, a standard format for articles, manuals, forms and more.

Adobe® PDF

QuickTime Player www.quicktime.com
Originally developed for the Mac, this program – the basic version of which is free – allows you to view pictures and play movie and sound clips in various file formats, including the special QuickTime format often used for compressed sound or movie excerpts.

Games

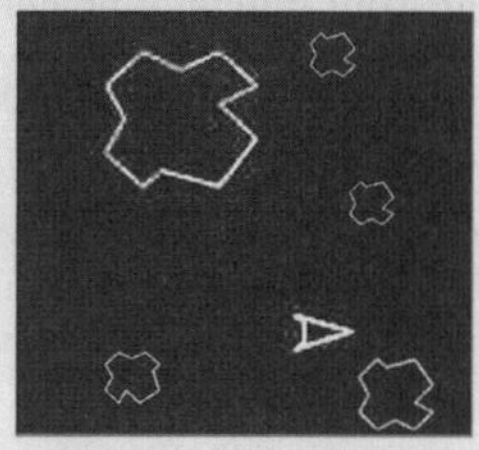

There are thousands upon thousands of games available for the PC, from rediscovered lo-fi classics of days gone by – such as Super Galaxians, Asteroids and PacMan – to modern action games with staggeringly sharp graphics. So whether you fancy fighting, driving, blasting or something a little more sedate – like Sim City, which lets you lord it over your very own metropolis – there's bound to be something out there for you. Though it's easy enough to find games in stores and read the blurb on the boxes, a far better way to cut through the hype is to check out *The Rough Guide to Videogaming*. You could also get hold of some PC gaming magazines or visit some of the countless gaming sites on the Web. To give you a head start, here are a few of the best:

AliveGames www.alivegames.com
Game Dex www.gamedex.com
Grrl Gamer www.grrlgamer.com
GameSpot www.gamespot.com
GamesRadar http://gamesradar.msn.co.uk
Games Domain http://gamesdomain.yahoo.com
PC Gamer www.pcgamer.com

RealOne Player www.real.com
Lets you watch and listen to online streaming audio and video in the common "Real" format.

Shockwave and Flash Players www.macromedia.com
These essential extras, downloadable for free, let you view and hear most Web animations and online audio.

Spybot S&D http://www.safer-networking.org
As described in the following chapter, this helpful tool piece of software clears your system of potentially privacy-infringing "spyware".

---

7 Zip www.7-zip.org
This freeware program for zipping and unzipping compressed files (see p.124) will come in handy if you are running Windows 98. Later Windows versions have basic zipping/unzipping functions built-in.

keeping it purring

19

Playing it safe

PC self-defence

Within weeks of getting a PC, most people will have a lot of stuff saved on their hard drive. And after a year or two, a single drive can contain thousands of hours of work as well as a huge library of downloads, pictures, music, contacts and Web links. The prospect of it all suddenly disappearing – or getting tampered with or spied on – is unpleasant to say the least, but unfortunately these things can happen. And, though seemingly lost data can sometimes be pulled back from the ether with suitable recovery software (see p.305), often when it's gone, it's gone. The first potential hazard is the hard drive itself: if a drive crashes, you're up digital creek without a paddle. Other risks includes malicious programs such as viruses and spyware, and the possibility of people accessing your machine through your Internet connection.

For all these reasons, the most effective thing you can do is also the most obvious: regularly back up your data – at the very least the stuff that would be a real pain to lose, and ideally everything on your whole system. But before we look at the backup process, here's a brief outline of the villains that threaten your files and privacy, and some tactics for keeping them at bay.

The bad guys

Malware

"Malware" is short for "malicious software", which pretty well sums up what it is: computer code written with the express purpose of doing something harmful or shady. Though people often use the word "virus" to refer to all of them, there are actually a number of different types of malware out there…

▶ **Viruses** are programs that infect other program files or floppy-disk boot sectors, so that can spread from machine to machine. In order to catch a virus you must either run an infected program (possibly without your knowledge) or boot your machine with an infected floppy disk inserted fully into the drive. There are thousands of strains, most of which are no more than a nuisance, but some are capable of setting off a time bomb that could destroy the contents of your hard drive. A **macro virus** spreads by infecting Microsoft Word or Excel documents.

▶ **Worms**, like viruses, are designed to spread. But rather than wait for an earthling to transfer the infected file or disk, they actively replicate themselves over a network such as the Internet. They might send themselves to all the contacts in your email address book, for example. That means worms can spread much faster than viruses. The "email viruses" that have made world news in recent years have, strictly speaking, been worms.

▶ **Trojans** (short for Trojan horses) are programs with a hidden agenda. When you run the program it will do something unexpected, often without your knowledge. While viruses are designed to spread, Trojans are usually, though not always, designed to deliver a one-off pay packet. And a custom-built Trojan can be bound to any program, so that when you install it the Trojan will also install in the background. There are dozens of known Trojans circulating the Internet, most with the express purpose of opening a back door to your computer to allow in hackers (see below) while you're online.

▶ **Spyware**, which may arrive via a Trojan, is software design that exists to snoop on your computing activity. Most commonly it's created by some kind of marketeer, who wants to find out about your online surfing and spending habits – usually to sell to someone else. But in theory it might also be someone with physical access to your computer who wants to keep an eye on you or even record the keystrokes when you log in to an Internet banking site.

▶ **Adware** is any software designed to display advertisements. Some of it is perfectly legitimate – you accept a program with an ad banner, say, in return for getting it for free – but other bits may be installed without your consent and have the sole purpose of bombarding you with pop-ups.

"Hackers"

The term "**hacker**" is somewhat fuzzy, as its original meaning – still in use among the computerati – is a legitimate computer programmer (see **www.happyhacker.org/define.shtml**). But it's the popular definition that concerns us here: someone who wants to break into, or meddle with, your computer. They may be a professional out to steal your secrets or a "script kiddy" playing with a prefab Trojan. They might be a vandal, a spy, a thief or simply just exploring. As far as you're concerned, it doesn't matter. You don't want them, or their handiwork, inside your computer.

Preventative medicine

As the above shows, most computer threats relate to using the Internet. But don't despair – and certainly don't let them put you off using the Net. Most people get by without any serious problems and there are various measures you can take to ensure that your data and privacy remain intact.

#1: Avoid running dodgy software

This includes steering clear of free downloads from websites which seem in any way untrustworthy, or which you reached via a pop-up or banner ad. It also means thinking carefully before opening opening suspicious **email attachments**, even from people you know (the message may have been sent by a piece of software without them ever knowing about it). Never touch any attachment described as a love letter, "sexy pic" or the like, and always check with the person who sent it before opening any attached file whose name ends with .EXE, .REG, .COM, .VBS, .INF, .BAT, .PIF or .SHS. Similarly, if you're surfing and Explorer offers you the option of accepting an **ActiveX Control**, press Cancel unless you know and trust the company offering it.

#2: Keep your copy of Windows up-to-date

This process, explained on p.246, is critically important, as an operating system without the latest security patches can be vulnerable in all sorts of ways. Unless you're up-to-date, simply connecting to the Internet or viewing a webpage could be enough to let in some kind of malware.

#3: Use scanners and a firewall

The above two steps, carried out consistently, should be enough to keep you safe from most computer threats. However, for more comprehensive security and privacy you'll need to use some software. First, download and run **SpyBot Search & Destroy**, which will clear your system of spyware.

SpyBot Search & Destroy security.kolla.de

Second, **hide behind a firewall**. This will prevent anyone from even being able to detect your computer on the Internet, let alone invade it. Windows XP comes with a basic firewall built-in, so be sure to enable it for your various Internet connections. In the **Control Panel** select **Network and Internet Connections**, followed by **Network Connections**. Right-click the icon for the connection you wish to protect and select **Properties** from the mouse menu. Under

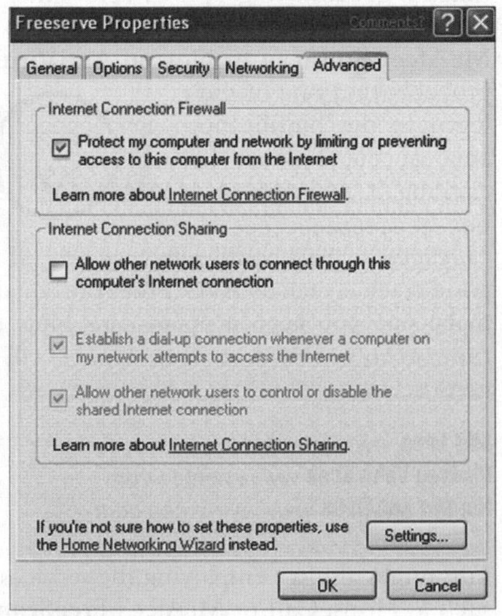

the **Advanced** tab you'll see a box that can be checked to activate your firewall protection.

If you're not running Windows XP, or you want a more powerful firewall, try a branded package such as **ZoneAlarm** or **Norton's Personal Firewall**. And if you want to find out more, visit the online **Home PC Firewall Guide**.

ZoneAlarm www.zonelabs.com
Norton Firewall www.symantec.com
Firewall Guide www.firewallguide.com

Finally, consider installing some antivirus software, which will allow you to examine suspicious files or scan your whole system to find and remove malicious software. They can also protect you in "real time", scanning emails as they arrive and disks as they are attached, though this can get annoying, as it all takes time.

You may find that your PC came with antivirus software – such as **McAfee VirusScan** or **Norton AntiVirus** – pre-installed. If so, you'll probably find one of their logos in the Notification area of the Taskbar. Try clicking it to bring up a box of options.

Otherwise, you could purchase one of these packages, or opt for a good freebie such as **AVG Free**. But whatever virus software you use, make sure you keep it up-to-date. New threats are developed all the time, so an out-of-date virus scanner will miss many of the most dangerous.

AVG Free www.grisoft.com
McAfee VirusScan www.mcafee.com
Norton AntiVirus www.symantec.com

You might also try employing the services of a free Web-based scanner such as **HouseCall** or McAfee's **FreeScan** (see p.305).

Internet Explorer Security Zones

Using the Web means striking a balance between flexibility (your browser allowing site makers to do fancy things with frames and built-in software) and security (stopping people using this fexibility to commit malicious acts). You can change the balance in Internet Explorer, both in general and for specific sites, to allow those you trust more flexibility than those you don't know.

You'll find these settings within the **Security** tab of **Internet Options**, which you can open from Internet Exporer's **Tools** menu. Here you'll find websites split up into various so-called **zones**.

▶ **Internet** This is where you can change your general security settings, using the slider toward the bottom of the panel. However, it's probably best left where it is.

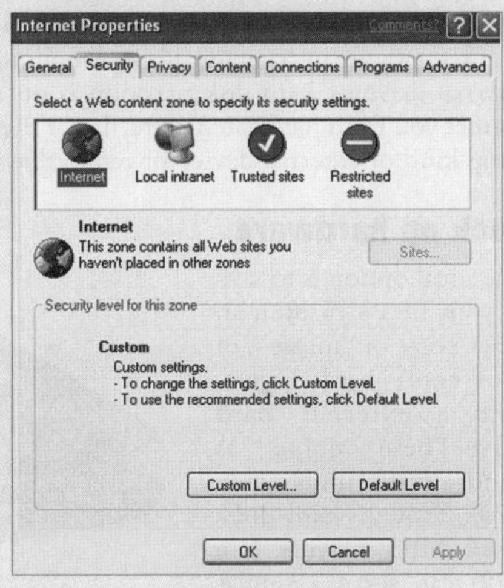

▶ **Trusted sites** If you trust a specific website, add it to this section. Then (assuming you stick with the default setting) the site will be treated with less suspicion by Internet Explorer, allowing its designers more freedom to do fancy things without first asking your permission.

▶ **Restricted sites** This is the sin bin: a place for adding sites you don't trust to minimize their potential for doing damage. Leave this one with the default high security setting.

▶ **Local intranet** is of less interest unless you happen to publish webpages on your home network.

In addition you can use the **Custom Level** button to fine-tune specific security settings, and there's also a button for returning all four zones to their **Default Level**.

Backing up

Following the advice on the previous few pages should be enough to leave you and your files pretty safe and secure. However, things can go wrong. Hard drives die, new viruses develop before virus scanners have time to recognize them, and, like anything else, computers sometimes get burned, flooded, stolen or struck by lightning. So if you want to stay one step ahead of Fate, get yourself into a routine of **backing up on a regular basis**. Once you're in the habit, it's not much hassle – so start today.

The basic idea is to create duplicate copies of your important files and keep them in a secure place. Duplicating them onto a separate internal drive or hard disk partition is not good enough, as it won't protect you from hardware failure, fire or theft. Instead, you need to use some kind of external device or removable media.

Back up hardware

The ideal option is to save all your files – or even an exact copy, or "image", of your entire hard drive – onto a **external hard drive**. These come as stand-alone units (see p.70), though hard-disk-based **MP3 players** (see p.78) can serve a similar function.

If you don't want to splash out on such as item, however, you can still carry out partial backups onto lower-capacity media such as writable **DVDs** (see p.40) and **CDRs** (see p.42), **Zip disks** (see p.69), or even an inexpensive and eminently portable **Flash drive** (see p.71). After all, much of your hard drive will be populated by programs which, as long as you have the original CDs, you could always reinstall later if necessary.

What to back up

Obviously you'll want to back up your **document files** – letters, spreadsheets, photos, music and so on – but some less obvious things are worth having a second copy of. Don't forget, for example:

▶ **Your emails** If you use Outlook Express you can use the **Export** function in the **File** menu to save your archive of emails as a folder of text files, which you can then back up like any other.

▶ **Your address book** If you use the address book, it can be a real pain to lose. Back it up by selecting **Export** from Outlook Express's **File** menu and then selecting **Address Book (WAB)** to save a copy in the Windows format, or select **Other Address Book** to save as a text document. You can then back up the copy like any other file.

▶ **Internet Favorites** A long and carefully cultivated Favorites list is a valuable asset, and it's easy to back up. If you Search for "favorites" on your C drive you will discover either one or several **Favorites folders** (there will be an individual folder for every user); these folders can be backed up like any other regular folder. Alternatively you can use the **Export** function in Internet Explorer's **File** menu.

▶ **Dial-up Networking** Especially if you have more than one ISP account, it's worth saving yourself the hassle of sorting out your various dial-up Internet connections should disaster strike. Simply drag the connection icons from Windows XP's **Network and Internet Connections** (or **Dial-Up Networking** in older versions) to your backup place of choice.

You can carry out a partial backup in various ways: with the program that came with your CD burner, for example, or just by dragging and dropping with a Zip disk or external drive. However, you could also use a special backup program, such as the one that comes bundled with Windows…

Windows Backup

Windows features a more than adequate backup tool that can be found in the **Start** menu by selecting **Programs, Accessories, System Tools** and then **Backup** – though you may find that in some versions of Windows this program is not present (see box).

In Windows XP, once the program is up and running you'll either be presented with a **Backup Utility Wizard** or a dialog box where you can initiate the process manually (under the **Backup** tab). In Windows 98 and Me, the wizard is simply called the **Backup Wizard**, but it works in much the same way.

Where's Backup?

If you can't find the Backup program in your version of Windows, dig out your Windows CD-ROM, pop it in the drive and select Browse This CD from the dialog box that should appear on-screen. Select the add-ons folder and then the MSBackup folder. You should see a icon called msbexp – double-click it to install the utility.

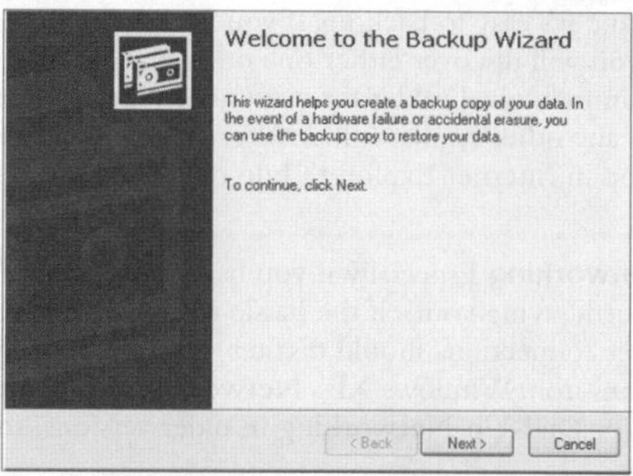

Whether you're using the wizard mode or regular mode to create your backup, decide which files you want to back up and select them by checking the boxes next to the files in the various layers of the folder tree. Then choose where you want the data to be backed up to – CDR, Zip, whatever – and whether you want to use compression to save space. You will also need to give the backup task a **name**. Next time you want to back up you can simply rerun your named backup process: the program compares your existing backup file with your current system and then resaves any files that have changed since the previous backup. There's no need to back up everything, every time – only the stuff that's altered.

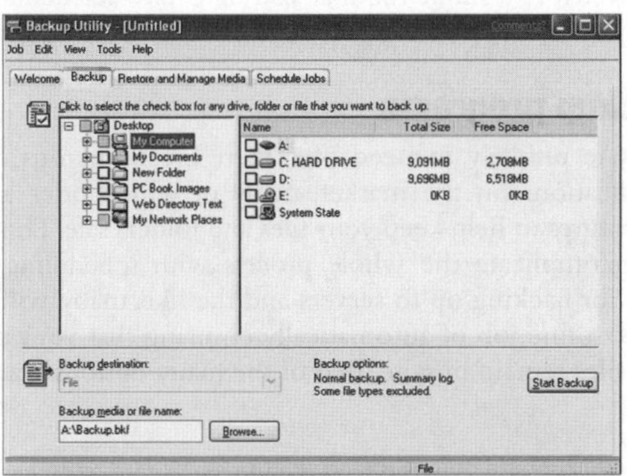

The first time you perform such a backup, it's called a full backup, while **subsequent backups** are known as **incremental backups**. With Windows XP you are also given the option to set up a backup schedule. As long as your machine is switched on at the specified time, your backup will be kept updated automatically – you could set it to go while you're asleep, for example.

If you ever want to retrieve all or some of the files from a backup,

Tips & Tricks

Wizardless backups

If your backup program always launches as a wizard, uncheck the **Always start in wizard mode** box on the first frame of the wizard; you'll find that the next time you run the program many more options will be available to you.

again use the Windows Backup, but this time click the **Restore And Manage Media** tab (or just **Restore** in earlier Windows versions). Browse your backup media for the files you're after, select them by checking the relevant boxes on the folder tree and hit the **Start Restore** button.

Remember, backups aren't just there for epic disasters. You can also use them to retrieve a single file that you may have accidentally deleted, or even just to compare a piece of work with its earlier version.

More backup programs

Though you're unlikely to need one, there are numerous dedicated backup applications on the market, many of which offer a stack of additional features to help keep your files and folders safe. Though they tend to overcomplicate the whole process with scheduling routines and features for backing up to servers and the like, many will, just like Windows, do a fine job of automatically ensuring that your main files and backup files remain in sync. Two of the many options you can find online are:

12 Ghosts www.12ghosts.com/ghosts/backup
HandyBackup www.handybackup.net

Online backups

Another option is to get yourself a chunk of space online (you might have received some for free with your Internet access account), and back up your files there. This way your data is well and truly out of harm's way, and you can access it from anywhere. However, without a high-speed Internet connection it's not a realistic option for anything more than a few small files.

Many backup programs, including Handy Backup (see above), now support online backups, and there are companies, such as **Data Backup Inc** and **Novastor**, that offer a complete service. But it's not cheap if you need any sizeable amount of online storage space.

Data Backup Inc www.backmeupoffsite.com
Novastor http://services.online-backup.com/homepc.asp

20 Troubleshooting

help is at hand

Like everything else, PCs occasionally go wrong. And even with endless technical refinements, they probably always will. Though your first instincts may be to panic, cry or take a sledgehammer to your machine, there are a plethora of tools and techniques at your disposal for tackling both minor niggles and major hassles. Whether hardware or software related, most of the problems you might encouter cna be solved without you having to send your computer away or running up a hefty phone bill calling technical support. And there's always the Internet, of course: if something's happened to you, it's no doudt happened to a thousand other people as well, and many of them are sure to have aired their woes and solutions online.

Hardware problems

Thanks to the advent of Plug and Play technology (see p.52), hardware connection problems are much rarer than they used to be. If you do encounter difficulties, they're most likely to be the result of something simple like a disconnected power cable or a plug that has become loose. But if you're still stuck after trying all the obvious possibilities, things can get frustrating. Here are a few of the most common problems and their solutions.

▶ My mouse is sluggish and jumpy

If your old-fashioned non-optical mouse is unresponsive and tends to stick, it probably needs a good clean. First, unplug the mouse, turn it over,

Windows XP Troubleshooters

Though this book arms you against many of the problems you're likely to encounter, Windows XP users should also consider turning to the built-in **XP Troubleshooters**. They work like wizards, walking you through a series of diagnostic questions in an attempt to isolate your problem – and, with any luck, suggest a fix. You might have already seen buttons for specific tools in dialog boxes, simply labelled "Troubleshoot", but the best way to find them is by looking in the **Troubleshooter** menus on the left-hand side of the various **Control Panel** category views. For example, within the **Appearance and Themes** category, you will see troubleshooters for **Display** and **Sound**.

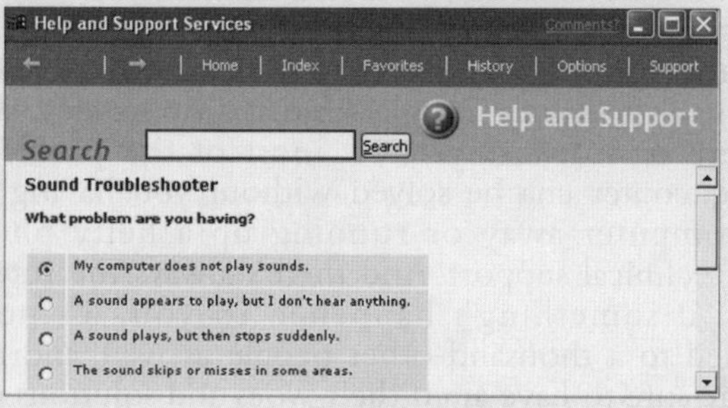

twist open the access panel and allow the rubber ball to fall out. Now take a look inside and you'll see three little rollers that may well be clogged up with grease, hair or some unidentifiable gunk. Use a cotton bud or some tweezers to remove the sludge, then reassemble your mouse and plug it back in. If your pointer still isn't as perky as you'd like, try adjusting its "motion" and "acceleration" settings in the **Mouse Properties** dialog box, which you'll find by clicking the **Mouse** icon in the **Control Panel** (within the **Printers and Other Hardware** category in Windows XP).

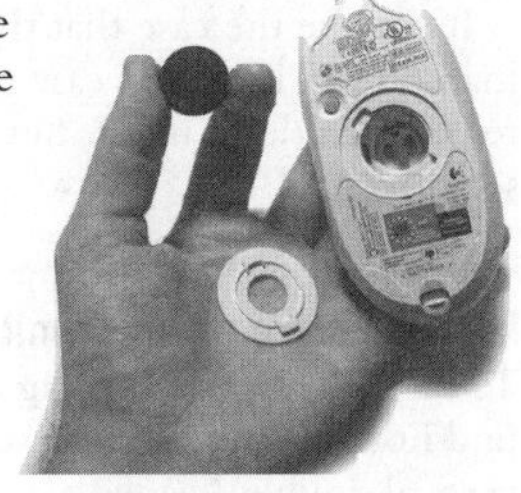

▶ My monitor flickers

If your CRT monitor is flickering, you could try resetting the monitor's refresh rate, if your hardware is up to it - anything less than 75 Hz can look pretty strobe-like. From the **Control Panel** select **Appearance and Themes** and then **Display**. Click the **Settings** tab, and then the **Advanced** button. Then click the **Monitor** tab (**Adapter** in some versions of Windows) and you'll find a list of available **refresh rate** settings. If several options are given, try a higher setting, but if possible check your manual to see what your screen can handle, because too high a refresh rate can damage a monitor.

If you are only offered one option (60 Hz), it could be that Windows can't find the monitor's Plug and Play configuration. To try and resolve this problem in XP, select the **Monitor** tab and click the **Properties** button: this will bring up a window that should tell you whether your monitor is working properly. It will also offer a button that launches the Windows **Video Display Troubleshooter**, which will help you to identify and correct any

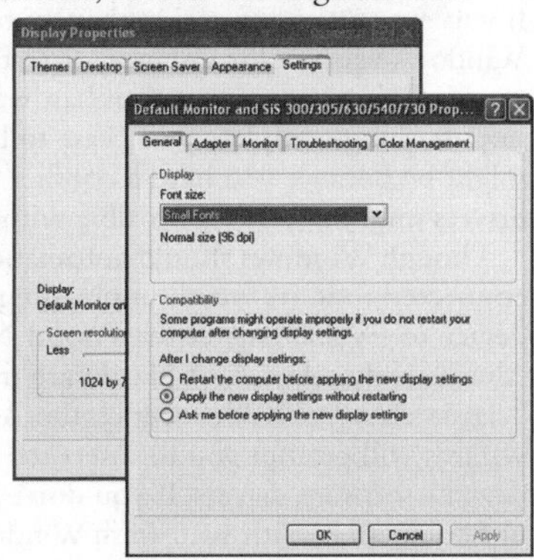

problems with your monitor and video card. In older versions of Windows click the **Monitor** tab, check the **Automatically detect Plug & Play monitors** box, and then restart your PC.

It may be the case that the monitor doesn't support any settings faster than 60 Hz, in which case try experimenting with different screen resolutions (look under **Settings** in the **Display Properties** dialog box; see p.133).

▶ The picture on my monitor doesn't fill the screen

To fix this you need to dig around in the controls on your monitor and find how to alter the two settings represented by little horizontal or vertical double-headed arrows. Tweak the settings until the on-screen image expands to fill the monitor's maximum viewing capacity.

If when you next turn on your computer the screen image returns to its old size, you may have a problem with your video card. If you know the manufacturer, try going to their website and searching for updated drivers. Alternatively, try opening a Command Prompt or DOS Prompt (in the **Start** menu under **Programs** then **Accessories**) and hitting **Alt+Enter** once, and then again. Oddly enough, this occasionally solves the problem.

▶ My PC can't find all my devices

If you ever make any major changes to your system – upgrading your Windows version, for instance, or installing a new expansion card – you may find that certain pieces of hardware (modems, printers and the like) stop working completely or cease to be recognized by your system. This might be because you have a conflict of resources, or your hardware drivers might not be compatible with the changes you've made.

Though Windows should automatically detect the presence of devices connected to it, it's worth unplugging and reconnecting a problematic device to try and trigger the **Found New Hardware Wizard.** Alternatively, select **Add Hardware** from the **Control Panel** (in the "classic view" in XP) to launch the **Add Hardware Wizard**. Both these wizards will prompt you to insert the disk or disks that contain the device's software drivers. If you don't have these disks, or the software is not compatible with your fresh Windows upgrade, you can use the wizard

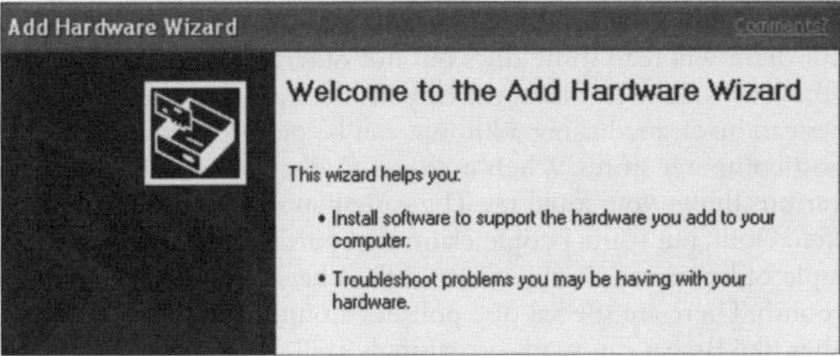

to search online for a newer version of the driver to download and install. If you're running older versions of Windows you will need to find your device's drivers yourself – have a look on the manufacturer's website.

If your hardware problems persist, it's worth checking the port settings. Right-click **My Computer**, select **Properties**, and click the **Device Manager** button under the **Hardware** tab (in pre-XP windows versions the **Device Manager** has its own tab). Find and double-click the icon for the troublesome device. Select the **Resources** tab, and look in the **Conflicting device list** box to see if this is the source of the problem. If there is a conflict you could try disabling the device that is causing it, by right-clicking its icon in the **Device Manager** list, selecting **Properties**, clicking the **General** tab, and selecting **Do not use this device (disable)** or **Disable in this hardware profile**. However, you won't be able to use the conflicting device until you re-enable it.

▶ Some of my USB connections won't work

The most common USB connection problems are with power. As well as actually connecting your PC to peripherals, USB ports sometimes send electricity to them. For many peripherals this isn't an issue because they have their own power supply; and, equally, USB ports on a PC's case or monitor base should have no difficulties delivering the juice when it's needed. But the USB ports found on some peripheral devices without power sources (like keyboards) shift far less power. Trying to use a USB device that needs a lot of energy – such as a scanner – with an unpowered port like this can be problematic. To solve the problem, either move the device to a self-powered port or invest in a **USB hub** with its own power supply.

▶ My CD or DVD drive won't read a disc

If your drive will read some discs but not others, the likelihood is either that the lens is dirty or that some of your discs are scratched or unclean. Lenses can be cleaned using a kit that can be picked up relatively cheaply in most computer stores. When it comes to dirty or scratched discs, there are various things you could try. The easiest approach is to use a clean, lint-free cloth, but some people claim that putting a CD in the freezer for a couple of hours can do the trick, while others swear by the application of a polish. There are special disc polishes around, but certain metal polishes like Brasso can work surprisingly well (though these should be applied with caution to discs containing important data). If the problem disc contains a piece of software, try contacting the manufacturer; they might be willing to swap your old copy for a shiny new one.

▶ I'm having problems saving files to a floppy disk, even though the disk appears to be empty

The first thing to check is that the little plastic write-protection tab on the corner of the diskette is closed: if you can see through the hole, slide the tab across to close it.

If you're still having trouble writing to the disk, try formatting it – but beware, as this will **irretrievably erase** all the data on the disk. Insert the disk into the drive, and then in **My Computer** right-click the drive's icon (almost always labelled **A:**), and from the mouse menu select **Format**. In the dialog box that appears, uncheck the **Quick Format** box – you need to perform a **Full** format that will not only delete any files but also check the disk for errors and return it to a totally blank state. In this dialog box you can also choose to give the disk a **Label** (a name that will appear alongside its icon in an Explorer window). When you're ready, click **Start**; it will probably take a couple of minutes for the process to complete. If you continue to have difficulties writing to a particular disk, it may well be physically damaged: the only option is to bin it and try a different one.

▶ I keep being presented with printer error messages

Printers are notoriously difficult to keep happy, so this is a relatively common problem. First, check that the printer is plugged into its power supply, connected to your PC properly, turned on and has paper in its tray. If all this seems fine, try turning the printer off, waiting a few seconds and then turning it on again – this will clear its memory, which sometimes does the trick. If you've recently upgraded your operating system it may be that you need to download a newer **driver** from your printer manufacturer's website. Equally, the driver you are using might be corrupted or suffering from a virus, so reinstalling drivers from the floppy or CD that came with the printer is always worth a try. To do this in Windows XP, open the **Control Panel**, click the **Printers and Other Hardware** category and select **Printers and Faxes**. In older versions of Windows open the **Printers** folder, which can be reached either from **My Computer** or the **Control Panel**. Now, right-click the icon for your current printer and click **Delete** in the mouse menu. Next click the **Add Printer** icon to launch the **Add Printer Wizard**, which will help you to reinstall your printer, either from the Windows built-in list or from the CD that came with the printer.

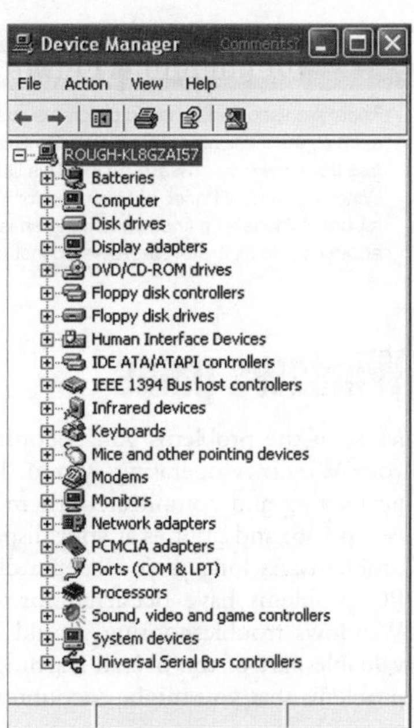

If you're still having problems, check the port settings. Right-click **My Computer** and select

Properties. In Windows XP select the **Hardware** tab and click the **Device Manager** button; in earlier versions of Windows just click the **Device Manager** tab. You'll see a list of all the ports and devices on your system. Double-click either **Ports (COM & LPT)** or **Universal Serial Bus controllers** depending on the sort of connection your printer uses (parallel or USB respectively). Double-click the icon for your printer port, select the **Resources** tab and look in the **Conflicting device list** box for **IRQ** (Interrupt Request Line) or **DMA** (Direct Memory Access) conflicts. If there is a conflict you could disable the device that's causing it. Find the device in the **Device Manager** list, right-click it and select **Properties**. When a dialog box appears, click the **General** tab and select **Do not use this device (disable)** or **Disable in this hardware profile**. This may make the printer work, but you'll have to re-enable the device that you've turned off when you next need to use it.

Diagnosing your hardware problems

There are various diagnostic programs available to help you with troubleshooting, such as the invaluable **SiSoft Sandra Standard**, which can be downloaded for free from www.sisoftware.co.uk. This little program looks very much like a Windows Control Panel, but it's used for running tests on your system and creating reports. Whenever it finds something amiss in your system, it makes suggestions about how to fix it with step-by-step instructions.

Windows pains

Most of the problems you encounter on your PC will be related to your Windows operating system. Though these difficulties can seem perplexing and complicated, there are various built-in **System Tools** (see p.166) and utilities at your disposal that can diagnose and fix many problems. As long as you keep a clear head and remember that most PC problems have occurred for a specific – and fixable – reason, Windows troubleshooting should be relatively straightforward and a valuable part of the overall learning process. Here are a few common problems that you might encounter:

▶ Windows has displayed an alarming error message with loads of codes and file names I don't understand

Though they often seem bewildering and it's tempting to ignore them, error messages generally appear for a good reason, so they're worth investigating. Make a note of everything that the message says and then visit the **Knowledge Base** section of Microsoft's website (**www.support.microsoft.com**). Here you should be able to find everything you need to know about your error message, as well as various tips about how to sort things out.

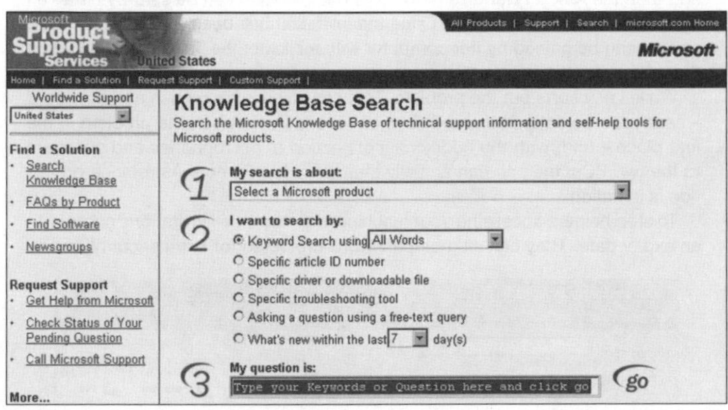

▶ My machine is having problems starting Windows

This kind of predicament is most likely due to a problem with your Windows registry or settings, perhaps caused by a bad software or hardware installation. In Windows XP and Me, such problems are often easily solved with the **System Restore** tool (see p.167). If you're running Windows 98 or earlier, you may be able to fix the problem by uninstalling the software or device driver that was installed before the problem arose.

But to try either of these solutions you obviously need to get your machine up and running again. Try rebooting your system in **Safe mode**, a special type of Windows start sequence that uses the minimum settings and drivers needed to get things going. To get most Windows versions to

Remote Assistance

If you're running Windows XP you can use the Remote Assistance utility to allow a trusted friend or technician to take complete control of your system from a remote location and try to deal with any problems you may be encountering. Equally, if you want to help someone else out with a problem, they could invite you to roll up your sleeves and rummage around in their system.

First, the party that needs aid (let's say Tom) has to issue an invitation to the individual that they think can help (how about Tom's cousin Lucy?). From the **Start** menu, Tom selects **Help and Support**, then clicks the **Support** button, and then the **Ask a Friend to help** task. The invitation can be sent by either an email or Windows Messenger. Once the invitation has been accepted by Lucy, control can be gained by her computer with a click of the **Take Control** button that she sees on her screen.

While Lucy sorts out the problem, Tom can still use his mouse and keyboard – handy for recreating the conditions or actions that caused the problem in the first place – and, with the additional connection of microphones and speakers to the two PCs, the pair can actually chat while the Remote Assistance operation is in action.

To stop helpers accessing your machine later, the email invitations come with an expiry date. They can also be password-protected for extra security.

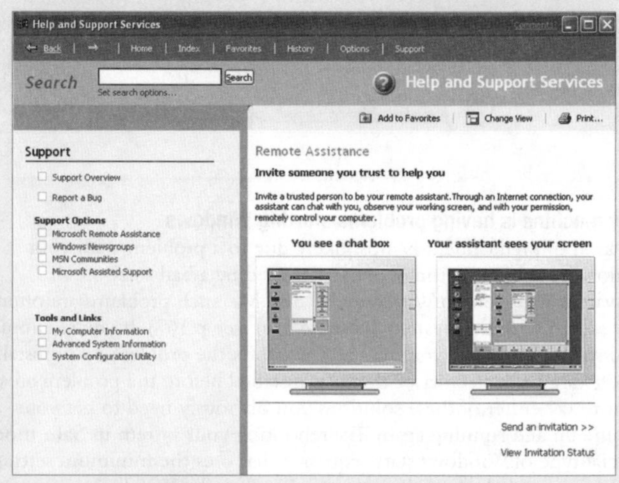

start in Safe mode, restart the computer and press the **F8** key during the boot sequence (in Windows 98, restart your computer and hold down **Control**). You might also discover that you are offered the Safe mode automatically when your machine repeatedly crashes.

During the Safe mode boot sequence you will be presented with a menu of Safe mode options, which will vary a little depending upon the version of Windows you are running. As a general rule, select the **basic Safe mode option**, though in Windows XP you could choose **Last known good configuration**. This will reboot your system as it was the last time a successful startup was recorded by the registry.

If you can't get Safe mode to work, try restarting your system with a boot disk (see p.245).

▶ I can't get Windows to boot because of an invalid "system disk"

Sometimes when you start your machine you might be confronted by a foreboding message questioning the validity of the "system disk" in drive A. Don't panic: this simply means that you left a floppy in the drive last time you used the machine. The PC gets confused because it detects the disk and assumes that it's found part of the boot-up information, when in fact it's probably nothing more than a letter to Great Aunt Edith. All you need to do is eject the disk, press the Enter key on your keyboard and the computer will continue as if nothing has happened.

If it seems to be something more serious, use Safe Mode (see p.301).

▶ I've adjusted some Windows settings and now things aren't working properly

If you have Windows XP or Me, this is the perfect time to try turning back the clock using the **System Restore** function, found under **Performance and Maintenance** in the Windows XP **Control Panel**, and **System Tools** in Windows Me. See p.167 for more.

▶ How do I stop programs starting automatically when I boot Windows?

Simply remove the offending programs from the Windows Startup folder (see p.190).

▶ Some of my files seem to have disappeared, while other text documents look like they've been put through a mincer

First of all back up any important data (see p.288) in case anything else disappears. The problem could be caused by a virus, so it's worth scanning your system (see p.286). Also try uninstalling any software or device drivers that you installed just before the problem arose.

However, it could conceivably be that your hard drive is on its last legs. Try opening **ScanDisk utility** (see p.167) and selecting the **Thorough** option to check the surface of your drive for bad or damaged sectors. You might well be prompted to delete detected **cross-linked** and **bad clusters**; this might be enough to solve the problem, but if files continue to vanish or be mangled, it could be that you'll soon need a new hard drive.

If something important seems to have permanently disappeared or if you can't find anything at all on your hard drive, you could try getting some **data recovery** software. If things are desperate you may even consider employing the services of a data recovery company.

▶ I'm having trouble with the setup of my Windows upgrade

In this situation, if you feel brave enough, the best thing to do is back up all your data, format your hard drive and make a **clean installation** (see p.244) of your new version of Windows.

▶ I'm missing the volume control icon from my Taskbar

This common niggle can be resolved by opening the **Control Panel**. In Windows XP select the **Sounds, Speech and Audio Devices** category and then click **Sounds and Audio Devices**; in earlier versions just click **Sounds** or **Sounds and Multimedia**. Click on the **Volume** or **Audio** tab of the dialog box that will appear, check the **Show volume control on Taskbar** box, and click **Apply**.

▶ My machine is running very slowly, crashing frequently, and it keeps displaying "Low Memory" error messages

You might need to add some more RAM to your system (see p.315), but there are several other things you could try if you don't fancy getting your hands dirty. First, try creating a little extra room for your **virtual memory** (also known as the **pagefile** or **swapfile**) – the special file on your PC that stores any excess data that your RAM can't accommodate. This file adjusts its size as required, but it's limited by the available space on your hard drive. To give your virtual memory a little more elbow room in Windows XP, right-click **My Computer**, select **Advanced** and then under **Performance** click the **Settings** button. In the next box, under **Advanced**, click the **Change** button under **Virtual Memory**: here you can adjust its size and location. In older Windows right-click **My Computer** and select **Properties**, go to the **Performance** tab and choose **Virtual Memory**. Select **Let me specify my own virtual memory settings** and try raising the maximum figure.

▶ I think my PC might have a virus, but I don't have any antivirus software

Though you should have an antivirus utility running at all times, don't worry too much: there is help to be found on the Internet. Try a free scan from **HouseCall** or McAfee Trend Micro's free virus scanning utility:

HouseCall http://housecall.trendmicro.com
McAfee FreeScan http://us.mcafee.com/root/mfs/default.asp

In some versions of Windows XP you also have the option of creating an **AVBoot floppy disk** – a special startup floppy disk utility that scans your computer's memory and all its local disk drives for known viruses. If a one is found, the AVBoot tool will try to get rid of it. To create an AVBoot disk, insert your Windows XP CD into your CD drive and click the **Browse this CD** option. Now double-click **VALUEADD** then open the **3RDPARTY** folder, then the **CA_ANTIV** folder, and double-click the **Makedisk** icon; insert a disk into your floppy drive and follow the on-screen instructions. To run the utility, insert the AVBoot startup disk into your floppy drive and restart your PC.

▶ I've deleted a file that I actually need

The first thing to do is check the **Recycle Bin**. But if you've permanently erased the file, it won't be there and you'll need to get hold of some recovery software from the Internet. Try downloading a free version of Ontrack's **EasyRecovery** (www.ontrack.co.uk/easyrecovery). It will show you which files on your drives and disks are recoverable with the EasyRecovery program, letting you decide whether it's worth purchasing the full package. There are loads of other similar applications available – use a search engine to see what you can find – and try not to save anything to the disk or drive in question until you have recovered the file, as this could make recovery impossible.

▶ I have forgotten my Windows password

In Windows XP you can create a new password for yourself by using the Password Reset Disk that you hopefully created a while ago: for more on these disks, see p.149.

In older Windows versions you might find you can simply press **Cancel** when prompted to enter your password, though this may not open your account with all settings in place. If this doesn't work, or if you really want to sort out the forgotten password, you'll need to restart your computer using a Windows Startup disk (see p.245). When you're presented with a menu of options, hold down **Shift+F5** to get a command prompt – a black background displaying something like **A:\>**. Type **c:** and hit **Enter**. Then type **cd windows** and press **Enter** again. Next, type **dir *.pwl**, press **Enter** once more – a list of the password files on your computer will appear.

Each password file will be named after the person who it relates to – if your username is "Elvis", for example, the password file will be named **ELVIS**. Though you won't be able to find the actual password this way, deleting the password file will allow you back into the machine, and you can set a new password later. To delete the ELVIS file, for example, type **del ELVIS.pwl** and press **Enter**. You can check that it's been deleted by once again typing **dir *.pwl** and pressing **Enter** – the list should be displayed without the relevant password file.

Remove the Startup disk and restart your machine (you may be asked to choose from a menu once more – select **Start in normal mode**). When Windows loads, you may be asked to enter a new password – do so if you want to, but it's fine to leave it blank. If Windows still asks for a password, simply click **OK** without entering anything in the password field.

▶ The sound from my PC sometimes clicks

This is quite a common problem, usually caused by misunderstandings between a graphics card and a sound card. Try right-clicking the Desktop and selecting **Properties** to open the Display Properties dialog box. Click the **Settings** tab, then the **Advanced** button, and a new dialog box will appear. Select the tab labelled **Troubleshoot** or **Performance**, and reduce the **Hardware Acceleration** setting. If you can't get a satisfactory result this way, try going to the website of your sound card manufacturer and download the latest drivers.

▶ The clock on my Taskbar doesn't keep the right time

In Windows Me and earlier the clock is pretty unreliable – you may find that it gradually drifts out over a few days or weeks, or perhaps it's correct when the machine is switched on but loses time over the course of a session. There's no perfect cure, but there are various programs downloadable for free from the Internet that will set your clock automatically whenever you go online. Try **Atomic Clock** (www.philex.net/clock).

▶ My Internet connection keeps cutting off

If you're constantly losing your Internet connection, especially at peak times, chances are that the fault is with your ISP rather than your machine. Try emailing your current provider to inform them of your difficulties or, if you don't get a satisfactory response, take your business elsewhere.

If it seems to happen after a set period of inactivity, however, it might be that your PC is set to hang up after a certain amount of "idle" time. To see if this is so, open the **Control Panel**, select **Network and Internet connections** and click **Network Connections**. (In earlier versions of Windows, click **Dial-up Networking** from the **Control Panel** or **My**

Computer). Right-click the icon for the connection you're having trouble with and select **Properties** from the mouse menu. Under one of the tabs you'll find an option labelled something like **Idle time before hanging up**; increase the time to an hour or so.

▶ Internet Explorer keeps crashing

Try clearing your browser of any old Web files and content that may be corrupted or troublesome. In Internet Explorer, select **Options** from the **Tools** menu to open the **Internet Options** dialog box.

Under the **General** tab, in the **Temporary Internet Files** section, click **Delete Files**. Further down, click the **Clear History** button. While you're there, consider reducing your History's memory to only a few days; this will limit the likelihood of corrupt files causing trouble in the future but will mean that your PC won't keep track of all the pages you've visited for as long. If problems persist, read on…

▶ My whole system seems buggy, slow and unstable

Windows – especially pre-XP versions – are notoriously prone to getting increasingly bug-ridden, crash-prone, slow and unreliable as time goes on. There are many things you can try, including sweeping your system for spyware (see p.283) and viruses (see p.305), defragmenting your hard drive (see p.167) and downloading the latest hardware drivers for the various components in your sytstem. However, it may be that the only real way to improve things is to **reinstall Windows** (see box).

Tech Info

Making a fresh start

If your system has grown annoyingly unstable, and nothing else seems to have worked, wiping your hard drive and reinstalling your current version of Windows could help.

However, this will **wipe your hard drive** so you'll first have to **back up** all your files (see p.288). And, once everything's up and running again, you'll have to reinstall all your programs and transfer your documents back onto the machine. It's a hassle, certainly, but worth it to make your system usable again.

Many PCs come with a **Restore CD** that will reinstall Windows on your behalf. Otherwise, you'll need to use a **Windows CD** (possibly with a boot disk), as explained on p.245.

Find help online

As mentioned above, there's truckloads of computer troubleshooting advice online. First try entering keywords (as specific as possible) into Google, both the standard **Web search** and the **newsgroup search**:

Google www.google.com
Google Groups http://groups.google.com

No luck? Try one of the many dedicated troubleshooting sites, such as:

Kelly's Korner www.kellys-korner-xp.com
ComputerHope www.computerhope.com
Windows-Help.net www.windows-help.net

For more pointers, see our website directory (see p.399).

21 Upgrades and self-builds

doing it yourself

If your PC no longer cuts the mustard and troubleshooting hasn't helped, it may be time for an upgrade. First, you'll need to work out what your weary system actually needs. Then you'll have to make a decision: either to take the PC to a computer store and get them to do the rest; or to be a bit more adventurous – buy a new component, find a screwdriver, get under the hood and perform the operation yourself. By choosing to upgrade rather than splash out on a whole new machine, you may well save quite a bit of cash, especially if you shop around for components online, and if you carry out your own PC surgery you're sure to learn loads about the workings of your computer.

What can be achieved?

If you have a specific computer problem, a one-part upgrade is often enough to solve it completely. If you've run out of storage space, for example, a new hard drive will do the trick; if your machine is struggling to run large programs, a bit more RAM could be enough to sort it out; and if you have a reasonable processor but 3D games aren't up to speed, then a new video card could make all the difference.

If, however, your intention is to turn a very old PC into a high-end multimedia powerhouse, you may find that practically every bit of the computer needs replacing – you'll need a fast processor, which will almost certainly necessitate a new motherboard, which in turn will probably mean getting a new case. You'll also need new RAM (your old stuff will probably be of the wrong sort), and a better graphics card. And you'll probably want a bigger hard drive for storing programs, music, video, games, etc. Some components might be reusable – the monitor, modem, sound card, mouse and keyboard, perhaps – but you'll essentially be building a new PC. This isn't necessarily a problem, but if you're going to all this trouble you should at least consider going for an entirely new machine.

Can I do it myself?

If you're of a relatively technical disposition and patient enough to do the necessary research, most upgrades aren't too difficult. Things can get tricky, though, especially if you're adding components to an old motherboard, and you may even **invalidate the warranty** of your PC if you start tampering within the case, leaving you with no comeback if you **accidentally break something**. But for many users, the pros substantially outweigh the cons. Not only can you **save money**, but getting under the hood of a computer is the best way to demystify the machine and gain a real knowledge of its bits and pieces.

This chapter runs through some basics of PC upgrading, but it's not designed to be a comprehensive or step-by-step manual. For one thing, **each system is different** and yours may require alternative treatment. If a **manual** came with your system, read it – you may find it describes the exact upgrade potential of the PC and offers advice about buying

Upgrading laptops

Although laptops are far less upgradeable than desktop systems, many do feature easily accessible RAM slots, interchangeable CD, DVD and floppy drives, removable hard drives and other do-it-yourself possibilities. And much more often than with desktops, laptops come with a manual specifying exactly what can be done in terms of upgrading and what types of components are required – perhaps even with detailed instructions about making the install. If your laptop didn't come with a manual, search for help online or contact the manufacturer for information.

components. And if your PC is a big-brand machine, it's worth visiting the **manufacturer's website** to see if they have an upgrading section. If they do, it may even provide step-by-step instructions for various types of upgrade. Finally, always read the **instructions** provided with the device you're adding.

Getting under the hood

You shouldn't be intimidated by the prospect of opening up your PC and carrying out some basic surgery. As long as you're careful and methodical you will probably be fine, and if you get stuck you can always take the machine to a shop and get the staff to rescue you. But there are a few things to consider before you open up a PC for the first time:

▶ **Safety first** Most important of all, you need to protect yourself from electric shock. **Never take the case off a PC before turning it off and disconnecting the power lead.** And, once the machine's open, don't touch anything unnecessarily: electrical components are easily damaged and some can carry a small charge even after the machine has been switched off.

▶ **Protect your components** Computer components, especially RAM chips and CPUs, are incredibly sensitive to **static electricity**. A static shock from a finger so small that you wouldn't even feel it can be enough to fry a high-quality stick of RAM. Though the chances of this happening are sometimes slightly exaggerated, before you unpack any new parts or touch anything inside, and then at regular intervals when you're handling components, be sure to touch some grounded metal such as an unpainted gas or water pipe. Or, even better, buy an anti-static wristband – they're inexpensive and are available from many electronic and computer stores.

▶ **Work in a sensible place** Before you begin, unplug everything from the computer and move it to a flat, stable and well-lit surface such as a table, with some small containers to hand for storing any screws you remove. If you don't have an anti-static wristband, avoid working on the PC whilst sitting or standing on a carpet, as this will increase the risk of picking up static electricity.

▶ **Equipment** There are some excellent PC toolkits available which include everything you could conceivably require for repairing a computer, but for a simple upgrade these aren't really necessary. Probably all you'll need is a small crosshead screwdriver – though some other tools may be required depending on the situation and the type of screws used on the case. A pair of pincer-nosed pliers can come in handy for removing power leads and other stubborn connections, though they should be used with care.

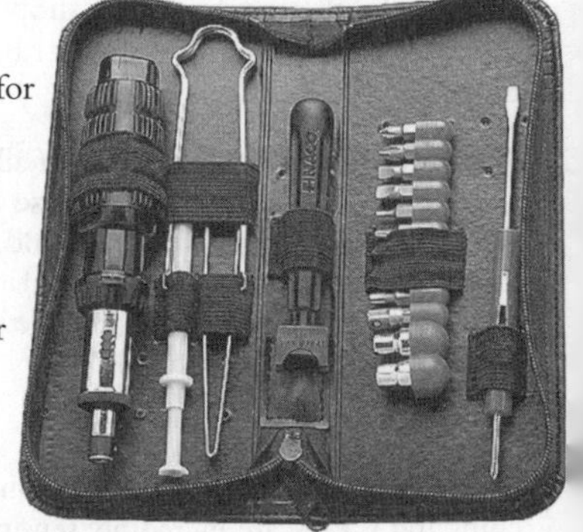

▶ **Opening the case** Opening up a PC is usually very simple. The sides (or the whole outer case) are usually secured by just a few small screws or clips at the back of the machine; remove these and the sides and/or top should simply slide off.

▶ **While you're in there...** When you open up the case to carry out an upgrade, you may be surprised at just how dusty everything is inside. This is largely due to the cooling fan or fans, which pull a lot of air through the case. If you have the hood off you may be tempted to give everything a quick clean. This is a good idea, but circuitry should only really be cleaned by carefully spraying with **compressed air**, which is available in cans from electronics stores. Make sure you blow the dust out of the machine rather than simply rearranging it, and never hold the can too near to the components.

Adding more RAM

This is the most common upgrade, and it usually gives the most notable performance increase for the amount of money you spend. You could take your machine to a shop and ask them to install the new RAM chips for you, but it's much cheaper – and usually surprisingly simple – to do it yourself. However, there are various different types, speeds, sizes and specs of RAM, so first of all you need to choose the correct sort for your system.

Choosing the right RAM

The easiest and most reliable way to find out what type of RAM your PC will take is to look at the manual that came with the system or motherboard. If you don't have a manual, ask the person you bought the PC from, check the manufacturer's website or – probably better still – use an online retailer's system identifier, which will guide you to the correct type for your PC and give the option of purchasing directly. One of the best sites for this is Crucial Memory, which also has good prices and an excellent delivery service.

Crucial Memory www.crucial.com

If none of these options work, have a look inside your PC's case to see what's currently installed (see p.313) and buy more of the same type. If you still can't work out what sort it is, remove the RAM that's there and take it to a computer shop. As a general rule, if you're not sure what you're buying, purchase from somewhere that will let you return it if it won't work with your system.

Aside from the actual amount of memory they hold (256 MB, 512 MB, etc), the main variables when it comes to RAM are **type**, **speed** and physical **size**.

▶ **Types of RAM** If you have a computer made in the last five years or so, the type will probably be either **DDR SDRAM** (the current standard) or **SDRAM** (standard from around 1998 to 2002). If you're running anything older (**FPM** or **EDO**, for example) you might want to consider upgrading your motherboard (see p.340) – or even your whole system – to take one of the newer standards. Old RAM types are not only less good, they're also usually more expensive.

▶ Speeds of RAM Both DDR SDRAM and SDRAM modules are available in different speeds, defined by a so-called "PC number". DDR SDRAM starts at PC1600 and PC2100 (operating at 200 and 266 MHz respectively) and goes up from there. With DDR you can mix different speed modules, though the system will run at the speed of the slowest component, whether it be one of the modules or the motherboard itself. SDRAM is available in PC66, PC100 or PC133 (transferring data at 66, 100, 133 MHz respectively) and can, again, be mixed, with the overall speed limited by the slowest component.

Because the speed doesn't affect the price much (faster is often cheaper, in fact) most people buy modules that run faster than their motherboard – the computer won't perform any quicker but a higher-spec strip of RAM is likely to be more useful in the future.

Tech Info

Other RAM jargon

▶ Non-parity, Parity and ECC (Error Checking and Correction) Parity and ECC refer to error-correcting technologies used on memory designed for "mission critical" systems. Always get non-parity RAM unless you already have some Parity or ECC RAM (you can check your current RAM by counting the rectangular chips on the memory module – if the total isn't divisible by three, you have non-parity RAM).

▶ NS speed This techie specification, which you don't really need to worry about, is an internal speed thing, measured in nanoseconds. A lower number means a very slightly faster speed. Different speeds can be mixed, though the whole lot will run at the speed of the slowest chip.

▶ Buffered or unbuffered? Buffers help RAM chips to deal with very large flows of data and are generally only used by servers, so most PC RAM you will come across will be unbuffered.

▶ CL number Another techie specification: this relates to latency, the amount of time the memory wastes when starting to send data. A lower number is better – CL2 being very slightly faster than CL3, for example. Usually you can ignore this spec, but some systems do require a specific CL number.

▶ **Sizes of RAM** Modern modules commonly come in two types of physical unit: DIMMs are long and thin and fit in regular desktop PCs, while SODIMMs are shorter and dumpier to fit in laptops and smaller desktop models. Older modules were known as SIMMs (see box).

As well as knowing whether you need DIMMs or SODIMMs, you may need to know how many pins (the little shiny teeth that make the connection to the motherboard slot) the strip has along its edge. DDR SDRAM, for example, may come with 184-pins or 240-pins.

Before you buy

First you need to see how many spare slots you have in your system. Unplug your PC, open up the case and have a look at your RAM slots and chips to see what's currently installed. The slots are easy to spot: they're plastic, about 10cm long, lined up in parallel, and generally there are between two and four of them. At least one will have a strip of RAM in it. If the RAM slots are obscured by lots of cables, expansion cards or drives, these obstacles may have to be temporarily removed. If you find this idea intimidating, you may decide at this point to take the machine to a shop; if not, remove each problematic item in turn, making sure you carefully note down where and which way round each cable or item went.

DIMM slots are black with plastic catches on the ends. If you're adding SDRAM, you'll probably want to simply add a single DIMM to a spare slot. If you don't have a spare slot, you'll have to remove your smallest current DIMM to make room for a bigger one.

If you want to add RAM to your **laptop**, refer to the manual to see how easily it can be done. Often a little screw panel on the bottom of the machine reveals the RAM slots, but in some models (especially older ones) they are difficult to get at. If your laptop's slots are full or inaccessible, you could consider buying RAM in the form of an easily insertable PC card (see p.8).

How much do you need?

All motherboards have a limit to the amount of RAM they can handle, so make sure you check your manual or an online system identifier if you're planning on adding a serious amount. At the time of writing, 256 MB is enough for most tasks, though 512 MB – or even a gig or two – is useful for serious multimedia activities such as video, music editing and high-end gaming.

Making the install

Make sure you're free of static electricity before touching the RAM module (see p.313). And never touch the metal teeth – while installing or removing modules, try to touch the edges only.

Your **DIMM** slots will be numbered – usually 0, 1, 2, etc – on the motherboard, and the lowest-numbered slots should be filled first. Also, the biggest module in terms of megabytes should be inserted in the lowest-numbered slot, so if you're adding a new DIMM that's bigger than those already installed you'll have to rearrange the modules to allow this. To remove a DIMM, simply open the little clips holding it in place (pull them away from the centre of the slot) and it will pop out. To install a DIMM, make sure you have the module the correct way around (align the two notches in the module with the ridges in

SIMM city

Some machines can take both DIMMs and older-style SIMMs, but you shouldn't mix them. SIMM slots work in the same way as DIMM slots, except that they are white (not black) and are numbered 0, 1 and so on in pairs called "banks", each of which has to be filled with a pair of identical SIMMs – **you can't add a single SIMM**.

As with DIMMs, SIMMs need to be inserted in the lowest available bank of slots, and your best bet is to stick the largest pair in terms of megabytes in the lowest-numbered bank, which will probably require you to move your old modules. To remove a SIMM you have to prise open the metal clips that are holding it in place. This can be quite tricky and is sometimes easier with the help of a pointed non-metal object. Once the clips are open, gently rotate the SIMM until it's at a 45-degree angle to the motherboard, and then pull it out.

To add a SIMM, make sure the clips aren't in the way, align it correctly with the slot (it will only fit in one way round because one corner is snipped off), and gently put it into the slot at a 45-degree angle. Then pull it to an upright position and the metal clips should close around it.

the slot) and press it into place with your thumbs until the clips snap shut. You might need to apply quite a lot of pressure – to make this easier, lay the case on the table in such a way that the motherboard is flat – but don't press too hard.

Switching on

Once your new RAM is in place, replace the case, plug everything in and switch on. You should see your memory being counted on the initial startup screen, and then Windows should load as normal. Right-click **My Computer** and select **Properties** to open the **System Properties** dialog box, which displays information about your computer. At the bottom of the box you'll see how much RAM is recognized – hopefully the correct new total. If there is less than you expected it could be because your graphics card uses "shared" memory. If you have 512 MB of RAM installed, for example, and your motherboard has in-built graphics with 32 MB of shared memory, only 480 MB will be recognized.

It doesn't work!

If after a RAM installation your PC won't start up, don't panic. Open up the case, make sure that the RAM is in the lowest-numbered slots and that the modules are securely held in place – if they wobble, take them out and put them in again. Also make sure that anything you moved or unplugged is back as it should be. And if you're mixing RAM speeds – PC100 and PC133, for example – try swapping them around so that the slowest strip is in the lowest-numbered slot. If the machine still won't work, remove your original RAM and try your machine with the new RAM on its own to rule out a conflict between the various modules. If it still doesn't work, it could be that your new RAM is incompatible with your motherboard – or possibly damaged. Hopefully you bought it from someone that guaranteed it would work with your motherboard, in which case you should be able to return it.

If your system has recognized the extra RAM but is actually running slower than it was before, it could be that your motherboard can't handle the new amount. This is very rare if you followed the maximums suggested in your manual, but it can happen. Remove the new RAM and think about investing in a new motherboard or system.

Adding expansion cards

Many PC upgrades take the form of adding an expansion card. The most common expansion cards are **graphics cards**, **sound cards**, **modems**, **TV cards** and **network cards**. But there are many other types, including SCSI, USB and IEEE 1394 **interface cards**, which add extra ports to your machine. Adding an expansion card is pretty simple, and in most cases should be relatively trouble-free. But before you attempt an operation there are a few things you should know.

▶ **1** Don't buy a card until you've checked that you have the necessary slot free on your motherboard.

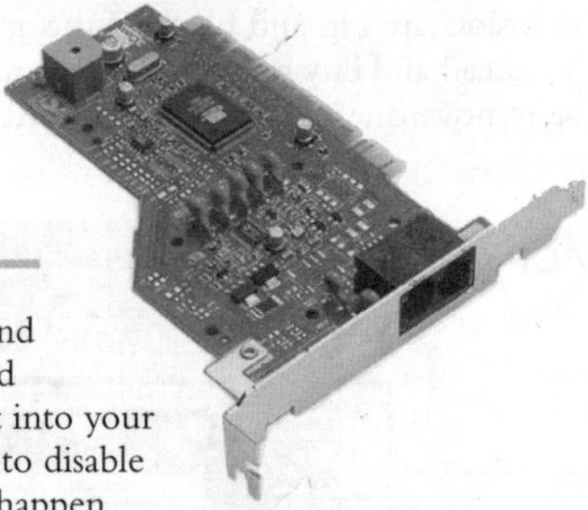

▶ **2** If you're adding a video or sound card to replace the graphics or sound functions that are "integrated" (built into your motherboard), you'll probably need to disable these in-built capabilities. This may happen automatically, but it can be a bit of a pain – for details, check your manual, contact the PC's manufacturer or search for help on the Internet.

▶ **3** If you're replacing a video card, you'll probably be in for a smoother ride if you reset the system to a standard Windows display setting first. Right-click the **Desktop** and choose **Properties**, then select the **Settings** tab, click the **Advanced** button and another dialog box will open. Click the **Adapter** tab, hit the **Change** button and a wizard will appear. When offered, choose **Show all devices**, select **Standard Display Adapter (VGA)** and click **OK**. Windows will prompt you to reboot – you're now ready to switch off your machine and swap the old card for the new one.

Locating the slots

Unplug the PC and open up the case (see p.313). Along the rear of the case you'll see a number of removable panels which will match up to plastic slots on the motherboard. Some – but hopefully not all – of these slots may already be occupied with expansion cards, which look like rectangular pieces of circuit board with a metal panel on the back. There are three types of slot: AGP, PCI and ISA.

If you have a newish motherboard, you'll probably have one AGP slot (for graphics cards), a number of PCI slots (for all sorts of devices) and either one or no ISA slots (these are for old devices). Each slot should be labelled on the motherboard – and in the motherboard's manual – to show you what type it is, but they're easy to tell apart just by looking: AGP slots are brown, PCI slots are white and slightly shorter, and ISA slots are big and black. If the appropriate slot is available, you can go ahead and buy the expansion card of your choice. If not, you'll have to remove one of your current cards or get a new motherboard.

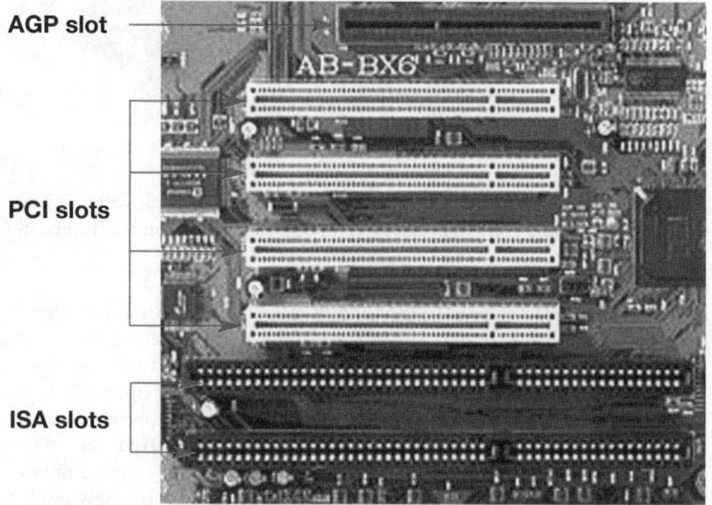

Installing the card

Before unpacking a new expansion card or touching an old one, be sure to rid yourself of static electricity (see p.313). Try to hold the cards only by their edges, and never touch the metal teeth that slot into the motherboard.

Choose a slot of the correct type – it shouldn't matter which if there is more than one of that type, so choose the one that will give you the most room – and remove the relevant panel from the rear of the case. This usually entails taking out the little screw holding it in place, though some old cases may have panels that need to be levered out with a screwdriver (be extremely careful not to touch any components with the screwdriver tip).

Once the panel is removed, press the card into the slot. Sometimes it's easier to insert one end first and then push the other end into place, but make sure you always keep the card at the correct angle, perpendicular to the motherboard. You should feel when it slots properly into place. You may have to apply quite a lot of pressure, but don't force it – pull the card out, check everything's aligned and try again.

Turning on

With the card in place, close up the case, plug everything in and switch on. If all goes well, Windows will start up, display a **New Hardware Found** message and open a wizard to guide you through the installation of the driver. When prompted, insert the CD or floppy that came with the expansion card – click the **Have disk** button if there is one – and guide Windows to the appropriate drive.

Problems

If you switch on but there's no sign that the new hardware has been recognized, open the **Control Panel** and select the **Add New Hardware** icon (select the **Classic view** first in Windows XP). This will prompt Windows to search for the new device.

If your system gives you trouble after you've added the card – it won't start up, keeps crashing and generally does weird stuff – it may be worth removing the new card and trying it in a different slot. If it still plays up, try swapping your cards around. This shouldn't be necessary really, but motherboards do sometimes accept cards in one order and not in another (a network card in a PCI slot next to the AGP slot can sometimes cause problems, for example). If that hasn't helped, try downloading an up-to-date driver from the website of the company that manufactured the card.

If you've added a new graphics card and when you switch on you don't see anything on the monitor at all, make sure that the card is properly "seated" in the slot – try taking it out and pushing it in again. And make sure the monitor is properly attached to the port on the back of the card.

Adding CD and DVD drives

Adding a CD or DVD drive to a system is generally fairly easy. This section assumes you'll be adding a standard ATAPI or IDE drive – one that will connect to an IDE port on the motherboard. There are other types of drives available – such as SCSI, for example – they're more expensive, less convenient and not as widely available.

Before you buy

If you plan to add a DVD drive to a machine that is around 450 MHz or slower, your PC may struggle to keep up, so you'll need to add an MPEG decoder card or a new graphics card with DVD support. The card will slot into an AGP or PCI slot and do some of the work. DVD upgrade packs are available, which include a drive, a card, installation instructions and playback software.

For CD drives there are no such problems, though if you're buying a CD burner for an old, sluggish computer, try to get one with BurnProof technology, which will reduce the chance of discs failing to burn properly.

Finally, whatever type of drive you're buying, make you have the appropriate **drive bay.** CD and DVD drives fit into 5.25" drive bays at the front of a PC (see picture below). You can tell if you have any spare just by looking – each bay will be occupied either by a drive or a removable plastic panel the same colour as the rest of the case. If you don't have a spare bay, you'll have to replace your existing CD drive (CD burners and DVD drives function perfectly well for reading CD-ROMs) or get a new case.

One final consideration is the amount of space inside your case. Some DVD and CD drives are quite "long", and if you have a relatively small case you may find these models won't fit. If you want to be sure, look inside your case and compare the space available with the advertised dimensions of the drive you're thinking of buying.

Making the install

The first thing to do is open up a 5.25" bay to put the new drive into. Unplug the PC, make sure you're free of static electricity and open the case (see p.313). If you're replacing an old drive, carefully pull the various leads from its back and take out the screws holding it in place (usually there are two on each side of the drive bay) while supporting the drive underneath if necessary. Then you should be able to simply slide it out of the front.

If you're opening up a new bay, you'll need to pop out the front panel using the little clips on the inside. To get to the panel, you may need to lever out an interior metal drive cover with a screwdriver – if so, be very careful not to touch the motherboard or other components with the tip. If you have a choice of bays, consider the length of the IDE cable that you'll be attaching to the back of the drive – if you're using it for two devices you may not have much slack. Also check you have a spare power connector: these flat-headed four-pin plugs come off the main power supply, connected by coloured wires. If you don't have a spare one, you can buy an inexpensive "Y-adapter" to add an extra plug.

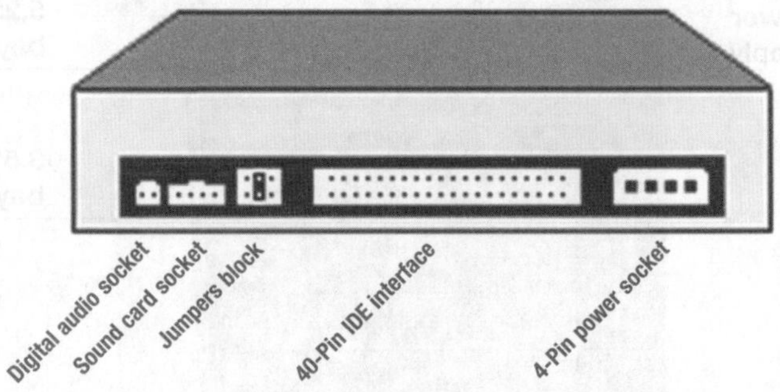

Before inserting the new drive, you need to decide whether to put it as a **slave** on the same channel as the hard drive or as the **master** or slave on the other IDE channel. And then you need to set the jumpers accordingly – this is all explained in the box overleaf. If attaching a DVD drive, it's generally best to put it as the master on the secondary IDE channel. If you're installing a CD drive it doesn't matter so much, though if you're adding a CD burner and intend to do a lot of copying from one CD drive to other CDs, your best bet is probably to put the CD burner as the secondary master and the CD-ROM as the primary slave. Some drives may come with instructions that suggest installing them in a particular position.

If you're installing a drive on an unused channel, you'll need to attach the IDE lead to the socket on the motherboard. The socket should be easy to spot – it's rectangular and about two inches long, usually dark in colour, and will be next to another similar slot with a cable already connected. When attaching the cable, be sure to line up the red edge with the pin 1 mark on the motherboard.

You're now ready to slide the new drive carefully into the bay from the front, giving it support from underneath if necessary. Line up the holes in the side of the bay with the holes in the side of the drive. Before securing the drive with screws, look to see whether there will be sufficient room to connect the cables in this position – if not, you may have to connect them with the drive half in and half out of the bay and then slide it into place and put the screws in. Assuming there is enough room, secure the drive with the screws that came with the drive, putting two on each side. Screw them down firmly, but **don't over-tighten** them.

Finally, attach the IDE cable to the back of the drive – being careful to line up the red edge with the **pin 1** mark on the drive – and insert the power supply plug. Assuming the drive will be used for music of some kind, you'll also need to connect the audio socket to the sound card (or to the motherboard if it has integrated sound). For this you'll probably be able to use the digital cable that ships with most drives – check your sound card, system or motherboard manual to find out where it needs to be attached. You can often only connect one drive this way, so you may have to remove the cable from your old CD drive.

If you're also adding an MPEG decoder card, you'll need to insert it into a spare slot of the correct type and connect it up. Follow the instructions that came with the card.

IDE basics

IDE, also called **ATA**, is the standard way of connecting internal PC drives. Most modern motherboards have two IDE ports, or "channels", and they're referred to as **primary** and **secondary**. Each port takes an IDE cable, similar to the one pictured, to which you can attach either one or two devices, making a total of four. If you require more than four IDE devices you can get special expansion cards to provide more ports.

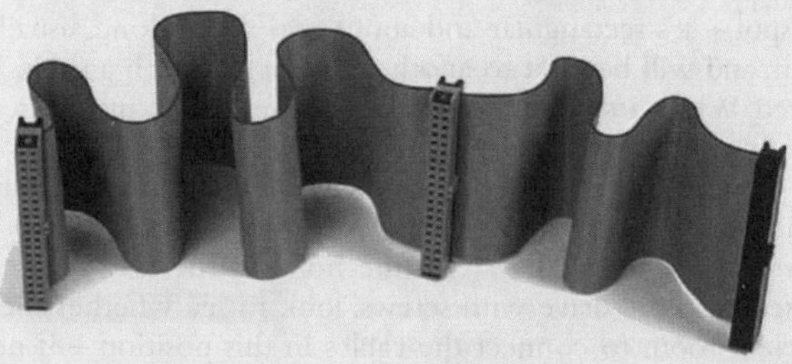

There are various types of IDE connection. As well as the old-school standard IDE, there's the newer **EIDE** and high-speed **Ultra ATA** varieties. Also known as **Ultra DMA**, Ultra ATA comes in three standard speeds, transferring data at up to 33, 66 or 100 megabytes per second. And, to add to the confusion, CD and DVD drives that attach via IDE are usually known as **ATAPI** devices. Despite all these different types and terms, all IDE devices can be attached to a standard motherboard IDE port. But to achieve the full speed of a fast device like an Ultra ATA/100 hard drive, you'll need a suitable motherboard. And Ultra ATA devices need an appropriate (80-connector) cable.

There are three plugs on an IDE cable: the one on the end furthest from the central one plugs into the motherboard; the other two are for the drives. One edge of an IDE cable is usually coloured red. When you insert the cable into the motherboard or drive you need to make sure that the red edge lines up with the **pin 1** mark on the port. This is very important, because inserting it the wrong way round can damage a drive – though today most sockets and cables are keyed (shaped asymmetrically) so that they will only fit the correct way round.

Each drive on an IDE cable must be set up as either a **master** or a **slave**. If there is just one device on the cable it should be set as the master; if there are two, one must be set as the master and the other as the slave. The primary hard drive – the one that Windows boots from – is attached as the master on the primary IDE channel. Apart from that, there are no strict rules about what should go where. Generally, a device on its own cable will work slightly more efficiently, as two drives sharing a cable have to take turns to send or receive data.

Drives are usually set as masters or slaves with jumpers – tiny plastic and metal connectors that connect two pins to complete an electrical circuit. Nearly all IDE drives have one or two jumpers on their back or bottom, and all you have to do is position the jumper(s) according to the option you want. In addition to master and slave there is usually a third option called **cable select**, though this isn't relevant for most users (you need a special cable and suitable motherboard). Often there is just one jumper and six pins, labelled CS, SL and MA, as shown in the diagram. In this case, the jumper should be placed vertically below SL for slave or MA for master. But often it's not as obvious as this, so always read the instructions that came with the device, or try the manufacturer's website if you don't have any. Hard drives usually come pre-jumpered to the master position.

Ultra ATA cables are colour-coded:

- The **blue** end is for the motherboard
- The **black** end is for the master device
- The **grey** plug in the middle is for the slave device

With a standard old-fashioned IDE cable, the slave device can attach with the plug on the end or in the middle.

Turning on

Make sure all the connections are secure, replace the case cover, plug in the monitor, mouse and keyboard if you removed them, then switch on. With any luck, Windows will load as normal, detect the new drive and prompt you to install the drivers for it – if so, insert the disc that came with the drive and direct Windows to it. From now on when you open My Computer you'll see an icon for the new drive, and you may find that the old drives are now relabelled – D may have become E, for example.

If the drive isn't detected, try running the **Add New Hardware Wizard**, which you'll find in the Control Panel (select the classic view to find it in Windows XP). If that doesn't work, open up the case and make sure everything is attached properly. And when you switch on again look at the initial screen – the white type on a black background – which will temporarily display a list of your various IDE devices.

If the new drive isn't included in the list, you could try entering the **BIOS setup program** (see p.337) and setting it there. All you'll have to do is find the relevant IDE channel and set it accordingly. If this seems too techie, or if you can't sort it out in the BIOS, it's probably time to call an experienced friend or a professional.

Adding an internal hard drive

If you're short of storage space there's no better solution than to add a new hard drive. And adding a hard drive that's faster than your old one can also make a difference to performance, too – especially for certain tasks such as working with video and recording music.

Installing a new hard drive and setting it up for use is manageable enough, but it's usually more complex than the other upgrades covered in this chapter. As well as physically installing the drive, you have to check that it's recognized in the BIOS setup (see p.337), and then go through the slightly frightening process of preparing it for use by partitioning and formatting it. If you don't fancy all this, you'll have to get a friend or store to do it for you. Alternatively, if you're only buying an extra drive to get some more storage space, consider buying an **external drive** (see p.70). These are more expensive, require no real installation, and can be very useful for backing up and transferring files between computers.

Before you buy

If you do decide to go for a new internal drive, there are a few things to consider before buying a drive.

▶ **1.** If you have a very old PC it may not be capable of handling the modern-sized drive. This could be because of the BIOS or the operating system. Early editions of Windows 95, for example, can only handle drives of up to 2 GB (you can use a bigger drive but you'll have to partition it into separate drives of 2 GB or less). These complications are beyond the scope of this chapter – check your system manual for information about what your system will take, or contact the manufacturer. Alternatively, search for further information on the Web.

▶ **2.** If you're choosing a drive for increased speed, be aware that an older system may not be equipped to exploit all the speed of the new drive. If you want to achieve the full data transfer rate from an ATA/100 drive, for example, you may need to get an expansion card with an appropriate IDE socket on it if your motherboard is more than a few years old.

▶ **3.** Ultra ATA hard drives require a suitable Ultra ATA cable, though this may come with the drive.

▶ **4.** Some drives come with clear instructions and special software for preparing the drive for use. You don't need this software but it may make everything a bit easier.

▶ **4.** When buying a hard drive, be sure to get some suitable screws to attach it to the case – using the wrong sort can cause damage.

▶ **5.** It's always worth backing up all your important files (see p.288) before moving or replacing your existing drive.

Add or replace?

If you're adding a new hard drive you have two options. The easiest thing to do is to keep your current hard drive in as the primary one – the one the operating system boots from – and use the new drive as storage space for programs and files. The other option is to set up the new drive as the primary drive and either remove the old drive or use it just for file storage or backup. This will usually result in the best performance, but it will require you to install Windows on the new drive (or copy the content of the old drive onto the new drive using special "disk image" software).

Bays and brackets

If you're planning on keeping your current drive and simply adding a new drive, you'll need to check you have a spare drive bay for it to live in. Standard hard drives live in 3.5" bays hidden away inside the PC (see illustration on p.325). Unplug your machine, open up the case (see p.313) and look inside. In standard tower cases, the 3.5" bays are most commonly located at the front of the case below the other bays used for CD, DVD and floppy drives. But in flat desktop cases and other types of design, the drive bays will be elsewhere.

If you don't have a spare 3.5" bay, you can get special brackets to allow you to insert a hard drive in a 5.25" bay, like those used for CD and DVD drives. Many drives come with such brackets.

Master or slave?

A hard drive has to be correctly **set with jumpers** as either a master or a slave before being attached to an IDE cable, as explained on p.328. If you're keeping your old drive as the primary drive you can either install the new one as the slave on the same cable as the old drive, or as the master or slave on the secondary channel.

Any position is fine, though if your new drive is faster than your old one its speed may be limited if installed as a slave on the primary cable. If you want to get the best out of your new, faster drive, put it as the **master** on the secondary IDE channel (though if you have a DVD drive this position may already be occupied) or consider making the new drive the primary master and installing the operating system on it.

Physical installation

Before installing a new primary hard drive, make sure that you have a working Startup disk (see p.245). Unplug your PC, remove the case and make sure you're free of static electricity (see p.313). If you plan to attach the drive to a currently unused IDE channel, you'll need to attach the IDE cable to the motherboard, being sure to line up the red edge of the cable with the pin 1 mark on the motherboard's port. Then you're ready to insert the drive.

If you have a choice of empty bays and you plan to install the drive on an IDE cable with another device, go for a bay near to the other device so the cable will reach. Gently slide the new drive, with its jumpers set correctly, into the bay, supporting it underneath if necessary but trying not to touch any circuitry. Line up the holes on the side of the drive with those in the bay and secure the drive with two screws on each side. Tighten the screws enough to hold the drive firmly in place (drives have been known to vibrate themselves loose) but **don't over-tighten** them – you don't want to damage anything.

Connect the IDE lead to the drive, being careful to line up the red edge of the cable with the **pin 1** mark on the drive's socket. If it's too awkward you may have to unscrew the drive, move it, connect the cable and then screw the drive back in. Next, attach the power cable: you'll probably find a spare plug on the multicoloured power lead coming from the main power supply and connecting to all your other drives. If you don't have a spare you can buy an inexpensive adapter to provide one.

BIOS settings

Check everything's secure and in the right place, put the cover on the computer and plug everything in. Switch on and read the white text that will briefly appear on the screen. You should see the machine counting its memory and also a list of all the IDE devices, labelled as primary master, secondary slave and so on. If the new drive appears correctly in the list, you're fine. Otherwise you'll have to enter the BIOS setup program (see p.337). Navigate through the various menus until you find the one that deals with the system's IDE connections – checking your system manual could be helpful here. When you find it, look at the setting of the appropriate position (primary slave, secondary master or whatever). If nothing is listed there, try setting it to **Auto** – this should help the motherboard to find it – and then save and exit the BIOS. If Auto isn't listed as an option, you may be able to input the information about the drive (number of sectors, etc) manually. This information may be written on the drive or the paperwork that came with it. If you feel out of your depth at this point, you may want to put the cover on the machine and take it to a computer store.

Preparing a new secondary drive

If you left your old hard drive where it was, Windows should boot as normal. You're now ready to partition and format the new drive to get it ready for use. If the drive came with special software, your best bet is to use it. If not, and you don't happen to have a friendly third-party program like **Partition Magic** (see p.340), you'll have to use either **Fdisk** (see below) or a **full Windows XP installation CD**.

In Windows XP

You can either use Fdisk via a boot disk (see p.245), or alternatively employ a full Windows Installation CD, as follows, being sure to quit the process once the partitioning is complete and before the XP installation itself kicks in:

▶ **1** Insert the Windows CD and follow the prompts to until the Installation Wizard detects your existing Windows installation and prompt you to repair it. At this point hit **Esc** on your keyboard as you do not want to make a repair.

▶ **2** You will now be presented with a list of partitioned and unpartitioned space on both your old and new drives. **Use the arrow keys** to select the unpartitioned hardware and then hit **C** to create a new partition (**D** followed by **L** can be used to delete selected partitions). If you are feeling brave you could at this stage create **multiple partitions** (see p.240).

▶ **3** At this point selecting the new partition and hitting **Enter** would begin the XP installation. But we don't want to do this: instead hit F3 twice to quit the setup.

▶ **4** Restart your machine, and when Windows loads, open **My Computer**. You should see the new drive – it will probably be designated as drive **D**. Right-click the drive's icon and click **Format** to prepare it for use (choose **NTFS** if you're asked what format you require).

In Windows 98 & ME

In Windows 98 or ME, use Fdisk as follows to prepare a new secondary drive:

▶ **1** Open the **Start** menu, click **Run**, type **Fdisk** and you'll be presented with a black DOS window.

▶ **2** If you're asked whether you want to **enable large disk support**, type y followed by Enter. You have to **tread extremely carefully** in this program as it has the power to completely blank any hard drive on your system. If you're not confident at any point, seek the help of an expert.

▶ **3** At the top of the window should be written **Current fixed disk drive: 1**, and underneath this there will be a list of options. **Hit 5** to select **Change current fixed disk drive**, and you'll be offered a list of the drives on your system. (If 5 isn't listed as an option, your computer probably hasn't recognized the new drive properly.)

▶ **4** Assuming that the new drive is the only hard drive in the PC other than the primary drive, you'll then see **Current fixed disk drive:** 2 written at the top, showing that you're now dealing with the new drive. Choose the first option, **Create DOS Partition or Logical DOS Drive**, and then choose **Create Primary DOS Partition**.

▶ **5** Fdisk will examine the drive, then ask if you want to use its maximum available size. Choose **Yes** and the program will verify the full drive integrity – this can take a while.

▶ **6** When it's finished, exit Fdisk by pressing **Escape** as many times as necessary.

▶ **7** Restart your machine and, when Windows loads, open **My Computer**. You should see the new drive – it will probably be designated as drive **D**, with the CD and any other drives pushed one letter up the alphabet.

▶ **8** Right-click the drive's icon and click **Format** to prepare it for action (choose **FAT32** if you're asked what format you require).

Partitioning and formatting a new primary drive

Installing an operating system onto a blank hard drive is usually pretty straightforward. Insert your full (not upgrade) Windows installation

BIOS setup

Pronounced "bye-oss" or "bye-ose" depending on where you're from, **BIOS** (Basic Input/Output System) is essential software stored on a PC's motherboard. It enables the machine to boot up, and acts as the bridge between the operating system and the hardware – but you'll probably hear the term most commonly in relation to the **BIOS setup utility**, a program that allows you to make various changes to your PC's settings. You'll need to access and tweak these settings when performing certain upgrades or building a PC, but otherwise they should be left alone – the BIOS contains some very techie options that can cause all sorts of serious problems if set up incorrectly.

Also sometimes referred to as **CMOS setup** (after the special memory chip that the configurations are stored in) or just "setup", the BIOS setup program is accessed differently on different systems. When you turn on your PC, some text will appear on the screen – the memory will be counted and the disk drives listed. Usually you'll then see a message towards the bottom of the screen inviting you to press a certain key or key combination to "enter setup" – most commonly **Delete** or some combination including **Escape**. If you don't get such a message, check any manuals that came with your system to find out the necessary key or do some research on the Web. BIOS setup programs are all different but they work in a very similar way: you browse through various menu options and make changes using the keyboard. Usually it's pretty clear which keys you have to press to select and change each option.

CD, switch on, sit back and see what happens. Everything should be pretty self-explanatory from there on – the CD will guide you through the formatting and installation process. If nothing happens, try entering your system's BIOS setup program and setting the CD drive as the primary boot device (see p.243).

Still no luck? Try using a Windows Me or 98 Startup disk (see p.245) to get the installation moving. Insert the floppy disk and boot up. Select **Start computer with CD-ROM support** from the menu that appears. You should be presented with a message (perhaps in the format **Drive E: = Driver MSCD001**), which shows you that your CD drive has been recognized. After a minute or two you may also be told that your CD drive has a new letter, probably E, and then you'll be presented with another A:\> prompt. Insert the Windows CD in the drive and type **e:\setup** then hit Enter. (If you were told that your CD drive was F: or some other letter, replace the "e:" in this command with the relevant letter.) If everything's OK, your blank hard drive will be checked by ScanDisk and the **Windows Setup Wizard** will walk you through the rest of the process. If your CD drive doesn't seem to be recognized, it could be that the Startup disk doesn't contain the suitable drivers for it. Refer to your CD drive or system manual, or contact your computer's manufacturer for advice.

If the floppy recognizes the CD drive but can't find the hard drive, you may need to partition and format the drive using the **Fdisk** utility that lives on the boot disk. Here's what you do:

▶ **1** Insert a working Startup disk, boot your machine, and select **Start Computer without CD support** when presented with a list of options.

▶ **2** At the **A:> prompt**, type **Fdisk** and press **Enter**. If asked whether you want to **Enable large disk support**, choose **yes** and you should be presented with a screen saying **Current fixed disk drive: 1** at the top.

▶ **3** Choose the first option, **Create DOS Partition or Logical DOS Drive**, and then choose **Create Primary DOS Partition.** When asked if you want to make use of all the disk space, answer **yes** and Fdisk will start to do its thing.

▶ **4** When it finishes formatting and partitioning, Fdisk then scans its handiwork for errors – this can take some time. When all is done, exit the program by pressing **Escape** as many times as necessary, and restart the machine, still with the Startup disk in place.

▶ **5** When the menu appears, select **Start Computer without CD support**; at the **A:> prompt**, type **format C:/s** and press Enter. (If you're told you've entered a bad command or file name, type **extract ebd.cab format.com** followed by **Enter**, and then try again.) After you've confirmed your decision by pressing **y**, the drive will be formatted and you'll be offered the option of naming the volume – do so if you wish, or just press **Enter** to skip this step.

▶ **5** You're then ready to retry the Windows install as described above.

Other upgrades

As well as the common upgrades described above, there are various other things you may want to do to bring your system up to scratch – inserting a better processor or motherboard, for instance, or getting a new case. We don't have the space to cover everything here – not because it's too complicated, but because there are many variables depending on your exact setup. Still, the following information should at least point you in the right direction.

Processors

Inserting a new processor can be a little fiddly but it's otherwise very easy. However, your motherboard defines the type and speed of processor you can use, so always refer to your system or motherboard manual before buying a new processor. As well as the brand and speed, you need to get a processor of the right **slot** or **socket** format (socket 7, slot 1, etc). And remember to buy a suitable heat sink and fan for the processor you're adding – your old one may work, but faster processors generally run hotter, so it's worth getting something suitable.

If you have a look in some magazines and e-stores you'll almost certainly come across various **processor upgrade kits**. These can include anything from a new processor and a tool to help you remove the old one to a special expansion card to improve your PC's computational power.

Motherboards

There are various reasons why you might consider getting a new motherboard: the old one may be damaged, for example, or you may want to add a faster processor and better RAM. Replacing a motherboard isn't really that difficult. First you have to unplug everything from the old one and remove it from the case (many cases have a motherboard panel that can be removed to allow easy unscrewing of the board). Then you attach the new board with a number of screws and spacers that should have come with it. The final stage is plugging everything in before going into your system BIOS to set the processor speed and ensure that the drives are recognized properly. Before buying a new motherboard, make sure it will be compatible with your processor and case – an old **AT** case won't take a new motherboard such as an **ATX** model.

Cases

Replacing the case can be a bit of a pain – if only because the motherboard, expansion cards and all the drives will need to be moved (you leave the processor and RAM on the motherboard). However, it's not usually very difficult.

Building a PC

If the upgrades described in this chapter don't strike you as too intimidating, building your own PC is unlikely to be a problem. A complete step-by-step guide to doing this is beyond the scope of this book, but the following paragraphs provide a rough outline.

The first thing you'll need to do, obviously enough, is buy all the components. The absolute essentials are: case; motherboard; CPU with fan and heat sink; RAM; hard drive; video card (unless the motherboard has in-built graphics); monitor; CD/CD-R drive; keyboard; floppy drive; and mouse. But you'll probably also want a modem and sound card. These components are discussed individually in Chapters 2 and 3, but for detailed information on the latest products and prices you may want to try the hardware review sites listed in Chapter 24 (see p.399). When selecting the body parts for your PC-to-be, you have to make sure they're all compatible. These days some items, such as CD drives, are pretty much compatible with any system, though with certain components you have to be careful – you'll need the correct motherboard for the processor, and the correct RAM for the motherboard, for example. If you buy all the bits from one supplier, you can ask about compatibility – and you may well also get a discount. Try and get a motherboard that comes with a good, clear manual that will guide you through the building process.

Putting it all together

Though different people have different views on the best way to put a PC together, basically it involves fixing the motherboard to the case – including attaching the connectors for the case's power supply, lights and buttons – and adding the RAM and CPU (with heat sink and fan, which will attach to the motherboard). Then you'll need to fix the hard drive, floppy and CD or DVD drives into the case's bays, and attach them to the motherboard with the necessary cables. Fit any expansion cards to the motherboard and run the audio cable (if there is one) from the CD or DVD drive to the sound card. Most of these processes are described individually earlier in this chapter.

When all this is done you can switch on, enter the BIOS to check that the motherboard knows which processor you have installed and that the IDE drives are recognized. Then finally you're ready to install your operating system (see p.243).

you the wrong way, the hardware features listed in Chapter 24 (see p.3[illegible]). When selecting the bits and pieces for your PC-to-be, you have to make sure they're all compatible. These days some items, such as CD drives, are pretty much compatible with any system, though with certain components you need to be careful – you'll need the correct motherboard for the processor, and the correct RAM for the motherboard, for example. If you buy all the bits from one supplier, you can ask about compatibility and you may get a discount. Try and get a motherboard that comes with a good, clear manual that will guide you through the building process.

Putting it all together

Though different people have different views on the best way to put a PC together, basically it involves fitting the motherboard to the case – including attaching the connectors for the case's power supply, buttons and indicators – and adding the RAM and CPU (with its heat sink and fan, which will attach to the motherboard). Then you'll need to fit the hard, floppy and CD or DVD drives into the case's bays, and attach them to the motherboard with the necessary cables. Put any expansion cards in the motherboard and run the audio cable (if there is one) from the CD or DVD drive to the sound card. Most of these processes are described individually earlier in this chapter.

When all this is done, you can switch on, enter the BIOS and check that the motherboard knows which processor you have and that the hard drives are recognized. Then finally, you're ready to install your operating system (see p. [illegible]).

contexts and resources

22 A brief history of the PC

the story so far

The modern PC is not the brainchild of any one person. No single cry of "Eureka!" heralded the beginning of its development. Instead its history is a tale of leaps, bounds and hold-ups stretching back at least five thousand years to the invention of the abacus in **Mesopotamia**. This brief history outlines some of the important people and events in the evolutionary passage from wooden bead counter to multimedia work-station.

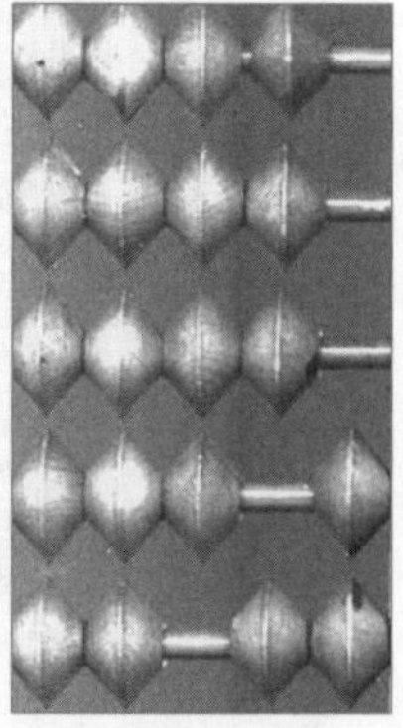

The mechanical era

In this age of microelectronics, computer components are not only powerful but also incomprehensibly small – it's atoms, not inches, that count. But the forerunners of today's computers were mechanical: they were made of cogs, shafts and sliders large enough to put together by hand, and were operated not by a keyboard and mouse but with dials and handles.

The earliest breakthroughs were made by the likes of **Leonardo da Vinci**, who designed a simple **mechanical calculator** in 1500, and **William Oughtred**, who in the early 1600s came up with the **slide rule**, a handheld tool for speeding up arithmetic which was still being used in schools three and a half centuries later. By the 1640s, the French mathematician **Blaise Pascal** had invented a machine capable of multiplication and division which was later improved by **Gottfried Leibnitz**, the same man who is credited with having laid down the principles of **binary** – the number system of 0s and 1s that is the fundamental language spoken by all modern computers.

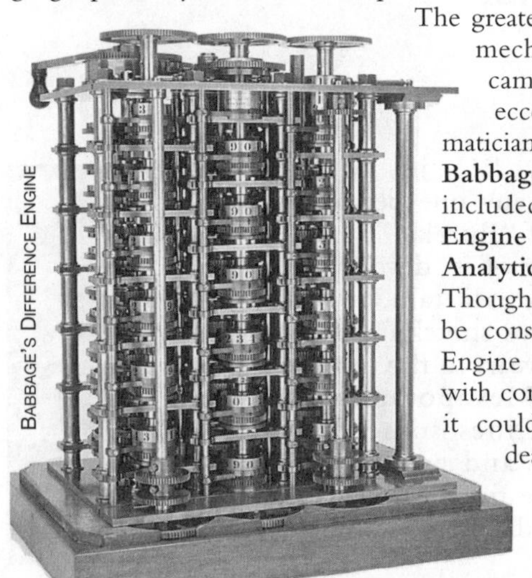

Babbage's Difference Engine

The greatest achievements of the mechanical era, though, came courtesy of the eccentric British mathematician and inventor **Charles Babbage**, whose inventions included the **Difference Engine** (pictured) and the **Analytical Engine** of 1833. Though he died before it could be constructed, the Analytical Engine could not only cope with complex mathematics, but it could be **programmed** to deal with various types of problem and make decisions based upon its own results – thus heralding the leap from calculator to "real" computer. Babbage's partner in crime was none other than **Ada Byron** – aka Lady Lovelace, the daughter of the poet Lord Byron – who is now sometimes described as the first ever computer programmer.

Punch cards and vacuum tubes

It wasn't until the end of the nineteenth century that computers actually started to prove themselves useful. Just before the 1890 census, the US government held a design contest to find an efficient way of counting the records of its exploding population. It was won by a German immigrant named **Herman Hollerith**, whose electric tabulating machine read data from paper punch cards, saving many years of manual counting and marking a significant point at which computing became as much to do with data management as performing calculations. Hollerith's Computing-Tabulating-Recording Company went from strength to strength, and in 1924 it merged with a rival to form International Business Machines – **IBM** – which grew into one of the most significant forces in computer design.

In the meantime the **vacuum tube** was being developed, from which a new generation of computers was to grow. The tubes did the same job as mechanical or electrical switches, but they were capable of switching on and off thousands of times faster, facilitating a whole new level of computing speed. This technology reached its zenith in machines designed on both sides of the Atlantic during World War II. The British utilized it in their powerful code-breaking machine, **Colossus**, but more significant was the American **ENIAC** (Electronic Numerical Integrator and Computer), developed between 1943 and 1945 to calculate missile trajectories. Containing nearly 17,500 vacuum tubes, ENIAC was the first multitasking computer, and it could add 5000 numbers or carry out fourteen ten-digit multiplications per second – making it about a hundred times faster that its closest rival.

While ENIAC was still being built, its designers **J. Presper Eckert** and **John V. Mauchly** joined forces with another key figure, mathematician **John von Neumann**, to work on a new machine. What they came up with was **EDVAC**, the first computer to have a **stored program**. This was a real breakthrough: instead of spending hours or even

ENIAC

days turning knobs and pressing buttons to instruct a computer to carry out a particular task, the commands could be written as numerical code and stored inside the machine. This made everything much faster, but more significantly it paved the way for the programming languages of the 1950s – which in turn led to the development of modern software.

Transistors and microchips

For all its speed, ENIAC highlighted the shortcomings of vacuum-tube technology: it was 150 feet wide, weighed 30 tons, produced so much heat that it regularly burned out and guzzled electricity in such quantities that the lights in the neighbouring towns dimmed each time it was switched on. These problems were soon to be overcome with the advent of the silicon transistor, which was better than the vacuum tube at controlling the flow of electricity while being much smaller and generating considerably less heat. Transistors were invented back in the 1920s, but it wasn't until 1954 that reliable silicon models were manufactured commercially, bringing small, reliable and affordable computers a significant step closer.

The ensuing years saw the birth of the **microchip** or **chip** – a single piece of board containing many transistors. As time went by, chips became increasingly powerful and ever more tiny, until in 1971 a company called **Intel** (Integrated Electronics) released their **4004** chip, the first **microprocessor**. The 4004 combined 2300 transistors and all the essential elements of a computer on a single chip, and in the space of a few square inches provided roughly the same computational power as the 17,500 vacuum tubes of ENIAC. These developments, combined with great advances in programming languages and other breakthroughs – such as the invention of the **floppy disk** – made it possible to produce smaller and faster computers, which were more flexible and less difficult to use.

Computers get personal

Despite all these advances, computers remained in the realm of big business, academics and governments, and it wasn't until 1975 that a vaguely personal computer, something that individuals could actually afford to buy, came onto the market. It arrived in the form of the **MITS Altair 8800**, which shipped with an Intel processor and 256 bytes of memory – around one millionth of the amount found in a decent modern PC. And it wasn't just in the memory department that the Altair was lacking: it had neither a keyboard nor a monitor. Instructions were fed in by small switches and results displayed by a pattern of little red lights – great for discos, but not a lot else.

THE ALTAIR 8800

But all this was soon to change. In 1977, **Stephen Jobs** and **Steve Wozniak** produced the **Apple II**, which, with its neat plastic case and video-out socket (allowing you to use your TV as a monitor), was an instant success. While the Altair was primarily of interest to hobbyists and enthusiasts, the Apple II was actually useful for non-giant businesses, and programs began to appear which could save hours of manual number-crunching, including the first ever spreadsheet program, **VisiCalc**.

THE APPLE II

During this time the price of components plummeted, and various bargain computers started appearing on the market. By the end of the 1970s, a variety of machines were available for a few hundred dollars, one example being the **Radio Shack TRS-80**, which became incredibly popular in homes and schools.

The PC is born

The next big turning point came in 1981, when IBM released their Personal Computer – the **IBM PC** – which was the blueprint of the modern PC. Though the design was strong, it was not just the computer that made IBM's new machine so popular: it was the company's decision to tell the world, in near-complete detail, how the PC worked and how it was built. IBM did this in the hope that other developers would produce extra pieces of hardware that would be compatible with the PC – which they did, by the truckload.

It soon occurred to these developers that they weren't limited to manufacturing add-ons; they could produce their own versions of the whole machine and sell them cheaper. This was possible because IBM only held a patent for the BIOS (basic input/output system; see p.337), and because most of the internal components of the PC had been bought off-the-shelf from other manufacturers. Very soon computer companies everywhere were manufacturing their own copies of the IBM design, and they could all the same programs, allowing data to be easily moved from one machine to the next. These computers were collectively known as **IBM-compatible PCs**, but it wasn't long before PC became a generic term used to describe any computer based on IBM's original.

The rise and rise of Microsoft

When IBM designed the PC they commissioned the young Micro-Soft company (later Microsoft) to provide the all-important operating system software, or OS. It was called the Micro-Soft Disk Operating System – **MS-DOS** – and, though it had been developed for IBM, Microsoft shrewdly retained the copyright. As PC clones began to spring up everywhere, nearly all were installed with MS-DOS and, though Microsoft's founder Bill Gates didn't know it at the time, this was soon to make him the world's richest man.

As time went by, it became increasingly difficult for new types of computer to get a decent foothold in the market. Inexpensive machines like the **Commodore 64** were very popular among home users, but any new system that set out to compete with the PC was faced with the problem of not being able to run all the software that

THE ORIGINAL IBM PC

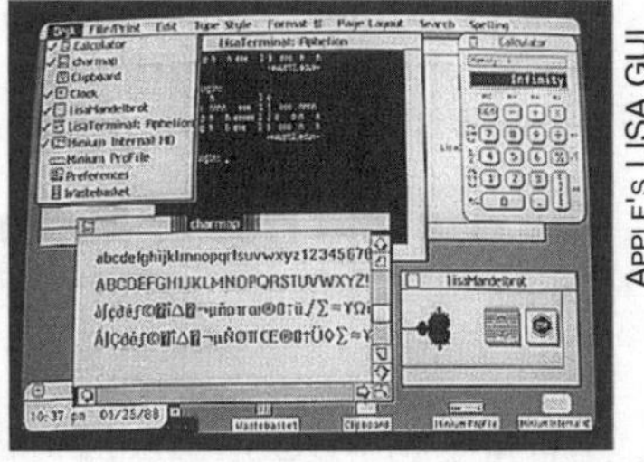

APPLE'S LISA GUI

had already been written for use with MS-DOS. Other operating systems were proposed by IBM and others, but they never really got off the ground or failed to gain the popularity of the Microsoft option. The MS-DOS PC still faced serious competition from established manufacturers such as Apple, however, who introduced the **LISA** and the **Macintosh** (the **Mac**) in 1983 and 1984 respectively. These were the first personal computers to use an operating system with a **Graphic User Interface** (GUI), meaning that the user, instead of typing coded instructions into the machine, could run programs and organize files by using a **mouse** to click on icons, windows and dropdown menus.

Soon afterwards, Microsoft released their own GUI operating system: a reworking of MS-DOS called **Windows**. Many of the features were very similar to those of the Apple system, and Apple promptly threatened to take Microsoft to court, claiming they had ripped off their design. In the end, Microsoft agreed to license certain elements of the Apple design to avoid court proceedings, and they managed to arrange it so that the features could be used in all future Microsoft programs. But when **Windows 2.0** came out in 1987, Apple thought Microsoft had overstepped the mark and this time actually took them to court for breach of copyright. Microsoft won the case, in part because of the previous licensing deal and in part because many of the original ideas for the Apple system had originally been developed by **Xerox** for non-personal computers. This made it easy for Gates and co take the line "Well, we may not have invented it, but neither did you..." – or words to that effect.

And the rest is history

As time went by, PCs and Macs held their ground as the most popular systems, and Windows – after the release of version 3.0 in 1990 – became the dominant PC operating system. Machines designed for things that PCs and Macs didn't do very well continued to enjoy success: the Atari ST and Commodore Amiga, for example, were popular for gaming until the early 1990s. But with the rise of specific gaming stations such as those made by Nintendo and the ever-increasing versatility of the PC, computers such as these started falling by the wayside, leaving a two-horse contest between Windows-driven PCs and Macs.

And for the time being this situation seems unlikely to change. Once a company or user has data and programs for one platform, switching to another can be a major, and potentially expensive, upheaval. Long-term change is in the air, however. A growing number of businesses and home users have started making the move towards free, open-source software, trading Windows for **Linux** and commercial applications for free ones created and updated by the wider programming community. Microsoft claim they're not too worried by the threat, but many of their recent actions – including flying top executives around the world to persuade government depertments and corporations to stick with Microsoft software – suggest otherwise. So, while the Windows monopoly isn't going to disappear quickly, it could be that the Microsoft heyday has been and gone.

As for the future of hardware, the tendency for ever-faster machines in ever-smaller boxes seems unlikely to lose pace. And neither does device "convergence", with the distinction between PCs, TVs, hi-fis, mobile phones and every other type of electronic equipment getting more blurred with every week that passes. The logical conclusion is that, at some point not too far off, there will be no concept of the "personal computer" as such – just high-tech, Internet-enabled bits and bobs of all shapes and sizes. That process is already happening, in fact, but it will doubtless be a few years, or even decades, before the concept of the PC dissolves into history.

23 Glossary

what does it all mean?

A

A The letter normally assigned to the primary floppy drive of a PC.

Access time Measurement of how long it takes a device, like a disk drive, to find a piece of data; measured in milliseconds (ms).

Active partition Part of a hard drive used to load the operating system at startup.

Active window The window that is currently being worked in, and which appears "in front" of any other open windows. See also *Foreground task*.

ActiveX Concept developed by Microsoft, allowing a program to run inside a webpage.

Adapter See *Expansion card*.

Add/Remove Programs Feature of the Windows Control Panel, primarily useful today for uninstalling programs.

Address bar The strip near the top of a Windows or Internet Explorer window where you can enter either a Web address or the path to a file on your computer.

Administrator A type of User account in Windows XP that allows full control of the computer.

ADSL (**A**synchronous **D**igital **S**ubscriber **L**ine) System for high-speed transmission of digital data over standard phonelines, used for Internet connections. Faster than ISDN. See also *DSL*.

AGP (**A**ccelerated **G**raphics **P**ort) Motherboard slot, designed for video cards, that can handle a much heavier data flow than PCI slots.

Alt (**Alt**ernative key) Standard keyboard key that can be used in combination with other keys to create characters or commands outside the normal keyboard range.

Analogue A signal that can be smoothly varied in strength or quantity, or a device that produces, records or stores such a signal. Contrast with *Digital*.

Antivirus software Program that detects, and sometimes removes, computer viruses.

Applet A small application program.

Application See *Program*.

Apply A dialog box button that enforces changes without closing the box.

Archive File that bundles a set of other files together under a single name for transfer or backup. Often compressed to reduce size, or encrypted for privacy.

ASCII (**A**merican **S**tandard **C**ode for **I**nformation **I**nterchange) Text format readable by all computers. Also called "plain text".

Aspect ratio An image's height divided by its width.

@ (At) This symbol separates the user's name from the domain name in an email address, eg **peter@roughguides.co.uk**

AT See *ATX*.

ATA (**AT A**ttachment) See *IDE*.

ATA-2 See *EIDE*.

ATA/33 ATA/66 ATA/100 See *Ultra ATA*.

ATAPI (**AT A**ttachment **P**acket **I**nterface) The standard interface used for attaching CD, DVD and tape drives to a PC. ATAPI is a type of IDE connection (or EIDE, to be exact). See also *IDE*.

Attachment File included with an email or other form of message.

ATX A modern standard specification for PC cases, power supplies and motherboards that superseded the older AT standard in the mid-1990s. The ATX layout supports USB, as well as integrated audio and video. Old motherboards won't fit in new cases and vice versa.

AUTOEXEC.BAT A file used by Windows each time a PC is turned on or restarted, running specific commands to get everything up and running.

B

Background task A task, such as a file download, which takes place behind the scenes while the computer deals with a foreground task (generally whatever you see in the active window).

Backup A copy of data or program files made for safekeeping, usually stored on a different device.

Backward compatible A product – hardware or software – that will work with certain older products, formats or media.

Bad sector Physically damaged or defective segment of a disk, marked by the operating system as not to be used.

Bandwidth The rate at which digital data flows through a cable or over a connection, usually measured in bits per second (bps). In analogue systems the bandwidth is the range of frequencies transmitted and is measured in hertz (Hz).

Binary Number system that uses only zeros and ones. When data is converted into binary code it can be dealt with electronically, with the zeros and ones represented by electrical charges being on or off (or high/low).

Binary file Any file that contains more than plain text, such as a program or image.

BIOS (**B**asic **I**nput/**O**utput **S**ystem) Pronounced "bye-ose" or "bye-oss". Set of essential software codes stored in a ROM chip on the motherboard. The BIOS tests hardware upon startup, kickstarts the operating system and supports the transfer of data between hardware devices.

Bit (**Bi**nary digi**t**) Abbreviated to b. Smallest unit of information that can be handled by a computer. One bit represents a 0 or 1 numerically, true or false logically, and opposing physical states in an electric circuit or magnetic disk.

Bitmap A picture file format that represents an image in the form of rows and columns of dots.

Bluetooth A short-range radio technology standard, designed to allow all types of desk-bound and portable devices, including mobile phones, to communicate with each other.

Bookmarks The Netscape equivalent of "Favorites" in Internet Explorer. The two terms are often used interchangeably.

Boot To start or reset a computer.

Boot disk A disk, usually a floppy, which is capable of launching an operating system. Also called a *Startup disk*.

Boot sector Space at the beginning of a diskette or partition reserved for the instructions that start the operating system.

bps (**b**its **p**er **s**econd) Basic measure of data transfer speed. Not to be confused with bytes per second (Bps), which is generally written with an upper-case B.

Bps (**b**ytes **p**er **s**econd) Measure of data transfer speed often used in relation to PC components like hard drives. Not to be confused with bits per second (bps), which is generally written with a lower-case b.

Broadband High-speed information connection; most commonly refers to cable or ADSL Internet access.

Browser Web viewing program such as Internet Explorer.

Buffer A temporary data storage area.

Bug Logical, physical or programming error in software or hardware that causes a recurring malfunction.

Burner Device that can write to certain types of CDs or DVDs. See also *CD-R*, *CD-RW*, *DVD-R*, *DVD-RW* and *DVD-RAM*.

BurnProof (**B**uffer **U**nder **Run-Proof**) A trademarked technology that drastically reduces the likelihood of errors occurring while burning a CD-R or CD-RW. Many CD burners now ship with BurnProofing features.

Bus A data transmission path on the motherboard that links the processor to various other components, such as expansion cards and disk drives. Or a set of conductors used to transfer data between two hardware components. See also *ISA* and *PCI* (two types of bus for attaching expansion cards).

Byte (**B**inary **Term**) Abbreviated to B. A small amount of memory consisting of eight bits. This is the amount needed to represent one character. Memory, file size and disk capacity are measured in bytes, kilobytes (roughly 1,000 bytes), megabytes (roughly 1,000,000 bytes) and gigabytes (roughly 1,000,000,000 bytes).

C

C: Letter normally assigned to the primary hard drive of a PC.

Cache Pronounced "cash". To cache data is to store it in a convenient place where it can be re-accessed quickly. The cache frequently mentioned in computer adverts is L2 (level 2) cache, a special piece of fast memory built into the processor. But operating systems also use system RAM for caching frequently used data, and when you visit a website it may be cached on your hard drive.

Card See *Expansion card*.

CD burner A drive that can write, or "burn" data to CD-Rs or CD-RWs (most can write to both). Also called a "CD writer".

CD-R (**CD R**ecordable) A special type of CD that can be written to by a CD-R drive. Once a section of a CD-R disc has been "burned" it cannot be changed. Each disc has a capacity of around 700 MB.

CD-ROM (**CD R**ead **O**nly **M**emory) Compact discs used for storing data. They can be read by a computer but not written to.

CD-RW (**CD R**ewritable) A special type of CD that can be written to by a CD-RW drive. CD-RWs can be rewritten on again and again like floppy disks. Has a capacity of around 700 MB.

CD writer See *CD burner.*

Chip See *Microchip* and *Processor*.

Chipset Any collection of chips designed to function as one unit. The term is mostly used to describe the all-important chips and circuitry of a motherboard, which determine many things, including the speed that information can pass between the processor and the RAM.

Click To position the mouse cursor over a screen object such as an icon or Web link, and press down on the left mouse button.

Client/server A type of networking relationship where one computer (the server) manages resources and access to data, while other PCs (the clients) simply run applications, relying heavily on the server for access to files and peripheral devices. This is sometimes called a "two-tier architecture".

Clip art Collections of graphics for pasting into documents, usually categorized into themes such as Christmas or Music.

Clipboard Special memory resource that holds the last piece of data Copied or Cut so that it can be transferred using the Paste command. See also *Cut*, *Copy* and *Paste*.

Cluster A section of a disk surface, consisting of various sectors. See also *Lost clusters* and *Sector*.

CMOS (**C**omplementary **M**etal-**O**xide **S**emiconductor) Pronounced "see-moss". This is an energy-efficient battery-operated memory chip in a PC that stores fundamental system information relating to the system setup, time and date.

Code Passage written in a programming language.

Codec 1. (**Co**mpressor/**Dec**ompressor) Any technology – hardware or software – used for compressing and decompressing data. MPEG and MP3 are both examples of codec file formats. 2. (**Co**der/**Dec**oder) A communications device such as a modem that translate analogue signals into digital and vice versa.

Combination drive A drive that combines functions usually served by two separate drives – most commonly a CD writer and a DVD drive.

Command line A line where you type instructions for your PC, such as the bottom line in a DOS window or the text input section of the Run box, launched via the Start menu.

Command prompt A string of characters (such as C:\>) inviting you type a command into a PC.

COM port See *Serial port*.

Configuration The way that a system – hardware or software – is set up.

Context menu See *Mouse menu*.

Control key A standard key on PC keyboards, usually marked "Ctrl". It can be combined with other keys to create characters or commands outside the normal keyboard range.

Control Panel Special Windows folder that contains applets to configure and adjust the system. Found in the Start menu (under Settings in Windows Me and 98).

Cookie A small file placed on your hard drive by a Web server so that it can recognize your PC when you return to the site.

Copy To duplicate the selected text, image, file or folder to the Clipboard so that it can be Pasted elsewhere. The shortcut is Ctrl+C. See also *Cut*, *Paste* and *Clipboard*.

Core logic Another term for a motherboard's chipset. See also *Chipset*.

CPU (**C**entral **P**rocessing **U**nit) The proper term for a PC's processor. See *Processor*.

CPU fan A little fan attached to a computer's processor to stop it from overheating.

Crack To break a program's security, integrity or registration system, or to fake a user ID.

Crash When a program or operating system fails to respond or causes other programs to malfunction.

CRIMM (**C**ontinuity **RIMM**) Pronounced "see-rim". A dummy RIMM module without any memory on it. Unused RIMM slots on a motherboard must always be filled with CRIMMs. See also *RIMM*.

CRT (**C**athode **R**ay **T**ube) Glass vacuum tube that forms the basis of the standard desktop computer monitor.

Ctrl See *Control key*.

Cursor Special screen character that usually looks like a flashing "I". It indicates where typed text will appear.

Cut Remove the selected text, image, file or folder from its current location, but keep it on the Clipboard so it can be Pasted elsewhere. The keyboard shortcut is Ctrl+X. See also *Copy*, *Paste* and *Clipboard*.

CYMK (**C**yan, **Y**ellow, **M**agenta, **B**lac**k**) These are the four colours of ink found in most standard colour printers. CYMK, or CYMB as it's sometimes known, describes the inks as well as the system by which they're mixed to make other colours.

Daisy chain A set of computers or devices connected "in series" – each one connected to two others like a set of Christmas lights.

Data Information in a form suitable for a computer.

Database A file designed to collect, store and retrieve information.

Daughterboard An expansion card that connects to the memory and CPU directly instead of shunting data via the expansion bus.

DDR SDRAM (**D**ouble **D**ata **R**ate **SDRAM**) Pronounced "dee-dee-are-ess-dee-ram", and often shortened to DDR RAM. A relatively new type of RAM that is twice as fast as normal SDRAM because it transfers data on both the rising and falling edges of each clock cycle. See also *SDRAM*.

Default The standard setting of an application or device.

Defragment Often shortened to "defrag". To rearrange the data stored on a hard drive so that it can be accessed more quickly.

Degauss To remove unwanted magnetic charge, usually from a monitor.

Delete 1. Remove a file or part of a document. Deleting a file in Windows normally sends it to the Recycle Bin. 2. The key that does this.

Desktop 1. The background space in an operating system such as Windows. 2. Any non-mobile computer – ie one that lives on a desk. 3. A computer in a case that sits flat on a desk, generally with the monitor perched on top of it. Contrast with *Tower case*.

Device name The operating system's title for a PC component.

Dialog box A box – like a window – that appears on the screen to ask or tell you something.

Dial-up connection Temporary network connection between two computers via a telephone line and modem.

Digital A signal that varies in steps rather than smoothly, or a device that produces, records or stores such a signal. Computers only work with digital information. Contrast with *Analogue*.

DIMM (**D**ual **I**nline **M**emory **M**odule) A type of strip-like circuit board that holds RAM. SDRAM and DDR SDRAM come on DIMMs. See also *SIMM* and *SODIMM*.

DIP switch (**D**ual **I**nline **P**ackage) A tiny switch built onto the circuit board of a computer component for configuring it to work with a certain piece of hardware or software. These days you will rarely need to worry about DIP switches thanks to Plug and Play technology.

Direct cable connection A means of connecting two PCs using just a cable (no network cards, hubs or other hardware). One machine is defined as the "host" and the other as the "guest".

Directory 1. See *Folder.* 2. Online guide that organizes Internet sites into categories.

DirectX A special system that allows programs to take full advantage of certain video and sound cards to improve multimedia capability.

Disk cache Area of a PC's RAM set aside for storing the data most recently transferred to and from the hard drive, so it can be quickly re-accessed by the processor if it's needed again.

Disk drive A device that reads and/or writes to magnetic or optical disks. The disks can be removable, as in the case of a CD-ROM, or fixed, as with a hard drive.

Display See *Monitor*.

Display adapter See *Video card*.

Display Properties Windows dialog box for configuring everything that relates to how things look on the screen, including the appearance of the Desktop and the resolution of the monitor. Found in the Control Panel or by right-clicking on the Desktop and selecting Properties.

DLL file (**D**ynamic **L**ink **L**ibrary) A set of software modules that can be used by a range of application programs to perform common tasks.

DMA (**D**irect **M**emory **A**ccess) A means of transferring data from a PC component, such as a hard drive, straight to the RAM, bypassing the processor. PCs with a DMA channel can transfer data faster than computers without, which is especially handy for fast backups, real-time applications, etc. See also *UDMA*.

DNS (**D**omain **N**ame **S**ystem) The system that translates Web addresses as used by humans (such as www.roughguides.com) into numeric IP addresses that computers understand (like 156.154.253.142). See also *IP*.

Docking station Device for connecting a portable notebook computer to a range of desk-bound external devices such as a printer, monitor and mouse.

Document A file (a letter, image, spreadsheet or anything else) that is created, saved and edited in a program.

Domain Part of an Internet address that specifies details about the host, such as its location and whether it's commercial (.com), governmental (.gov), etc.

DOS (**D**isk **O**perating **S**ystem) 1. An abbreviation of MS-DOS, the forerunner of Windows. 2. Any operating system loaded by disk devices at startup, as opposed to the operating systems of early computers which were permanently stored in the circuitry.

DOS prompt A command prompt in MS-DOS, showing that the machine is ready for input. Typically, it looks something like C:\>.

Dot pitch A measure of the maximum image sharpness that a monitor can achieve. It describes the minimum size of a pixel in millimetres (though in some cases it is used to refer to the gap between the pixels). A smaller dot pitch normally means a sharper image.

Double-click To press and release the left mouse button twice quickly in succession. In Windows, double-clicking a file or folder opens it.

Download To copy files from a remote computer to your own. Contrast with *Upload*.

dpi (**d**ots **p**er **i**nch) A measure of printer, scanner or monitor resolution, defined by the number of dots a device can print or display in a linear inch.

Drag-and-drop To move an object, such as a file, icon or passage of text, by selecting it and moving the mouse with the left button held down. Releasing your finger drops the object in its new location.

DRAM (**D**ynamic **R**andom **A**ccess **M**emory) Pronounced "dee-ram". Family of RAM types, which need to be periodically topped up to stop them "leaking" their electronic charges. There are many types, including EDO, FPM, SDRAM, DDR SDRAM and RDRAM.

Driver Small program that acts like a translator between a hardware device and the operating systems or programs that use that device.

DSL (**D**igital **S**ubscriber **L**ine) An "always on" data transfer system that allows high-speed transfer of digital data over standard phonelines. There are various types, such as ADSL and SDSL, sometimes collectively referred to as xDSL.

DTP (**D**esktop **P**ublishing) Software, such as QuarkXPress, PageMaker or Publisher, used to produce documents containing positioned text and images – a brochure or book, for example.

DV (**D**igital **V**ideo) Video footage stored as digital code on tape or disk, or a camera that captures such footage.

DVD (**D**igital **V**ersatile **D**isc or **D**igital **V**ideo **D**isc) High-capacity optical storage disc that looks like the CD and which is likely to supersede it. Currently used mostly for storing movies, DVDs can be only read by DVD drives, not standard CD drives.

DVD burner A DVD drive that can write information to one or more types of DVDs. See also *DVD-R*, *DVD-RW* and *DVD-RAM*.

DVD-R (**DVD R**ecordable) A type of DVD that can be written to by a DVD-R drive.

DVD-RAM A type of DVD that can be written to again and again. It usually comes in a protective plastic case that slots into a DVD-RAM drive, or as a permanent internal unit. They cannot currently be read by standard DVD drives and players.

DVD-RW (**DVD R**ewritable) A type of DVD that can be written to by a DVD-RW drive. They cannot currently be read by most standard DVD drives and players. A newer, more compatible standard called DVD+RW is currently being developed.

E

eBook (**e**lectronic **book**) A "book" in the form of a file that can be bought and downloaded from the Web. There are various formats available that can be read on computers, notebooks or PDA devices with the appropriate software. See *eBook reader*.

eBook reader A program for reading titles saved in a particular eBook format. The two most commonly used programs – both downloadable for free – are the Adobe Acrobat eBook Reader (www.adobe.com/products/ebookreader) and Microsoft Reader (www.microsoft.com/reader/download.asp).

Edit To change the contents of a document.

EIDE (**E**nhanced **IDE**) A faster version of the standard IDE connection. Also known as Fast ATA. See also *IDE*.

EISA See *ISA*.

Email (**E**lectronic **mail**) A system of sending messages, sometimes with files "attached", from one computer to another.

Email address A unique private Internet address to which email is sent. Takes the form user@host.

EPS (**E**ncapsulated **P**ost**S**cript) File format that can contain two versions of an image: a bitmap for displaying on the screen and a PostScript for high-resolution printing on a laser printer.

Error message A message displayed by a program or operating system reporting that a problem has occurred.

Ethernet Very popular type of local area network (LAN) that connects devices using coaxial cable. The protocol was developed by Xerox in the 1970s.

Ethernet card Expansion card that lets a computer hook up to an Ethernet network.

Exit To quit a program. This option is normally found at the bottom of the File menu. The shortcut in Windows is Alt+F4.

Expansion card A rectangular circuit board, usually with a back panel, that slots into a computer's motherboard to expand its features or add extra sockets. Examples include sound cards, video cards and SCSI interface cards.

Expansion slot A slot on a motherboard where expansion cards (video, sound, modems, etc) are inserted. The three types are AGP, PCI and ISA.

Explore An option in Windows when you right-click a folder or drive icon. If selected, the contents of the folder or drive are displayed in an Explorer window with the folder tree displayed on the left.

Explorer See *Windows Explorer* and *Internet Explorer*.

Extension See *File extension*.

External A computer device not housed within the PC's case, such as an external hard drive or external CD-ROM drive.

F

FAQ (**F**requently **A**sked **Q**uestions) Document that answers the most commonly asked questions on a particular topic.

Fast ATA See *EIDE*.

Fast user switching A feature of Windows XP that allows users to switch between their accounts without having to close applications or documents.

FAT (**F**ile **A**llocation **T**able) A system that Windows and other operating systems use to keep track of exactly where each file on a disk is stored – quite complicated, as a single file can be spread across many locations. There are various versions of FAT. The term on its own is generally used to describe FAT16, the system used up until the first edition of Windows 95, which could only support tiny hard drives by today's standards (maximum 2 GB). Windows XP, Me, 98 and later versions of 95 also support FAT32 (meaning the entries in the allocation table can be 32 bits long) – this allows bigger hard drives and uses disk space more efficiently. See also *NTFS*.

FAT32 See *FAT*.

Fatal error Program failure for which the only remedy is to restart the system.

Favorites A system in a Web browser such as Internet Explorer that allows you to store a list of webpages you wish to return to again. (In reality it's a folder on the hard drive containing a file for each website listed.) The term is used interchangeably with "Bookmarks", the equivalent in the Netscape Navigator browser.

Fax modem A modem capable of sending and receiving fax messages. Most modern modems are fax modems.

File A chunk of data stored on a computer, such as a program, image or document. Programs tend to be made up of many files, while a document is contained in a single file.

File attributes Certain properties of a file – such as whether it's read-only or editable, shared or private and visible or hidden. To view the attributes of a file in Windows, right-click its icon and select Properties.

File compression *Zip file*.

File extension Set of characters added to the end of a filename (after a dot) which identifies the file as a particular type. For example, the extension .txt identifies a text file. In recent versions of Windows, known file extensions aren't shown unless you unhide them in Folder Options. For a list of extensions and their file types, visit: www.webopedia.com/quick_ref/fileextensions.html

File format See *Format*.

Firewall A security system – hardware, software or both – which restricts unauthorized access to a computer or network, especially from other computers connected to the Internet.

FireWire See *IEEE 1394*.

Firmware Operational software stored in the ROM (Read Only Memory) chips of a hardware device. This software is put in place by the manufacturer and cannot be altered by the user.

Flash memory A special type of RAM that retains data even in a device that's switched off. It's often used on motherboards to store BIOS code or in digital cameras for holding image data, and can be bought on little sticks or cards for use with portable computers, MP3 players and other devices.

Flat panel See *LCD monitor*.

Floppy See *Floppy disk*.

Floppy disk A removable magnetic storage medium. The term is almost always used to refer to the 3.5" diskettes that have hard square plastic cases (they're floppy inside) and which are used in a standard PC A: drive.

Folder A container for files in a graphic user interface (GUI) system such as Windows.

Folder tree A graphic representation of the folders and drives of a PC, laid out as in the folder view of Windows Explorer.

Font A typeface, such as Times New Roman or Arial. Technically, the font includes factors such as size (in points), style (italic, outline, etc) and weight (bold).

Footprint The amount of space a PC system or device takes up. Most commonly used in relation to the depth of monitors.

Foreground task The activity or program displayed in the current active window. See also *Background task* and *Active window*.

Format 1. Every file is saved with a particular "file format", which determines which application or applications can be used to open, view and edit it. There are thousands of different file formats – simple text format, rich text format and JPEG being a few examples. See also *File extension*. 2. The structure or appearance of a document, font, paragraph, number or any unit of data. 3. To initialize a disk so that it can be used to store information. When a disk is formatted, all previously stored data is lost.

Freeware Copyrighted software that is available for free for your own personal use. Countless freeware utilities and programs are downloadable from the Internet.

fsb (**f**ront**s**ide **b**us) The bus within a processor that connects it to the RAM, determining the speed at which data can be sent or received. See also *Bus*.

FTP (**F**ile **T**ransfer **P**rotocol) A standard for sending and receiving files over the Internet. FTP is commonly used for sending webpages from the computer where they were created to the server where they will live and be accessible from the rest of the Internet. It is also used for downloading files. FTP sites are like Internet storage depots where people send files for others to download, thus avoiding having to send large files as email attachments.

Full duplex Capable of transmitting data in two directions simultaneously. A full duplex sound card can record and play back sound at the same time, for example.

Function keys Keys labelled F1, F2 and so on, running along the top of a computer keyboard. They do different things in different programs, though F1 nearly always activates Help.

G

Game port Socket for connecting a joystick or other gaming device to a computer.

GB See *Gigabyte*.

GIF (**G**raphic **I**nterchange **F**ormat) A compressed graphics format frequently used for images on the Web.

Gigabyte Abbreviated to GB. Roughly 1 billion bytes of data – 1,073,741,824 to be exact. This is the most common means of describing the capacity of a hard drive.

Graphics card See *Video card*.

Graphics tablet A special input device (an alternative to the mouse), which is favoured by illustrators. It uses a pen, or "stylus", and sensitive pad to duplicate the action of a regular pen or pencil.

GSM (**G**lobal **S**ystem for **M**obile Communications) The leading digital wireless communication system technology in Europe and Asia. It allows multiple calls to be made on a single radio frequency.

Guest 1. A type of Windows XP User account that allows an individual to use a PC without already being registered as a user. 2. The name given to a PC that accesses the resources of a host PC using a Direct cable connection. See also *Direct cable connection*.

GUI (**G**raphic **U**ser **I**nterface) Pronounced "gooey". Any system with which you operate a computer using graphics rather than text. In Windows, for example, the GUI lets you enter instructions with a mouse pointer, icons, menus and windows.

Hacker A computer user who breaks into networks or servers by various means, such as decrypting user IDs and passwords. The term is also used in computer circles to describe a legitimate programmer.

Hard disk See *Hard drive.*

Hard disk controller An expansion card that controls one or more hard drives.

Hard drive The primary storage device in modern PCs. All PCs have at least one hard drive (usually labelled C: in Windows), though they can have two or more. Hard drives, which are also referred to as hard disks, consist of a stack of magnetic disks housed in a dust-proof shell. A modern hard drive's capacity is usually measured in gigabytes (GBs).

Hard reset Turning a computer off completely before restarting, as opposed to simply pressing the reset button. This gives the components a chance to discharge.

Hardware The physical components of a computer.

Hidden file A file not displayed in the normal listing (such as in Windows Explorer) to protect it from deletion or modification. See also *File attributes*.

Hi-Speed USB The successor of the original USB connection, this connection standard shifts data at up to 480 Mbps – 40 times faster than a standard USB. Also known as USB 2.

Home page 1. The page automatically loaded by your Internet browser when you start it up. 2. The entry page of a particular website.

Host Computer that offers some sort of service to users via a network or a direct cable connection. See also *Direct cable connection*, *Client/server* and *Guest*.

HTML (**H**ypertext **M**ark-up **L**anguage) A programming language used to create Web documents. It's also a file format: behind most webpages there's an HTML document that determines what it looks like.

HTTP (**H**ypertext **T**ransport **P**rotocol) The Internet's communication protocol. Most Internet addresses begin with "http://", though you don't need to type this when entering Web addresses into a modern browser.

Hub A cable junction box: types include a USB hub (which turns one USB port into two or more), and a network hub (which each computer connects to in certain types of network).

Hypertext links Bits of text, often in blue and underlined, that when clicked take you to another webpage, window, etc.

I

Icon Small image used to represent an object (document, program, etc) in a graphic user interface system. Individual programs and file formats generally have their own unique icon.

IDE (**I**ntegrated **D**rive **E**lectronics) Also known as ATA. An interface for connecting disk drives and other devices (its name comes from the fact that IDE devices have their controller built-in rather than on a separate card, as with SCSI). Standard IDE was superseded by EIDE and Ultra ATA, but the term "IDE" is used to describe all these different standards. Most modern PCs have two IDE ports on the motherboard, each of which can take two devices. See also *EIDE*, *Ultra ATA* and *SCSI*.

IEEE (**I**nstitute for **E**lectrical and **E**lectronics **E**ngineers) 1. A body that classifies and promotes computer standards such as interface types, and gives them numbers like IEEE 1394. 2. An abbreviation for IEEE 1394. See also *IEEE 1394*.

IEEE 1394 High-speed type of computer connection developed by Apple and used for peripherals such as digital video cameras and external hard drives. It supports Plug and Play, lets you attach 63 devices to a single port, allows you to plug and unplug devices without turning the computer off ("hot swapping"), and transfers data at up to 400 Mbps. Often abbreviated to IEEE, and also known as FireWire and (in some Sony products) i.LINK.

i.LINK See *IEEE 1394*.

Infrared A type of wireless PC connection that uses a line-of-sight beam to transmit data in the same way as a conventional TV remote control. Though not commonly used on desktop systems, Infrared ports are often found on notebook PCs.

Inkjet printer The most commonly used type of home printer, which works by spraying tiny droplets of ink onto the paper. Contrast with *Laser printer*.

Insertion point See *Cursor*.

Input device Any device that allows a user to instruct a PC to perform tasks. Mice, keyboards and joysticks are all examples of input devices.

Install 1. To integrate a program into a computer's setup so that it's ready to be used. 2. To add a new piece of hardware, usually an internal component such as an expansion card or hard drive, to a computer.

Internal Any computer device, such as a disk drive, that lives inside the PC's case.

Internet A cooperatively run global computer network with a common addressing system.

Internet connection sharing Using one Internet connection for two or more PCs on a network.

Internet Explorer Microsoft's Web browser, which comes bundled with Windows. It's also downloadable for free from: www.microsoft.com/ie

Internet Favorites See *Favorites*.

I/O (**I**nput/**O**utput) 1. The selection of ports on a computer. 2. Any devices or programs that send or receive a flow of data to the PC's core components. Two examples are the keyboard (an input device) and the monitor (an output device).

IP (**I**nternet **P**rotocol) Every computer connected to the Internet, including the servers where webpages live, has a unique numeric IP address that allows computers to find each other. Whenever you request a webpage online, your PC's IP address is sent to the computer where the webpage is stored so it can send the page to your machine. See also *DNS*.

IP address See *IP*.

IRQ (Interrupt Request Line) The path that a PC device, such as a printer or expansion card, uses to send messages to the processor. If two devices try to share the same IRQ, a conflict may occur and neither device will operate.

ISA (Industry Standard Architecture) Pronounced "eye-sa" or as separate letters. A type of internal slot (technically a bus) used for connecting expansion cards to the motherboard. However, despite the development of EISA (Extended ISA), ISA has now been almost completely superseded by PCI and AGP. Many new PC motherboards, though, still feature one or more ISA slots. See also *PCI* and *AGP*.

ISDN (Integrated Services Digital Network) An international standard for sending digital data over telephone lines. Commonly used for Internet connections.

ISP (Internet Service Provider) Company that provides access to the Internet. When you connect to the Internet, you actually connect to your ISP's computer, which feeds the webpages you request to your machine.

IT (Information Technology) Anything relating to computers and their development. People who work in computing are often said to work in IT.

J

Java A programming language often used to create applications for use on the Web, as the language is compatible with all major operating systems.

Jaz drive A type of high-capacity SCSI-connecting removable storage device built by Iomega (www.iomega.com). See also *Zip drive*.

Joystick A type of gaming device.

JPEG/JPG (**J**oint **P**hotographic **E**xperts **G**roup) Pronounced "jay-peg". A compressed graphics file format often used in webpages.

Jumper A small plastic and metal block used for configuring a piece of hardware. A jumper connects two metal pins, and can be removed or moved to change the setup of the device.

Justified Text which has each line expanded to fit the full width of a page or column.

K

Kbps (**K**ilo**b**its **p**er **s**econd) A standard measure of how fast data is transferred by cables, ports, connections, etc. 1 Kbps is the same as 1000 bps.

Kernel The underlying program code on which an operating system is based.

Keyboard One of the two main input devices of a PC, the other being the mouse. Various different types of keyboard are available, but almost all feature the traditional QWERTY key layout.

Kilobit (**Kb**) 1024 bits when referring to data storage and 1000 bits when referring to data transfer.

Kilobyte (**KB**) 1024 bytes when referring to data storage and 1000 bytes when referring to data transfer.

L

LAN (**L**ocal **A**rea **N**etwork) Computer network that spans a relatively small geographical area, such as in a home or office. Contrast with *WAN*.

Landscape The view or print option for a document where the width of a page is greater than its height. Contrast with *Portrait*.

Laser printer High-resolution printer that creates images by rolling a charged drum through a reservoir of toner and then over the paper. Contrast with *Inkjet printer*.

LCD monitor (**L**iquid **C**rystal **D**isplay **monitor**) The thin, light but expansive monitors used in notebook computers. They are also available for desktop systems as a thinner alternative to the CRT monitor. Most LCDs sold today are of the TFT (Thin Film Transistor) type.

Link Any clickable text (technically "hypertext"), icon, button or image in a webpage (and sometimes elsewhere) that takes you to either another webpage or another location within the same page. Links on webpages are also sometimes used to trigger a download or play music and video clips. See also *Hypertext links*.

Linux A version of the UNIX operating system that is becoming an increasingly popular alternative to Windows for both home and business users. Unlike Windows, the source code for Linux is freely available, allowing programmers to tailor the OS for their individual needs. Many versions of Linux are available, either to buy or download for free.

Local Describes the drives and folders on your computer, as opposed to those on a computer connected via a network or the Internet.

Logical drive See *Partition*.

Log off To disconnect from a network or website, or end a session on a computer to make way for another user. Contrast with *Log on*.

Log on To connect to a network or Website, or start a session on a computer as a particular user – generally the term implies entering a username and possibly also a password.

Lost clusters Small sections of a hard drive that have been labelled by the operating system as being in use even though they are not associated with a particular file. Lost clusters can be identified and reassigned for use in Windows using the ScanDisk utility. See also *ScanDisk*.

Macro A sequence of actions, within an application, that has been assigned either a keyboard shortcut or toolbar button so that the actions can be executed with a single click or keystroke.

Magnetic storage The collective term for storage devices that hold their data magnetically, such as hard drives, floppies and Zip disks. Contrast with *Optical disc*.

Mainboard See *Motherboard*.

Mass storage Hardware and related media used for storing large quantities of data. Common examples are hard drives, Zip disks and optical discs such as CD-Rs.

Maximize See *Minimize/Maximize/Restore*.

MB See *Megabyte*.

Media Player 1. The built-in Windows utility for playing CD audio, sound files and video files. 2. Any media playback program.

Megabyte Abbreviated to MB, and often referred to as "meg". When used to refer to disk space, a megabyte is roughly 1 million bytes (1,048,576 to be exact); when used to refer to data transfer it describes exactly one million bytes. See also *Byte*.

Megahertz Abbreviated to MHz. A measurement of frequency, equivalent to one million cycles per second. Commonly used to describe the speed of computer processors and other components.

Memory Generally refers to system RAM, or the RAM on video cards and other components. But there are also various other types of removable and non-removable memory. See also *RAM*, *ROM* and *Flash memory*.

Menu bar A strip towards the top of a window that contains dropdown menus. Usually includes File, Edit and View menus.

MHz See *Megahertz*.

Microchip Dense electronic circuit fabricated on a single piece of silicon. A chip smaller than a thumbnail can contain millions of transistors. Also called an "integrated circuit" or "silicon chip".

Microprocessor See *CPU*.

MIDI (**M**usical **I**nstrument **D**igital **I**nterface) A standard adopted by the electronic music industry for controlling devices such as sound cards and synthesizers. MIDI files contain synthesizer instructions rather than recorded sounds.

Minimize/Maximize/Restore Windows options for resizing and hiding windows. They can be executed in many ways, such as by using the buttons on the right-hand side of a window's Title bar.

Mobo Techie slang for Motherboard.

Modem (**mo**dulator/**dem**odulator) Device that allows one computer to communicate with others, usually over a telephone line. It converts digital data into analogue signals and vice versa.

Monitor Computer screen.

Motherboard The PC's main circuit board that all the other components connect to.

Mouse One of the two primary PC input devices, along with the keyboard.

Mouse menu A useful little menu that pops up when you right-click screen items such as icons, Web links and the Windows Taskbar. Also called a "shortcut menu" or "context menu".

Mouse wheel See *Scroll wheel*.

MP3 (**MP**EG Audio Layer **3**) A compressed music file format.

MP3 player A small portable Walkman-like device for playing compressed music files downloaded from a computer.

MPEG/MPG Pronounced "em-peg". A compressed video file format.

MS-DOS (**M**icro**s**oft **D**isk **O**perating **S**ystem) The forerunner of Windows. It's a single-tasking operating system where the user types in coded commands rather than clicking icons and menus with a mouse pointer. Usually referred to just as "DOS".

Multitasking An operating system such as Windows that can run many applications, and perform various tasks, simultaneously.

N

Net See *Internet*.

Network 1. To connect a computer to one or more others. 2. A set of connected computers. See also *LAN* and *WAN*.

Network card See *NIC*.

Newsgroups Internet-based message forums, or discussion groups, organized into subjects.

NIC (**N**etwork **I**nterface **C**ard) Expansion card that enables a computer to be linked to a network.

Notebook Portable computer. Used interchangeably with "laptop".

Notepad A very basic text editor built into Windows.

Notification area The right-hand end of the Windows Taskbar where system utility icons and the Windows clock reside. Sometimes called the "System tray".

NTFS (**N**ew **T**echnology **F**ile **S**ystem) A type of disk drive filing system favoured for its stability and security features. XP is the first home version of Windows to use this system. Contrast with *FAT*.

OCR (**O**ptical **C**haracter **R**ecognition) Software that enables a computer to convert a bitmap image containing text into an editable text file.

Offline The state of being disconnected from a network, typically the Internet. Contrast with *Online*.

Online 1.The state of being connected to a network, typically the Internet (contrast with *Offline*). 2. Any resource located on the Internet, such as an online directory.

Operating system A special program – such as Windows, DOS or Linux – that acts as a bridge between the hardware of a computer and the software on it. Among other things, it allocates system resources to specific tasks and determines the way in which you view, move and open files and programs. Often abbreviated to OS.

Optical character recognition See *OCR*.

Optical disc (or **disk**) Any disc – such as a CD or DVD – that is read or written to by means of a laser in an optical drive. Unlike magnetic storage media, optical discs have data physically burned onto them. Some are read-only, some can be written to once and others can be written to again and again. See also *CD-ROM*, *CD-R*, *CD-RW*, *DVD-R*, *DVD-RW* and *DVD-RAM*.

OS See *Operating system*.

Overburning A technology that allows you to squeeze a little more data or music onto a CD-R or CD-RW by burning beyond the official capacity of the disc.

Overclocking Setting a PC to run the processor faster than its theoretical maximum speed. This requires you to know what you're doing and involves an element of risk (processors fry if pushed too far). For more information, see: **www.tomshardware.com/overclocking**

Palmtop A small handheld PC with a stylus instead of a keyboard. Also called a "PDA".

Parallel port A type of PC input/output connection often used for printers or scanners. A PC's parallel port is often referred to as the "printer port".

Parent folder The folder that a particular file or folder is stored in.

Partition A hard drive (or other disk) can be divided into various sections called partitions that work as if they were separate physical drives. Partitions can be created to help organize data, or install more than one operating system on a computer. A partition can also be referred to as a "logical drive" (as opposed to a physical drive).

Paste To insert text or graphics that have been Cut or Copied to the Clipboard. The standard shortcut is Ctrl+V. See also *Copy*, *Cut* and *Clipboard*.

Patch Temporary add-on to fix or upgrade software.

Path name The location of a particular file or folder on a PC, expressed as the drive and folders you have to would go through to find it. For example: **C:\Documents and Settings\Bob\My Documents\My Music\Bach**

PC card See *PCMCIA*.

PCI (Peripheral Component Interconnect) A standard type of internal connection (technically a bus) for expansion cards such as modems, video cards, etc. PCI devices attach via PCI slots on the motherboard.

PCMCIA card (Personal Computer Memory Card International Association) A computer device about the size of a thick credit card used primarily for adding devices to notebook PCs. PCMCIA devices can be either self-contained components or external devices that attach via a cable with a card on the end. Also called a "PC card".

PDF (Portable Document Format) A file format frequently found on the Web. Can be viewed with Adobe Acrobat Reader, freely downloadable from: www.acrobat.com

Pentium Frequently updated CPU series produced by Intel. The Pentium superseded the 486 in 1993.

Peripheral device Any external hardware device attached to a computer, such as a printer, scanner, keyboard or mouse.

PIM (Personal Information Manager) An appointments and contacts management program.

Pirated Software that is illegally copied and distributed.

Pixel (pix – picture – element) Bitmap images and everything you see on a computer screen are made up of small squares of colour called pixels. The size and number of pixels displayed depends upon the resolution of the image and the screen.

Platform Another name for a computer operating system. The most common examples are Windows, Linux and Mac OS.

Plug and Play A system, often abbreviated to PnP, that simplifies hardware installation by having the PC detect the new device and configure it automatically.

Plug-in A small program or utility that adds additional features to a bigger program.

POP3 (**P**ost **O**ffice **P**rotocol **3**) A standard email protocol. If you have a POP3 mail account, the messages are stored on a mail server until you download them to your machine (or someone else's).

Port A socket for connecting a cable. There are many different types, including serial, USB and PS/2.

Portal Website that specializes in leading you to others via links.

Portrait The view or print option for a document where the width of a page is narrower than its height. Contrast with *Landscape*.

POST (**P**ower-**O**n **S**elf **T**est) The self-diagnostic sequence that a PC runs when it's turned on to check that everything is working correctly.

PostScript An industry-standard language and file format for printing high-resolution text and images on compatible laser printers. Developed by Adobe, PostScript treats letters and images as scalable shapes rather than bitmaps.

PPM (**P**ages **P**er **M**inute) The maximum number of pages a printer can churn out in a minute.

Printer port See *Parallel port*.

Print preview Shows how a program expects a document to look when it's printed. This option is normally found in the File menu.

Processor Also called the CPU or the "chip", this is the component that does most of the work in a PC and determines the system's maximum speed. The Intel Pentium and AMD Athlon are examples of PC processors.

Program A piece of software that tells the PC how to perform certain tasks, such as word processing or photo editing.

Protocol Agreed way for two devices to communicate.

Proxy server A computer that sits between a client, such as a home user, and the actual ISP server. Most often used to improve performance by delivering stored pages (in a similar way to browser cache) and to filter out undesirable material.

PS/2 A little circular port used for attaching mice and keyboards.

Q

QuickTime A multimedia standard commonly used to preview movie clips online. You can download the QuickTime player from: www.quicktime.com

R

RAID (**R**edundant **A**rray of **I**nexpensive **D**isks) A type of hard disk setup that employs multiple drives running in combination – frequently used in servers.

RAM (**R**andom **A**ccess **M**emory) Memory used for short-term data processing rather than storage. The term generally refers to the main system RAM, but sound cards and other components can also have their own RAM. Usually, when a PC is turned off the memory is drained of its data.

Rambus A company best known for producing RDRAM. See also *RDRAM*.

RDRAM (**R**ambus **DRAM**) Pronounced "are-dee-ram", and often referred to simply as "Rambus memory". A recently developed type of high-speed RAM capable of very high data transfer rates. Comes on RIMMs and SORIMMs.

Readme file A document included with a program that provides installation instructions or other information. Sometimes useful when things go wrong.

Read-only A file or piece of data that can be accessed (read) but not modified. See also *ROM*.

RealPlayer A program, downloadable for free from www.real.com, for playing streaming audio and video from the Web.

Recycle bin Special Windows system folder where deleted files are stored until you choose to delete them permanently. You can view the contents of the Recycle bin by clicking its icon on the Start menu or Desktop.

Refresh rate Generally refers to the rate at which a monitor renews its image, measured in Hz (number of times per second).

Registry A database in Windows where system and software configuration settings are recorded. It can be viewed and edited by typing **Regedit** in the Run command in the Start menu – but altering anything incorrectly can cause major problems.

Rename To assign a new name to a file or folder. In Windows, select an icon, click the nametag and type the new name; or right-click the icon and choose Rename from the mouse menu.

Reset To restart a computer, either via the operating system (in the Turn Off or Shut Down options in the Windows Start menu) or with the small button on the case.

Resolution 1. The degree of detail in a printed or displayed image, usually expressed in dpi (dots per inch). The resolution of an individual image can be altered using an image editing program – reducing the resolution should reduce the file size. 2. The number of pixels on a screen. See also *Pixel*.

Restore See *Minimize/Maximize/Restore*.

RIMM Pronounced "rim". A module of RDRAM. See also *RDRAM* and *CRIMM*.

ROM (**R**ead **O**nly **M**emory) Computer memory chip or disc on which data has been pre-recorded. Once data has been written onto a ROM chip, it can only be read, not removed or altered. Unlike RAM, ROM retains its contents even when the computer its in is turned off.

S

Save To transfer data from short-term memory (RAM) to a more permanent storage place such as a hard drive, floppy or tape drive. Found in the File menu of most applications.

Save As The same as Save, except this option lets you choose a different filename or file type. Found in the File menu of most applications.

ScanDisk A Windows built-in utility that checks the surface of a hard drive or floppy disk for errors and lost clusters. See also *Lost clusters*.

Scanner A peripheral device used to transfer "hard copy" such as photos and documents on paper into digital images in order to edit, save, print or send them with a computer.

Screen resolution See *Resolution.*

Screen saver Utility that blanks the computer screen, or displays an animated loop, after a certain period of user inactivity.

Scroll bar Horizontal or vertical bar at the side or bottom of a window allowing you to view parts of the document, webpage or list not currently displayed. Either click on the arrows at either end of the bar or drag the slider to scroll up, down, left or right.

Scroll wheel Small wheel positioned between the right and left buttons of a mouse, and used for scrolling through webpages, among other things. Also known as a "web wheel".

SCSI (**S**mall **C**omputer **S**ystem **I**nterface) Pronounced "scuzzy". A type of high-speed connection for internal and external PC devices. Several devices can be attached to a single SCSI port, but you need a SCSI interface expansion card to get the port.

SDRAM (**S**ynchronous **DRAM**) Pronounced "ess-dee-ram". A type of RAM found in most machines built in the last few years, though it's starting to be superseded by DDR SDRAM and RDRAM. See also

DRAM, *DDR SDRAM* and *DRDRAM*.

Sector The smallest unit of disk space, usually 512 bytes.

Serial mouse Mouse that plugs into a serial port. Such mice can often also be plugged into in a PS/2 port with the aid of an adapter.

Serial port An old-school PC socket that allows data transfer 1 bit at a time. Can be used for many different peripherals.

Server Computer that makes services or files available on a network or on the Internet.

Shareware Software with a free trial period, generally downloaded from the Internet and often produced by a single programmer. Users are encouraged to send the programmer a token payment if they like and use the program.

Shortcut An icon that opens a program, folder or file that lives in another location on the computer. Shortcut icons generally have little arrows on their lower left corner to differentiate them from "real" files.

Shortcut menu See *Mouse menu*.

Shut down To close down a program, operating system or computer in a way that ensures no data is lost. Windows should always be shut down via the option on the Start menu (Turn off computer in Windows XP or Shut Down in earlier versions).

SIMM (**S**ingle **I**nline **M**emory **M**odule) Pronounced "sim". A type of RAM memory module, typically containing FPM or EDO RAM. SIMMS have now been almost completely superseded by DIMMs and RIMMs. See also *DIMM* and *RIMM*.

Slot A long thin socket on a computer motherboard or elsewhere for inserting an expansion board or RAM module.

SODIMM (**S**mall **O**utline **D**ual **I**nline **M**emory **M**odule) Pronounced "so-dim". 1. A small type of DIMM memory module often found in notebook computers. See also *DIMM*. 2. A Mac user.

Software General term for the various kinds of programs used to operate computers and related devices. Software consists of coded instructions rather than physical ("hard") components.

SOHO (**S**mall **O**ffice/**H**ome **O**ffice) A category of computer users who run small and home offices – and any product designed for such users.

SORIMM Pronounced "so-rim". A smaller type of RIMM memory module sometimes found in notebook computers. See also *RIMM*.

Sound card Expansion card that allows a PC to play and record sound.

Spam Junk email or newsgroup postings.

S/PDIF (**S**ony/**P**hilips **D**igital **I**nterface **F**ormat) Pronounced "ess-pee-diff". Digital audio connection found on some sound cards, used for attaching surround-sound speaker systems, DAT players and effects racks.

Spreadsheet Document based on a grid of rows and columns, or a program that creates such documents. Spreadsheets are used for organizing information, manipulating numbers and producing graphs.

Start button The button on the left of the Windows Taskbar that launches the Start menu. See also *Start menu*.

Start menu The main Windows menu, which is accessed by clicking the Start button in the lower left-hand corner of the screen.

Startup disk See *Boot disk*.

Storage A device that stores data. Sometimes storage is divided into "primary" (RAM, cache, etc) and "secondary" (hard drives, tape drives, etc), though generally the term is only used to describe mass storage devices. See also *Mass storage*.

Streaming A process that allows you to view movie files or hear audio files (generally on the Web) in real time. Whilst you watch or listen to the first segment of a file, your computer is downloading and preparing the next segment, so you don't have to wait for the whole file to arrive before playback can begin.

Subwoofer Speaker specifically for dealing with low-frequency sound, which often comes in a set with small "satellite" speakers for treble.

Surf Skip from page to page on the Web by clicking links.

Surge protector A device that stops surges in an electrical power supply from reaching a device such as a PC.

Swap file See *Virtual memory*.

System disk See *Boot disk*.

System RAM See *RAM*.

System tray See *Notification area*.

T

Tape drive A type of mass storage device that utilizes magnetic tape – often used for backing up data.

Taskbar The long thin strip that generally spans the bottom of the Windows Desktop, with the Start menu at one corner and the Notification area (or System tray) at the other.

TCP/IP (**T**ransmission **C**ontrol **P**rotocol/**I**nternet **P**rotocol) The basic communication protocols that make the Internet possible.

Temporary Internet Files Special system folder used by Internet Explorer to store the content of webpages for quick recall when backtracking.

Text file A simple document that contains nothing but plain text (ASCII characters, to be exact). Can be read or created with Windows Notepad.

TFT See *LCD monitor*.

Thumbnail A small preview image of an unopened image file. One of the View options for files and folders in Windows.

TIF or **TIFF** (**T**agged **I**mage **F**ile **F**ormat) One of the most popular bitmap image file formats.

Title bar The uppermost strip of a window, where you'll find the name of the program or document running within the frame.

Toner cartridge Disposable unit that supplies toner, the equivalent of ink, in a laser printer.

Toolbar A strip in a window – usually on one of the edges – that contains icons, dropdown menus and so on. It can sometimes be detached from the window to become an independent floating palette.

Touchpad The pointing device used in most notebooks. Operated by moving your finger around a small, flat touch-sensitive pad.

Tower case A computer case that stands upright – is taller than it is wide. Contrast with *Desktop*.

Trackball An input device resembling an upside-down mouse. Instead of moving the mouse, you roll the ball around with your fingers.

Trackpad See *Touchpad*.

Trojan (horse) A malicious and destructive program that hides its true (usually sinister) intentions.

Troubleshooter In Windows XP this is a diagnostic tool that asks you various multiple-choice questions to try and locate, and help you fix, a problem.

TV card A type of expansion card that allows your PC to receive and display television signals. Equivalent external devices are also available.

TWAIN Standard interface protocol used to bridge software and image capture devices such as scanners. (From the saying "Ne'er the twain shall meet", not "Technology Without An Interesting Name", as is often claimed).

UDMA (**U**ltra **D**irect **M**emory **A**ccess) A high-speed interface protocol governing the flow of data to and from EIDE hard drives; it vastly improved upon the DMA standard. See also *DMA*.

Ultra ATA A high-speed IDE hard drive interface that supports the UDMA protocol. The three types are Ultra ATA/33, Ultra ATA/66 and Ultra ATA/100; the numbers represent the theoretical maximum data transfer rate expressed in megabytes per second, though most drives don't achieve the stated speed. These terms are often written differently – Ultra ATA/33 is the same as a UDMA ATA33, UDMA33, DMA33, etc. Ultra ATA devices can generally be plugged into standard IDE ports, though the speed will be limited.

Uninstall To remove all parts of an application from a PC.

Update To bring a program, operating system or data file up-to-date by installing a patch, revision or complete new version. See also *Patch*.

Upgrade To improve a computer system by adding hardware, or to update a program.

Upload To send files to a remote computer. Contrast with *Download*.

UPS (**U**ninterruptible **P**ower **S**upply) A power source incorporating a battery that kicks in when the mains supply is disrupted, providing at least enough power to shut down the PC properly.

URL (**U**niform **R**esource **L**ocator) The technical name for a Web address.

USB (**U**niversal **S**erial **B**us) A popular type of connection that allows the connection of up to 127 devices to one port, supports Plug and

Play and lets you "hot-swap" devices – plug and unplug them without shutting down the computer. See also *Hi-Speed USB*.

USB 2 See *Hi-Speed USB*.

Usenet (User's network) A collection of networks and computer systems that exchange messages, organized by subject into newsgroups.

Utility A small program which serves a specific function – usually as part of a bigger program or operating system.

V

Video adapter See *Video card*.

Video card An expansion card that sends signals to the monitor, though video capability is sometimes built into the motherboard. Also called a "video adapter", "video board" or "display adapter".

Virtual memory The concept of using part of a hard drive – called a "swap file" – as pretend RAM. When the real RAM is full, some of the data is temporarily moved to the swap file, where it stays until it's needed or until there is some free RAM.

Virus A small program or piece of program code that finds its way onto a computer and then causes havoc. Viruses are most commonly spread from machine to machine via infected floppy disks or email attachments.

Voice recognition software Application that attempts to interpret the user's voice, either to turn spoken text into type or to respond to commands.

W

Wallpaper Background image on the Windows Desktop.

WAN (**W**ide **A**rea **N**etwork) A network of geographically diverse computers connected via satellite or telephone. Contrast with *LAN*.

Warez Pronounced "wares" or "ware-ez". Slang for software, usually pirated. See also *Pirated*.

Web (or **World Wide Web**; the "**www**" in Web addresses) A globally spread collection of graphic and text documents published on the Internet that are connected by clickable links and which share a common programming language (HTML). A webpage is a single HTML document; a website is a collection of related HTML documents.

Web authoring Designing and publishing webpages.

Webcam A small digital video camera that perches on top of a PC monitor, primarily used for video conferencing and image capture.

Wi-Fi A family of radio technologies that allow computer devices to communicate wirelessly over a range

Window A self-contained rectangular portion of the screen in which a particular document or program is dealt with.

Windows A series of GUI-based operating systems designed and published by Microsoft.

Windows CE A slimmed-down version of Windows designed to be run on handheld computers.

Windows Explorer The special Windows program that is used to browse through the files on a PC. My Documents, Control Panel and so on all open in Windows Explorer. Confusingly, it's sometimes used to describe only those windows with the folder tree showing, and it's sometimes muddled up with *Internet Explorer*.

Windows key A special key found on most modern PC keyboards, used for various shortcuts in Windows.

Wizard A special Windows program that walks you through the various stages of a particular task – installing a new printer, for example.

WMA (**W**indows **M**edia **A**udio) A compressed file format supported by the Windows Media Player and many MP3 devices.

WordPad Simple word processor bundled with Windows. Found under Accessories in the Programs menu.

Word processor Software used for creating and manipulating text-based documents such as letters. Some popular examples are Microsoft Word and Corel WordPerfect.

World Wide Web See *Web*.

Worm A type of virus that self-replicates and consumes system resources. They spread very quickly via emails and the Internet.

WYSIWYG (**W**hat **Y**ou **S**ee **I**s **W**hat **Y**ou **G**et) Pronounced "wiz-ee-wig". A program, such as a Web design package, that lets the user see what the finished document will look like, rather than forcing them to work in code and view the results later.

Z

Zip drive Like a floppy drive, but takes much higher-capacity disks. Made by Iomega (www.iomega.com). See also *Jaz drive*.

Zip file A file compression format with the extension .zip. Files are "zipped" to reduce their size for transfer or storage, or to bundle numerous files onto into one archive file.

Windows key A special key found on most modern PC keyboards, used for various shortcuts in Windows.

Wizard A special Windows program that walks you through the various stages of a particular task: installing a new printer, for example.

WMA Windows Media Audio. A compressed file format, created by the Windows Media Player and many MP3 players.

WordPad Simple word processor bundled with Windows, found under Accessories in the Programs menu.

Word processor Software used for creating and editing text-based documents such as letters. Some popular examples are Microsoft Word and Corel WordPerfect.

World Wide Web See Web.

Worm A type of virus that replicates and consumes system resources. They spread very quickly via email and the Internet.

WYSIWYG What You See Is What You Get. Term used to describe a program, such as a word or desktop publishing package, that lets you see what the finished document will look like, rather than just the code which will be converted into a printable later.

Zip drive Like a floppy drive, but uses much higher capacity disks made by Iomega (www.iomega.com). See also Jaz drive.

Zip files A file compression format with the extension .zip. Files are compressed to reduce file size for transfer or storage, or to bundle multiple files into one archive file.

24 Some websites

PCs and Windows online

News and reviews

Anand tech

www.anandtech.com

Good techie site dealing with all kinds of hardware news and reviews. Includes weekly prices for memory, motherboards, etc.

CNet

www.cnet.com

"The source for computers and technology", as it calls itself, is a massive computer portal, containing everything from hardware reviews and downloads to how-to guides and an effective price comparison tool.

Dan's Data

www.dansdata.com

Contains in-depth reviews of all kinds of hardware, from heat sinks to DVD-RAM camcorders, as well as some good how-to articles. Dan really knows his stuff, and also reviews model tanks.

Maximum PC

www.maximumpc.co.uk

A nice-looking and user-friendly site with loads of reviews, downloads, links, tips, forums – definitely worth a click or two.

Motherboards.org

www.motherboards.org

As well as reviews, it includes info on BIOS upgrades and overclocking, and the "Mobot", for identifying and comparing motherboards.

The Register

www.theregister.com

The best place for general technology news. Sign up for the daily email update and you'll know what Gates and chronies are up to before they do.

Sharkey Extreme

www.sharkeyextreme.com

Very similar in layout to Tom's (below), and again a little on the techie side, this site is overflowing with articles and product reviews. Includes weekly CPU and memory price guide.

Tom's Hardware

www.tomshardware.com

This large but easy-to-navigate site has made Tom something of a living legend. Though techie in places, you'll find hundreds of informative articles about all things hardware.

ZDNet

www.zdnet.com

Another giant computer site, this time with a business focus.

Magazines

Magazine sites are a great place to find out what's hot and what's not, and many offer downloads, tips, forums and links for purchasing the kit you've read about. Some of the best include:

Computer Shopper www.computershopper.co.uk
PC Answers www.pcanswers.co.uk
PC Buyer www.pcbuyer.com
PC Format www.pcformat.co.uk
PC Magazine www.pcmag.com
PC Plus www.pcplus.co.uk
PC Pro www.pcpro.co.uk
PC World www.pcworld.com
Personal Computer World www.pcw.co.uk
What Laptop www.whatlaptop.co.uk

Reference

About

www.about.com/compute

About.com is a mammoth site where you can find resources – and links – relating to almost every subject. Their computing section is excellent, covering everything from downloads to computer history.

How stuff works

http://computer.howstuffworks.com

Learn how processors process, operating systems operate, and much, much more.

Old Computers

www.oldcomputers.co.uk

One for nerds trying to rediscover old computing flames. Maintained by a chap called Brian, this site will help to put everything in perspective – a work of genius. Please pay Brian a visit.

The PC Guide

www.pcguide.com

Though the presentation is a little old and cold, and the content not always cutting-edge, this is an unbelievably comprehensive site that offers in-depth information for both advanced and uninitiated PC users. The only problem is that there's simply too much here to read.

The PC Technology Guide

www.pctechguide.com

Similar to the PC Guide, this site offers in-depth info about all elements of PC components and operation. Contains lots of links and illustrations.

PC911

www.pcnineoneone.com

This good reference site is geared toward troubleshooting and tutorials for upgrading. There's also regular articles, usually focusing on hardware.

Webopedia
www.webopedia.com
This is a great reference tool, overflowing with easy-to-understand definitions with good links for most entries.

What Is?
http://whatis.techtarget.com
Probably the best definitions site around, What Is? provides in-depth but easily digestible articles on everything from AAA Servers to ZV Ports.

Wikipedia
www.wikipedia.org
One of the greatest things to have appeared on the Web in the last few years, this open-content, user-editable encyclopedia features a plethora of PC-related entries. Either search for something specific, or start browsing from http://en.wikipedia.org/wiki/Computers

PCs and components

Stores

The Web is probably the best place to shop for PCs, components and software, and many online stores do more than just flog stuff, offering feature reviews, articles and product comparisons.

Amazon (US) www.amazon.com
Amazon (UK) www.amazon.co.uk
Aus PC Market (AU) www.auspcmarket.com.au
CNet Shopper (US) http://shopper.cnet.com
Computers 4 Sure (US) www.computers4sure.com
Dabs (UK) www.dabs.com
eCost (US) www.ecost.com

Insight (US) www.insight.com
Insight (UK) www.insight.com/uk
Insight (Canada) www.insight.com/canada
The Laptop Shop (UK) www.thelaptopshop.co.uk
MicroDirect (UK) www.microdirect.co.uk
Outpost (US) www.outpost.com
Ozbuy.com (AU) www.ozbuy.com
PC Mall (US) www.pcmall.com
Simply Computers (UK) www.simply.co.uk

Auctions

Internet auctions are often a good place to pick up real bargains, but be warned: it's possible to get your fingers burned, so try to limit your bids to products that claim to be boxed or sealed, have a full description that you're happy with and which offer a picture of the goods. Many auction sites also offer vendor ratings if you want to check credentials before you buy. For the full story on Internet auctions, see *The Rough Guide to the Internet*.

Ebay (AU) www.ebay.com.au
Ebay (UK) www.ebay.co.uk
Ebay (US) www.ebay.com
Yahoo (US) http://auctions.yahoo.com/computers

Manufacturers

Here's a list of some manufacturers' sites worth looking at, for browsing and comparing, if nothing else. Many will sell to you direct, though you're unlikely to save much money by cutting out the middleman. For country-specific sites, look for links of these homepages…

Acer www.acer.com
AJP www.ajp.co.uk
AMD www.amd.com
Carrera www.carrera.co.uk

Creative www.creative.com
Dell www.dell.com
Dragon Systems www.dragonsys.com
Evesham www.evesham.com
Fujitsu www.fujitsu-computers.com
Gateway www.gateway.com
Hewlett Packard www.hp.com
Hi-Grade www.higrade.com
Hitachi www.hitachi.com
IBM www.ibm.com
Intel www.intel.com
Iomega www.iomega.com
LaCie www.lacie.com
Mesh www.meshcomputers.co.uk
Packard Bell www.packardbell.com
Psion www.psion.co.uk
Samsung www.samsung.com
Sony www.sony.com
Texas Instruments www.ti.com
Time Computers www.timecomputers.com
Tiny Computers www.tiny.com
Toshiba www.toshiba.com
Umax www.umax.com
Watford Electronics www.watford.co.uk

Windows sites

Microsoft

www.microsoft.com

Home of the all-powerful creators of Windows. Once you've cut through the corporate spin, there are loads of useful resources to be had: downloads, updates, forums, tips, troubleshooting, links and loads more.

Paul Thurrott's SuperSite for Windows
www.winsupersite.com
Serious site focusing on the future of Windows. Every beta and release candidate examined in full.

Toejumper
www.toejumper.net
Though the address suggests a foot-fetish website, it's actually a good troubleshooting and resource guide for Windows, full of sound, well-written advice and easy-to-follow troubleshooting instructions.

Win Drivers
www.windrivers.com
Great site containing every Windows driver you ever needed, as well as tips, troubleshooting, news and reviews.

World of Windows Networking
www.wown.com
An extremely detailed guide to networking with Windows. Covers everything from the basics to customizing your own cables.

For more general tips, tricks and Windows troubleshooting advice, see:

PC Guide www.pcguide.com
Kelly's Korner www.kellys-korner-xp.com
ComputerHope www.computerhope.com
Windows-Help.net www.windows-help.net

Free and nearly free Windows software

Most people don't realize quite how much free software is available online – from tiny utilities to whole applications. See Chapter 18 for some specific pointers, or browse some online archives:

Download.com www.download.com
Nonags www.nonags.com
PC Plus Downloads www.pcplus.co.uk/downloads
Review Now www.reviewnow.com
TuCows www.tucows.com

More links...

For millions more PC- and Windows-related sites, try one of these online directories:

Computer Hardware Links http://users.erols.com/chare/hardware.htm
Google Directory http://directory.google.com/Top/Computers
Looksmart www.looksmart.com
Yahoo www.yahoo.com/computers

index

Index

As well as references to equipment, people and other subjects, this index contains important functions and features of Microsoft Windows. These appear capitalized, and can also be found under the entry for Windows.

a

index

c

d

index

g

h

i

j

k

l

n

o

p

q

r

s

t

v

Z

notes

notes

notes

notes

notes

notes

notes

notes

notes

notes